The
REALLY USEFUL
MATHS BOOK

The Really Useful Maths Book has been written for all those who want children to enjoy the challenge of learning mathematics. It presents teachers, students and home educators with exciting and varied ideas for introducing mathematics to primary aged children. With suggestions about the best ways to use equipment and resources to support learning, it describes in detail how to make learning the easy option for children.

This accessible book is split into two comprehensive sections. The first covers the practical side of mathematics and is packed with ideas and activities. The second concentrates on theory and practice of mathematics teaching and will help you to improve your teaching strategies. Topics covered are:

Part I
- numbers and the number system;
- operations and calculations;
- shape and space;
- measures, statistics and data handling.

Part II
- what teachers need to know about interactive teaching;
- teachers and children interacting to sustain learning;
- children making sense of mathematics;
- consolidating new ideas and developing personal qualities;
- consolidation and practice for accuracy, speed and fluency, application and automaticity.

This practical guide to making maths meaningful, challenging and interesting is invaluable to teachers in schools, students on primary teacher training courses, tutors and mentors, home educators and others interested in mathematics education programmes.

Tony Brown is currently based at the Graduate School of Education, University of Bristol, and was previously Head of the Centre for Learning Development at the University of Hull.

Henry Liebling was Senior Lecturer in Primary Education at the College of St Mark & St John in Plymouth prior to his retirement.

We shall only be able to serve as educators
when we reach deeper and deeper into the
mystery of the mind at work on itself.
(Gattegno, 1963)

The

REALLY USEFUL MATHS BOOK

A guide to interactive teaching

Tony Brown

and

Henry Liebling

 Routledge
Taylor & Francis Group

LONDON AND NEW YORK

First edition published 2005
by Routledge
2 Park Square, Milton Park, Abingdon, Oxon, OX14 4RN

Simultaneously published in the USA and Canada
by Routledge
270 Madison Ave, New York NY 10016

Routledge is an imprint of the Taylor & Francis Group

Transferred to Digital Printing 2009

© 2005 Tony Brown and Henry Liebling

Typeset in Palatino and Gill Sans by
Florence Production Ltd, Stoodleigh, Devon

British Library Cataloguing in Publication Data
A catalogue record for this book is available from the
British Library

Library of Congress Cataloging in Publication Data
A catalog record for this book has been requested

ISBN 0–415–25208–3

Contents

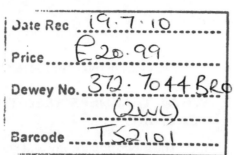

Contents

Resource pages

LIST OF RESOURCE PAGES FOR PHOTOCOPYING

Acknowledgements

It is impossible to individually name and thank all those who have contributed to our thinking. We have gained enormously from the generosity and enthusiasm of teaching colleagues, students and, of course, the children we taught over many years, who gave their time generously to educating us while we went about our teaching.

We especially want to thank all those colleagues at Marjon, in Plymouth, who have supported, challenged and encouraged us in our work. Richard Harvey, our maths colleague for many years, deserves a special mention. Thanks, too, to our families and friends in England and in France who have been supportive, patient and unstinting in their enthusiasm for our various projects. We have referred to and used unpublished work from the following maths education colleagues: Zöe Evans, David Fielker, Kris Turner and Helen Williams.

If we had to pick out a single individual it would have to be Caleb Gattegno, whose profound and sometimes controversial views have had a continuing influence down the years.

We would like to thank Network Educational Press Ltd for permission to use some of the material and ideas from *Getting Started: An Induction Guide for Newly Qualified Teachers* (1999) by Henry Liebling.

We are also grateful to RoutledgeFalmer for permission to use some of the material from *Meeting the Standards in Primary Mathematics: A Guide to the ITT NC* (2003) by Tony Brown.

Thanks are also due to Susan Leaper and Sarah Moore for careful editing and typesetting; any remaining errors are probably all our own work.

This book is dedicated to teachers who create rather than react, take risks rather than play safe, and experiment with their teaching.

Bristol
January 2005

Using *The Really Useful Maths Book*

Mathematics is a hard subject both to learn and to teach. Throughout the following pages, we address the challenges for both learners and teachers.

This book is intended to be helpful to those who want to try out some interesting activities with primary school-age children. It has also been written for those who wish to extend and further develop the ways in which they work with children.

We provide a wide range of mathematical activities. We also discuss why particular activities are useful and how they can be made more effective by thinking carefully about teaching strategies. This means using a dual approach of discussing the activities themselves and teaching effectiveness.

In Part I the emphasis is on the activities themselves rather than the pedagogical approach. It is about trying some activities with children to see what happens. In contrast, in Part II the emphasis is on more complex teaching strategies and ways of working with children. The activities in this part are provided to illustrate the approaches we discuss. The sections in Part I follow a fairly conventional order, which match the National Numeracy Strategy (NNS) strands:

- numbers and the number system;
- operations and calculations;
- shape and space;
- measures, statistics and data handling;
- problem-solving and investigation activities appear throughout the book and their role is discussed in Part II.

Part II opens with a look at the NNS and how to maximise the effectiveness of its philosophy of interactive teaching. We comment on research from the science of learning and use it to discuss how to get the most from practical resources and equipment. We look at interactive teaching from several perspectives, particularly the role of questioning and the influence of informal assessment and giving feedback to children.

We argue for a diversity of experience and suggest the inclusion of real world-focused and classroom-focused activities, activities based on fantasy and reality, and problem-focused and rule-focused work.

Drawing on recent ideas from the new science of learning we argue that children need opportunities to exercise choice and independence if they are to be successful learners of mathematics. We look at the work of Reuven Feuerstein and his ideas for making *links* or *bridges* between different areas of mathematics, and between new and previously acquired knowledge and skills, before taking a brief look at the origins of children's errors and misconceptions in mathematics.

Those who are most likely to find the book really useful are those who have sufficient freedom to experiment with their own teaching.

Tried an activity or resource and want to comment on it? You can contact us and post your comments at: really_useful_maths_support@hotmail.com. Tell us what worked for you and share your ideas with other users.

Suggested dialogue to illustrate effective interactions between teacher and children. These snippets of dialogue offer ideas to get things going and to keep them going. They also highlight and exemplify key interactions that will scaffold thinking and develop understanding.

N9 Taking ideas from 'floor to head'

STARTING WITH LARGE OBJECTS ON THE FLOOR

'Floor to head' is a simple model to help you think about using a variety of resources to enable children to internalise mathematical concepts and make these concepts both meaningful and available.

Especially with younger children, you might start with large-scale objects such as number tiles on the floor or with the children each holding a different number card. Get the children to associate physical movements with problem-solving and decision-making.

> Which two children have cards with numbers that add up to make 7?
> Come and stand together.
> 3 and 4? Yes, 3 and 4 make 7.
> 5 and 1? Yes, well done!
> Stand inside the set ring if you are wearing trousers. Everyone else stand outside.
> Where should Seema stand?
> Who is holding a number that is less than the number on my card? Wave your card in the air!
> Even number people, take your even number card and put it on the floor tile that is one more than your number. Ready, steady go. Now odd number people ...

The activities could move through intermediate sizes and orientations, starting with large numbers pegged onto a washing line, moving to large wall number lines and grids. These large physical resources can be used by the teacher, an individual child or a group to demonstrate an idea that can then be repeated with table-top versions of the same or similar resources.

This model is not just arguing that large resources are good because they can be seen by everyone in the classroom. Nor is it arguing that the move from floor to table top to head, should take place over weeks – they could all be part of the same lesson!

S3 p. 112
A p. 148

Thinking about floor to head
Children learn best by being involved in activity within a language-rich environment. The most successful learning is achieved when activities are firmly associated with higher-order language skills, where children are:
- explaining their reasoning
- applying logical arguments
- questioning each other
- predicting possible events
- exploring consequences
- elaborating an argument
- interpreting ideas.

From: Washing lines, floor tiles, Brio, Duplo, Action Mats, hopscotch, skipping ropes as Venn diagrams, playground 100 squares, interactive whiteboards
To: Cuisenaire, Play People, Multilink, dominoes, jigsaws, personal computers and laptops
To: Paper grids and 100 squares pasted into books, 30 cm rulers, angle measurers, compasses, hand-held calculators

Where appropriate, we offer prompts, commentary, key points and summaries, resource lists, background information, advice and suggestions for follow-up activities.

THE EFFECT OF RESOURCES ON THINKING

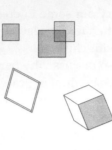

- A paper square shows squareness by virtue of its edges.
- Four equal length Geostrips have their squareness determined by the interior angle.
- Two pieces of gel can be used to illustrate squareness in their overlap.
- The faces of a cube have a squareness that can be imagined, even when the eye does not see a square.
- Combining resources is a powerful strategy, e.g. a number line with Cuisenaire Rods or Play People.

Resources emphasise different mathematical attributes
- When we look at a paper square, its squareness is strongly visible in the 'edgeness' of the paper.
- When we use four equal-length Geostrips, hinged at the four corners, the squareness appears as a special position obtained only when the internal angles are held carefully at 90 degrees.
- When we use two pieces of gel and form a square in the overlap, the squareness appears in the darker shade of the overlap.

Only by using different resources in a range of contexts do we realise that:

- Squares are solid – except when they are not.
- Squares are skeletal – except when they are solid.
- Squares are two dimensional even when they are the faces of a three-dimensional cube.
- Squares can be seen as a special case of a rhombus, and so on.

The ability to recognise squareness builds up in us, together with an awareness of the contradictions, until we gain a robust and persisting view of the generality of squareness. In the physical world most views we get of the faces of a cube are not square – we abstract the squareness despite what our visual sense tells us we are seeing.

The conclusion to draw is that we should use a range of resources within lessons and teach children to move between them. We need to point out how each resource shapes our perceptions and our thinking, by allowing certain viewpoints while limiting others.

The tired discussion about whether to start teaching 2D or 3D to young children is irrelevant. Children need to be taught to 'see' the 2D in the 3D and vice versa: they need to print triangular patterns with the face of a tetrahedron dipped in paint, and to guess an object's shape from its shadow cast by an OHP.

N9 p. 50

S3 p. 111

Developing interactive teaching strategies

Links show connections between simple and more complex ideas, between activities and pedagogical discussion, between brief and more detailed explanation of pedagogy. Add to our links by writing in your own when you find them. You can also annotate the book with self-adhesive bookmarks.

Part I

N1 Counting and counting out

p. 152

CIRCLE COUNTING

Reception children sit in a circle with their teacher. In the simplest form there are 9 children in the group, each with their own numeral card. The teacher or helper makes the 10th person. The teacher chooses a 'decade', for example sixty: forty, sixty and eighty are all good ones because they sound like four-ty and six-ty; and you can cheat with five-ty. (But miss out the 'Silly Teens' until the children have learned and practised all the other decades and can say them smoothly, backwards and forwards.) Then the children take it in turns, starting with 1, repeating the teacher's decade number (sixty) and adding their own number (sixty-one). The teacher just works on a single decade for 10 minutes.

The children get used to saying their number in the right order but they also hear the other numbers being spoken. Ask them what comes before and after their number. At first they may tell you *who* comes before and after them, rather than what is said. Counting forward and back can be helped by the teacher pointing at each child in turn, although this shifts the focus from listening to the number count and focuses on a visual, non-mathematical stimulus instead. You could try holding hands in the circle and each person can gently squeeze their left hand as they speak. That will prompt the next person to speak.

When this is working well, get the children to close their eyes and repeat the activity. After plenty of practice, finally try it with eyes closed and no hand-holding: this is totally aural, and you can get the children to begin to put their focus on all the sounds they hear, rather than just listening out for when it's their turn. This helps them learn to listen to counts up to 99, and of course the children can be given plenty of opportunity to count back. With older children, various counting chants can be tried, using software such as ATM Counter.

PEOPLE MATHS

Thirty children have A4 cards with a number from 1 to 30 pinned to their front and back. In a large indoor or outdoor space they can play different people maths games. Encourage, and insist on, looking, thinking and walking! Later on, when children are familiar with the game, the set of numbers can be any positive integers or decimals, and can be written on individual wipe boards.

'Two More Than Me'
Tell the children to hold the left hand of the person who has a number 2 more than theirs with their right hand. What other instruction gives the same result?

'Chains'
Tell the children to hold hands with someone whose number is 1 less than their own number. Similar instructions would be: 'double, or half their number'; '2 more or 2 less than their number'; '10 more or 10 less than their number'.

Some tools for numeracy
- Fingers
- Circle counting
- Counting stick
- Cards or tiles on the floor, wall, washing line, table or child
- Number line
- Number track
- Number grids (counting, addition, multiplication, other systems)
- Numdrum
- Target boards
- Gattegno number charts for saying and making numbers
- Place value arrow cards
- Real money
- Abacus
- Soroban
- Cuisenaire Rods
- Base 10 materials

'Odds and Evens'
Tell the children to divide themselves into two sets: one set of children holding odd numbers, and one set holding even numbers. Then tell them to line up in ascending (or descending) order. Use any convenient floor lines in the hall or playground, or use skipping ropes to divide the space. Make big labels for odd and even, or use coloured flags or traffic cones as markers.

'Multiples'/'Tables'
Tell the children to find the other people who belong to the same set of multiples as them. Then tell the children to try holding hands with them. This can get complex.

COUNTING GAMES

The 'Giver of the Rule'
The 'Giver of the Rule' can be a child or an adult. They have a set of A4 cards with some or all of the following on (+1, +2, 0, −1, −2, double, half, → and ← to change the direction of the chant). The children sit in a circle. Start the game with the +1 card (which means add one to the previous number) and the 0 card (which means add nothing to the previous number, just say the same number).

The 'Giver of the Rule' can either *select* the card they want to show or take a card at random (in which case the pack should contain multiple copies of some of the cards). They draw a card and hold it up so that everyone in the group can see the current rule. The next person in the circle has to work out and say what the consequence of each new card is on what has already been said. Make sure you keep the chant moving round the circle and help the children with the rules if needed.

Try changing the starting number or picking it from a pack of number cards. This game can be used for any age by changing the level of difficulty to match what needs to be consolidated ($\times 10$, $\times 5$, $\div 5$, $\div 10$, $\times 0.1$, $+3$, $+5$, $+7$, $\times 3$, $\times 4$ . . .). Interestingly, starting at one and 'doubling' halfway round a circle of 30 and then continuing round with 'halving' can be enough of a challenge for most adults. This can easily be adapted into a tables circle game such as 'Fizz Buzz'.

COUNTING STICK

You can make counting sticks from bamboo canes, beechwood broom handles, dowels or square section timber. Mark the divisions with coloured insulating tape, which can be cut into thin strips or arrow points. You can use a wooden metre rule with 10 cm sections coloured alternatively red and white.

The stick represents a small part of a continuous number line with clearly marked points at regular intervals along the stick to represent specific points along the number line. You can put numerals on the stick with Blutack or Velcro. In fact having a blank stick with a strip of Velcro along its length can be a good way to encourage children to decide where numbers should go. Some teachers hold the stick horizontally at one end, others put it down or suspend it so that everyone can see it clearly.

Garden cane or broom handle counting stick

RESOURCES

Bloomfield (1990) *People Maths*; Mosley (1990) *Quality Circle Time*; ATM (2004) *Developing Number 2* software

CONTEXTS FOR COUNTING

A standard procedure with a new set of numbers might be as follows:

- Point to and name one end of the stick 'zero' and the other end 'ten'.
- Move your finger or a pointer along the stick, pausing just long enough at each mark or division to let the children say the number.
- Reinforce any anchor points such as *halfway, five*.
- Count forwards and backwards a few times until both the children and you sound and feel confident.
- Point to any mark at random.
- Go forwards and back one or two marks either side of the chosen number.
- Ask what might be found halfway between two marks.
- Ask what numbers might exist beyond both ends of the stick.
- Encourage children to take on your role.
- Start with a different number for one end of the stick.
- Work with each group in the class using different sets of numbers.
- Give children the opportunity to run their own groups.

It is easy to vary the task and the children enjoy being in control. Counting sticks are good for learning and visualising tables, fractions, decimals and large numbers.

You can change the orientation of the stick as well as the direction of the counting and also consider applied contexts, such as money and temperature, as reasons for counting.

Horizontal

• Frogs hopping on lily pads • Swimming in metres • Rowing races • Walking steps (use paving stones and playground chalk) • House numbers up and down the street • Olympic track and field events, such as hurdles and hop, step and jump • Journeys and route planning.

Vertical

• Ladder rungs • Jack and the Beanstalk • Steps, stairs, floors and lift stops • Shelves • Mountain climbing • Hot air balloons • Diving and submarines.

Nursery & Reception
• Counting in ones 0 to 10

Years 1 & 2
• 0 to 10; 5 to 15; 0 to 20; 0 to 100

Years 3 & 4
• Counting in 2s, 3s, 4s, 5s and 10s
• Find and name mid-points 0 to 1000; −10 to 0; 0 to 10 000, 0 to 1
• Counting in 7s, 8s and 9s . . .

Years 5 & 6
• 0 to 1 fractions, decimals and percentages, tenths and hundredths
• All tables
• 0 to 1 000 000

NUMBER CYLINDER

This is now commercially available as 'Numdrum', but can also be made by either printing out a grid on card and bending it so that the numbers form a continuous set, or taking a paper or plastic number line and winding it round a suitable cardboard cylinder. You could make one from cardboard with the circumference the same length as the number grid from 0 to 9, however this is tricky because you need to get 9 next to 10.

We make numerous links within this book to resources for numeracy, and explain why we believe that tools to think with are so important. Look in the index and contents as well as at the explicit links.

OBSERVING CHILDREN COUNTING

What is going on when we count?

Can you make sense of these stories from Kris Turner? What do these children understand? What can they do already? What else do they need to know?

Girl:	(putting stones in a bag and counting) 'One, two, three, four.'
KT:	'Can you show me two?'
Girl:	'I don't know which is two.'

KT:	(to James, new in Reception) 'You're five now aren't you, James?'
James:	'If I'm five, where are the other four?'

Observing Gillian, Caroline and their auntie sitting on the school bench.

Gillian: 'One, two, three, . . . that's wrong, I'm four. I'll try again. One, two, three, . . . but I'm still four. You do it.'

Pamela can orally count to ten. She was carefully counting out objects into a tray. She counted three bricks, three pine cones, three conkers, three bobbins and then dropped a large handful of peas into the tray.

Seema was asked to show her teacher two, three and four of all the objects on the table. She did this accurately without hesitation. She was unable to say the counting words in order.

Assim wanted a watch with, 'one of those hands what goes round quickly'.

KT:	'A second hand?'
Assim:	'No. It's a third hand, it's already got two!'

What was counting like when you were young? Can you recall a personal counting episode? What is it like now to listen to and watch young children working with numbers, counting and talking about mathematical things? What things do *we* count?

A

p. 152

When do children learn to name things such as cows, dogs, dolls, etc.? Consider names such as car, bus, man, flower, door. They are used as the name for a particular object and also for a class of objects. A young child can say 'that's a dog' (knowing therefore it cannot be a cat). Compare this naming of a *class of objects* with *one, two, three, four, . . . , seventy-eight, . . . which can be attached to different sets* containing *any* class of objects. What's going on? What is being learned?

Adults often spontaneously count when they are with children. We count when we are going up or down stairs and steps, doing up buttons on a child's coat, tickling toes and fingers, feeling fingers in a glove, etc. Children hear the special set of counting words and most of them quickly learn that counting is a special ritual.

When children start school, many know the counting words and the order in which to recite them. Many can also count small numbers of objects accurately. They don't necessarily do all these things in English.

CARDINALITY AND ORDINALITY

Cardinality is the name given to *what* is actually countable – sets of 'things'. If the question is 'How many?', then the answer is a cardinal number. One, two, three, etc. are written using numerals which, in Western Europe look like this: 1, 2, 3, . . ., etc. These same numerals are of course used with a variety of collections of objects. We can use the numeral 5 as a label for five elephants, five hats, five moons – which does not seem much to us now, but at some time in our lives was a stunning surprise!

Ordinality refers to the *position* of an object within a set of things. Ordinal numbers are: first, second, third, etc. For example, third time lucky, sixth floor flat, the thirty-fourth year of her reign. If the question is 'What comes next?', then the answer is derived by ordinal counting. We can count up to a million and beyond if we want to. We don't use cardinal counting because collecting a million objects might be inconvenient! Instead, we use what we know about our counting system to say what comes next.

Children need to make links between cardinal and ordinal counting. This is achieved when they realise that stopping the count on reaching the 5th object (in a set of more than 5) means they have counted 5 things so far and they've stopped on the 5th one. At about the same time, they need to learn that the order in which we count the objects in a set doesn't affect the count. The move from counting to calculation requires that we stop counting objects and focus on using the structure of the number system to manipulate the symbols.

Distance effect

This refers to how we see numbers which are very different, for example 1 and 9, and numbers which are close together, for example 8 and 9. Our brains can compare two quantities of food and distinguish between the larger and the smaller. Distinguishing between a plate with 1 sandwich and a plate with 9 sandwiches is easy, but when the quantities are similar, such as one plate with 8 sandwiches and one with 9, we find it harder. And it doesn't really matter that much anyway – or does it? It could depend on what's *in* the sandwiches – and then it will take us longer to decide.

Magnitude effect

This refers to how we see small numbers, for example 1, 2, 3, and large numbers, for example 1 000 000 or 2 222 000. When the numbers are small we are very good at distinguishing between them, for example between one apple and two apples. As the quantities get larger we find it increasingly difficult to tell the difference, and we take longer or make mistakes. There appear to be 'a lot'.

Both these effects have been observed in a variety of tasks and also in many species, including pigeons, rats, dolphins, apes and, of course, humans. We should be aware of these two effects when we work with children (Dehaene, 1997).

Signing

The British sign language used by the deaf employs a finger counting method of conveying numbers. In the diagram below, the arrows indicate movement. For example, to show ten, the hand is moved in a circular manner. For 13, the three fingers are shaken from side to side.

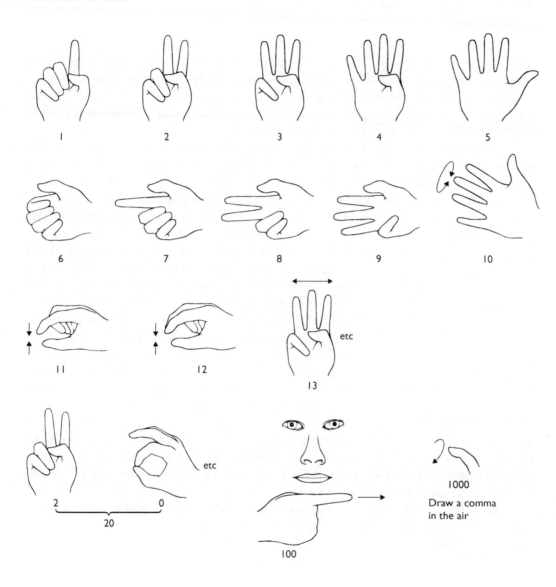

N2 Saying and making numbers

Geoff Faux has reintroduced Gattegno's number chart to teachers (Faux, 1998). These activities work on number structure using children's spoken language, with the teacher remaining silent as much as possible. The activities work well as a starter or plenary activity with the whole class. The activities build on what children know, encouraging them to 'have a go', to probe the as yet unknown.

Sit the children fairly close together facing a number chart. You stand to one side with a pointer (a garden cane with coloured tape bound round the end is useful). You can use a projector, and it is easy to cover up any rows of numbers that you do not want to use. A piece of paper can be stuck over the irrelevant parts of a poster version of the number chart. You can start with just units or hundreds, tens and units.

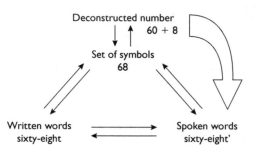

Deconstructed number

60 + 8

Set of symbols

68

Written words
sixty-eight

Spoken words
sixty-eight'

Be aware that you are pointing to a symbol, for example '7', but you expect them to say the word, in this example 'seven'. Chorus work supports the new learner by revealing what needs to be said. The chanting encourages children to have a go even if they are not confident. This work helps the learners make the link between the symbol '7' and the sound of the word 'seven'.

If you need to, point to the symbol and say the correct word, pronouncing it correctly, with the correct intonation, but do this *once and only once*. Otherwise, point to the symbol, tap it and gesticulate to indicate that you want some response from the children. This is the scary bit, but be brave – someone *will* reply, hopefully with the correct word. If you hear a correct and an incorrect word spoken at the same time, then stop by letting the pointer point downwards and move towards the person who gave the correct answer.

Signal them to speak again and for everyone to listen, then go back to the chart, signal them again as you tap and confirm that they are giving the right response. Remember, don't criticise a wrong response (even by looking).

ATM (2004) *Developing Number 2* software supports this set of activities.

O1

p. 57

O6

p. 91

S4

p. 114

Caleb Gattegno (1988) created his 'Silent Way' activities around teaching and learning languages and mathematics. The principle is that the learner speaks the most, practising the language or mathematics, and the teacher speaks the least – since it is the learner who has to do the work of learning. The teacher's role is first to give the culturally dependent information to the learner. For example:

In English we call this symbol, '8', 'eight' and this decade symbol '60' is called 'sixty'. When we put them together we say the decade symbol first. So (60, 8) actually looks like this '68'. Now say it . . . using the rules I've given you. (Sixty-eight.) This symbol '9' is called 'nine'. What do you say when you see '69'? (Sixty-nine.)

After giving the learner the necessary cultural information, the teacher can remain silent and just point to, for example, 61, 62, 63, 64, . . . while the learners practise applying the rules of the count.

'SILENT WAY' AND THE GATTEGNO CHART

Reward behaviour that you want repeated; ignore wrong responses because you *do* want everyone to try, but you will only respond to the correct response.

Tap again and encourage others to join in. As long as at least one person says the correct sound 'seven', look encouraging and positive. You really need to express your wishes and responses non-verbally. Don't say anything: just use facial expressions, gesture and body language. This is why it's called 'Silent Way': the teacher is teaching in a *silent* way. You will find your attention is directed at the children's responses and you will be thinking about where to point to next. It is a bit like teaching when you have lost your voice. Strangely the children feel in control. You will hear their confident voices probing the unknown while watching for signs of your approval. This feedback loop is a powerful learning tool.

1	2	3	4	5	6	7	8	9
10	20	30	40	50	60	70	80	90
100	200	300	400	500	600	700	800	900
1000	2000	3000	4000	5000	6000	7000	8000	9000
10 000	20 000	30 000	40 000	50 000	60 000	70 000	80 000	90 000
100 000	200 000	300 000	400 000	500 000	600 000	700 000	800 000	900 000
1 000 000	2 000 000	3 000 000	4 000 000	5 000 000	6 000 000	7 000 000	8 000 000	9 000 000

A Gattegno chart from 1 to 9 999 999. See Faux (1998)

Point to the next number, in this example the symbol '8', and encourage the whole class to respond. Your awareness needs to be with the class. Who is actually responding, even very quietly, but correctly? Point to the correct respondent with your free hand, and encourage them to repeat the answer, more clearly or perhaps louder. Nod in agreement. Gradually more children will get the idea of the game and start joining in. You point, they speak. Don't worry if only a few children respond initially. Gauge the speed of your pointing to the next number by the speed of their responses. Rhythm and pace are important, but on their terms rather than yours. Go as fast as the majority of respondents, neither too fast nor too slow. Go forwards 1, 2, 3, 4, 5, ..., 9 in simple sequence at first. Then go backwards 9, 8, 7, 6, ..., 1. Then move about from one number to another in a pattern: $1 \rightarrow 3 \rightarrow 5 \rightarrow 7 \rightarrow 9 \rightarrow 8 \rightarrow 6 \rightarrow 4 \rightarrow 2$. Now you can be fairly sure about assessing their responses. Then try a completely random order.

You can go on to the tens next and emphasise 'times ten' along one row, or move to the hundreds. Gattegno's logic is to provide the smallest piece of information necessary for a logical step. The children only need to learn to say one new word, 'hundred'. They need to recognise the two zeros after the hundred digit as a signal to say the word hundred after you have spoken the unit digit name. So '400' is 'four hundred'.

To introduce 'hundred', tap 1 in the units row and then immediately tap the stick *beside* the hundred row to the left of the '100', so it is clear that you are not pointing to any particular number. As you do this, say 'hundred'. Now try pointing at '2' in the units row and again tap to the left of the hundreds row and say 'hundred'. As the chorus of voices grows stronger, reduce your spoken input. Go through from 3, 4, 5, 6, 7, 8, to 9. Each time you point to the units number, follow it by tapping the hundreds row to signify hundred.

SAYING LARGER NUMBERS

Now make a big gesture and change the routine. This time point directly and exaggeratedly at the '1' in '100', then at the '00', so make two taps in quick succession as you speak ('1' '00', 'one' 'hundred').

> With the standard chart you can make and say all the numbers from 1 to 9 999 999, from 10^0 to 10^{+6}.

Practise working along the hundred row with 100, 200, 300, 400, . . . , 900. Repeat the procedures above and be amazed at how quickly the children respond now they know the game. You will find that *they* are pushing *you*. You will need to point carefully, clearly and accurately. You can tap the number and quickly remove the cane gazing at them eagerly for an answer. They need to watch carefully where you tap, this is a 'Zap Tap'.

What is very dramatic is the response you get when, part way through a lesson with children who are very familiar with this activity, you slip a piece of blank paper over the chart so that nothing is visible to them, or you. Carry on working (but you have to pay careful attention to placing your taps accurately). The children will hesitate for a few seconds only, and will then carry on as if the chart is still there, showing that they have internalised it as a visual image.

Since this can be a playful introduction to a 'virtual' Gattegno chart, why not go to the imaginary row above the (now virtual) chart? The power of the chart is really being demonstrated when they begin to offer 'point one', point two' because that shows they have internalised both the layout and the structure of the 'powers of ten' that makes the Gattegno chart so useful. After this, and with the chart visible again you can still 'go virtual', by tapping '34' followed by a glide to produce '3.4' and '0.34' above the existing chart.

Now make up your own repertoire of moves. Ask the children for suggestions.

THE TEACHER AS CONDUCTOR

Your initial shyness with this new way of working will be swept aside by the children's enthusiasm. You will develop new ways of using the chart – and probably new charts.

Do encourage children, especially a child who is a clear step ahead of the class, to take on the role of conductor for a few numbers. In one session with a group of colleagues, as part of their CPD (continuing professional development) for the NNS. a very talented music teacher was also a lightning mathematician who thought he was poor at maths! And so the only way to give some of the hesitant English specialists a chance to respond was to hand the musician the baton.

You will develop your own repertoire of movements for the pointer/stick/cane/baton.

- Sometimes, for just one number, *hover* over one set (e.g. units), then point and *quickly* remove the pointer. This builds tension and encourages attention.

- *Tap gently* on the component parts of a number, moving from the largest to the smallest with a rhythmic flourish between each and rest the pointer on the final part. For example, for 437:

    $$(400 \rightarrow +30 \rightarrow 7)$$

- You can sky-write the 'AND' as '&' or '+', or wiggle the stick. You will be listening for 'four hundred *and* thirty seven'. Your pace and rhythm determines theirs and vice versa.

- You might *circle* each '×10'. For example, if you are reinforcing '7 → 70 → 700', go to '7', wait for a response; then down and once round '70', wait for a response; then down and twice round '700', waiting for a response. This works well when you have built up the chart from scratch.

- The *stroke* is useful to remind the children what each row represents. So stroke from 1 to 9 expecting 'units', i.e. what all these numbers have in common is that they are units; repeat for 'tens', 'hundreds' and so on. When might a vertical stroke be used?

- Indicate a number such as '34', by pointing to '30' then '4'. But move quickly, laying the pointer across both numbers, and before children can say the expected 'thirty-four', *glide* down to '340' (300 + 40) and wait for 'three hundred and forty'; then glide again to 'three thousand four hundred'. Of course you can glide back up to '34'. This is a very economic and powerful demonstration of multiplying and dividing by 10.

After working on the hundreds, you can combine hundreds and units and expend one unit of the class's mental energy to learn where the word 'and' is placed for numbers such as 305, 'three hundred *and* five'. American counting does not require an 'and' in this type of number.

You will need to acquire a new cane-tapping skill as you will need to move from the '300' to the '5' with a halfway flourish for the 'and'. You need to watch the class at the same time as tapping the cane on the right numbers. Tricky.

'DODGY TENS' AND 'SILLY TEENS'

Next attack the 'Dodgy Tens' which can be called 'one-ty', 'two-ty', 'three-ty', 'four-ty' (nearly okay), 'five-ty' (oops), 'sixty', 'seventy', 'eighty' and 'ninety'. To be able to be most logical, start with 90. You can do any number, e.g. 493 or 795. Note where the 'and' comes (after the hundred). Discuss the not-quite-right names such as thirty, forty and fifty. Twenty is harder and the teens are downright silly.

The 'Silly Teens' will require a separate session when you and children are feeling confident about what has been learned so far. Eleven and twelve have to be treated as special words (Ifrah, 1998). The suffix '-teen' is in the wrong place logically, as we normally say the larger value first, e.g. '65' is 'sixty-five', whereas '16' is not 'teen-six' but 'six-teen'. The 'thir-' and 'fif-' are the same irregular roots as for the tens. Note when spelling that '40' is 'forty', but '14' is 'fourteen'. To make any sense of the teens you need to point to the ten and units in quick succession. Once you have made it this far then the rest of the chart is easy.

Note that the Gattegno chart includes a double line between hundreds and thousands, and between hundred thousands and millions. This is where the spaces or commas go when you are writing the symbols, e.g. 1 367 429 or 1,367,429. However, it is also where the logic starts again when you say the number. It is where you breathe. Here goes. 'One million, three hundred and sixty seven thousand, four hundred and twenty nine.' Phew! Oh, by the way, look where the 'ands' are.

> How do I say this? Three hundred and forty eight thousand and five

348 005

You can use place value cards to reinforce the '60' + '7' making '67'.

300 and 40   4 0 >   3 0 0 >

Knowing the underlying rules that govern the chart, and making these rules explicit through actions of the pointer and your discussion with the children, can help their understanding of the structure of the number system, because it closely resembles the algebra of the Gattegno chart. Each time you move the pointer down a row the number gets ten times bigger and conversely, perhaps inversely, each time you move up a row the number gets ten times smaller or a tenth of its previous value. You can emphasise this by a circular action with the end of the pointer on the number you have moved to.

> What is this number? Four hundred and five thousand

405 000

THE ALGEBRA OF THE CHART

Note that horizontally the numbers always start with the symbols 1 to 9 in the same order. So three, thirty, three hundred and three thousand are all under one another. Although apparently obvious, these facts need sharing, pointing out and discussing.

$\times$ 10 $\downarrow$	$\div$ 10 or $\times$ $^1/_{10}$ $\uparrow$
$\times$ 100 $\downarrow\downarrow$	$\div$ 100 or $\times$ $^1/_{100}$ $\uparrow\uparrow$
$\times$ 1000 $\downarrow\downarrow\downarrow$	$\div$ 1000 or $\times$ $^1/_{1000}$ $\uparrow\uparrow\uparrow$

- You can vary the chart by reducing the scope or changing it.
- You can make the numbers as large or small as you wish.

1	2	**3**	4	5
10	20	**30**	40	50
100	200	**300**	400	500
1000	2000	**3000**	4000	5000

Stressing powers of ten up and down

10^{-3}	0.001	mill-
10^{-2}	0.01	centi-
10^{-1}	0.1	deci-
10^0	1	–
10^1	10	deka-
10^2	100	hecto-
10^3	1000	kilo-

Following the same rules, you can make a grid from 1/1000 or 0.001 through the units to 9000, i.e. from 10^{-3} to 10^{+3}.

This scale links clearly with the metric system.

0.001	0.002	0.003	0.004	0.005	0.006	0.007	0.008	0.009
0.01	0.02	0.03	0.04	0.05	0.06	0.07	0.08	0.09
0.1	0.2	0.3	0.4	0.5	0.6	0.7	0.8	0.9
1	2	3	4	5	6	7	8	9
10	20	30	40	50	60	70	80	90
100	200	300	400	500	600	700	800	900
1000	2000	3000	4000	5000	6000	7000	8000	9000

RESOURCES

Gattegno chart available in pull-out supplement (Faux, 1998), overhead projector (OHP) or interactive whiteboard (IWB), a pointer such as a garden cane, ATM (2004) *Developing Number 2* software

N Numbers and the number system

CHANGING THE RULES FOR THE CHART

You could work out how the rest of the chart would look or how it would continue a few rows above the chart. The chart shown here is good for practising doubling and halving in a different way. Notice how some numbers appear more than once. Is there a pattern?

Can we change the rules?

1	2	3	4	5
2	4	6	8	10
4	8	12	16	20
8	16	24	32	40

What are the rules for this grid?

The following charts are essentially enhanced number lines with equivalent values above and below the line.

D

p. 187

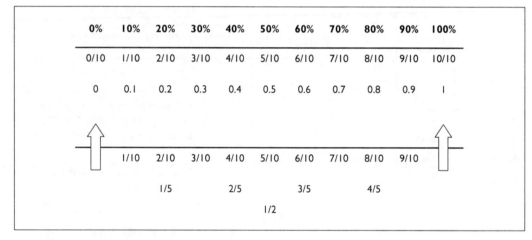

0%	10%	20%	30%	40%	50%	60%	70%	80%	90%	100%
0/10	1/10	2/10	3/10	4/10	5/10	6/10	7/10	8/10	9/10	10/10
0	0.1	0.2	0.3	0.4	0.5	0.6	0.7	0.8	0.9	1

	1/10	2/10	3/10	4/10	5/10	6/10	7/10	8/10	9/10	
		1/5		2/5		3/5		4/5		
					1/2					

This chart allows you to make explicit links between equivalent fractions and decimals and percentages. It also works as a probability scale.

The number line can go between any values you choose. So you can work on positive and negative numbers by creating a line from say $^-9$ through 0 to $^+9$.

You could use a chart with 0 pence to 100 pence (or £1), with all the values in pence and as decimal parts of a pound. If you put the equivalent percentage of £1 above these values, this will be useful when teaching decimals – you can say, 'Imagine it is money'.

0%	10%	20%	30%	40%	50%	60%	70%	80%	90%	100%
0/10	1/10	2/10	3/10	4/10	5/10	6/10	7/10	8/10	9/10	10/10
£0.00	£0.10	£0.20	£0.30	£0.40	£0.50	£0.60	£0.70	£0.80	£0.90	£1.00
0p	10p	20p	30p	40p	50p	60p	70p	80p	90p	100p

EQUIVALENCE GRIDS: USING A BLANK SCREEN

One of the most exciting ways of using 'Silent Way' is to present the children with a blank screen or board and start pointing, preferably at an imaginary '1' or some other suitable starting point.

This can be done, at first, with one chart. But when you have used a number of different grids and number lines with the children, they will have to work out which chart is in your mind, and decode the positions and rules.

There are some pieces of software that foster this kind of approach. The children have to *hypothesise* what is going on.

- Which way do the numbers increase?
- From left to right or right to left?
- Do they increase by a simple addition to form a straightforward arithmetic series, or is it more complicated?
- What happens vertically?
- The rules might be different.

I				16
	4			
3		12		
				64

Guess the rule!

USING OTHER LANGUAGES AND NUMBER SYSTEMS

Some languages, such as Spanish and Italian for example, have a similar logic to English. French has some interesting idiosyncrasies such as 'quatre vingt quinze' (4 × 20 + 15) for 95, and 'soixante dix neuf' (60 + 10 + 9) for 79. German is highly logical although the teens are similar to our teens. The units are said before the tens, 51 is 'one and fifty', 325 is 'three hundred five and twenty'. Chinese is the most logical and closely follows our Arabic number system. The Celtic tongues have their own logic: look at Irish, Welsh or Cornish. When chanting counting in another language the logic rings through, producing an awareness and insights that we cannot always realise in our own tongue. Here are five sets of European counting words to try out.

COUNTING IN FIVE EUROPEAN LANGUAGES

	English	French	Welsh	Irish	German
1	one	un	un	amháin	eins
2	two	deux	dau	dha	zwei
3	three	trois	tri	tri	drei
4	four	quatre	pedwar	ceathair	vier
5	five	cinq	pump	cuig	funf
6	six	six	chwech	se	sechs
7	seven	sept	saith	seacht	sieben
8	eight	huit	wyth	ocht	acht
9	nine	neuf	naw	naoi	neun
10	ten	dix	deg	deich	zehn
11	eleven	onze	un deg un	aon deag	elf
12	twelve	douze	un deg dau	do deag	zwölf
13	thirteen	treize	un deg tri	tri deag	dreizehn
14	fourteen	quatorze	un deg pedwar	ceathair deag	vierzehn
15	fifteen	quinze	un deg pump	cuig deag	funfzehn
16	sixteen	seize	un deg chwech	se deag	sechzehn
17	seventeen	dix-sept	un deg saith	seacht deag	siebzehn
18	eighteen	dix-huit	un deg wyth	ocht deg	achtzehn
19	nineteen	dix-neuf	un deg naw	naoi deag	neunzehn
20	twenty	vingt	dau ddeg	fiche	zwanzig
21	twenty-one	vingt et un	dau ddeg un	aon is fiche	ein und zwanzig
22	twenty-two	vingt-deux	dau ddeg dau	dha is fiche	zwei und zwanzig
30	thirty	trente	tri deg	triocha	dreißig
40	forty	quarante	pedwar deg	daichead	vierzig
50	fifty	cinquante	pump deg	caoga	fünfzig
60	sixty	soixante	chwe deg	seasca	sechzig
70	seventy	soixante-dix	saith deg	seachto	siebzig
80	eighty	quatre-vingt	wyth deg	ochto	achtzig
90	ninety	quatre-vingt-dix	naw deg	nocha	neunzig
100	one hundred	cent	cant	cead	hundert

THIS PAGE CAN BE PHOTOCOPIED FOR USE WITH YOUR CLASS

ONE TO NINE MILLION GATTEGNO CHART

1	2	3	4	5	6	7	8	9
10	20	30	40	50	60	70	80	90
100	200	300	400	500	600	700	800	900
1000	2000	3000	4000	5000	6000	7000	8000	9000
10 000	20 000	30 000	40 000	50 000	60 000	70 000	80 000	90 000
100 000	200 000	300 000	400 000	500 000	600 000	700 000	800 000	900 000
1 000 000	2 000 000	3 000 000	4 000 000	5 000 000	6 000 000	7 000 000	8 000 000	9 000 000

ZERO TO ONE EQUIVALENCE CHART

0%	10%	20%	30%	40%	50%	60%	70%	80%	90%	100%
0/10	1/10	2/10	3/10	4/10	5/10	6/10	7/10	8/10	9/10	10/10
0	0.1	0.2	0.3	0.4	0.5	0.6	0.7	0.8	0.9	1

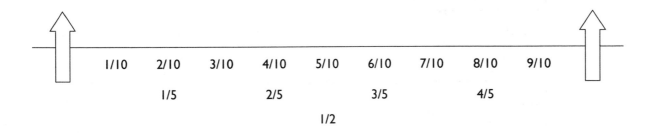

	1/10	2/10	3/10	4/10	5/10	6/10	7/10	8/10	9/10	
		1/5		2/5		3/5		4/5		
					1/2					

THIS PAGE CAN BE PHOTOCOPIED FOR USE WITH YOUR CLASS

N3 Arabic and other number systems

THINKING ABOUT NUMBER SYSTEMS

Britain is a multicultural society in which we need to appreciate and understand both ourselves and others.

No single culture has a monopoly on mathematical achievement. . . . Mathematical experience can be enriched by examples from a variety of cultures.

(Nelson *et al.*, 1993: p. 19)

Exploring the history of mathematics:

- provides access to a rich cultural heritage;
- shows the origins of ideas from different continents and times;
- shows how women as mathematicians have been systematically sidelined;
- reveals how ideas spread, were modified, developed and passed on;
- can encourage a world-view rather than a Eurocentric-view dominated by Greco-Roman thought and ethnocentrism.

We need to recognise the importance of mathematicians from around the world in order for mathematics to progress as a practical and universal language. Hearing the way counting is organised in other languages and cultures can help us to understand our own spoken counting system better. For example, which other languages have 'Silly Teens' as in English? Are they really so silly, or is there good reason for special words for 11 and 12? Linguistic similarities abound, e.g. many Arabic and Hebrew words for numbers are the same. The links between cultures can be heard and seen. Looking for patterns and the underlying logic in the way numerals are written deepens our understanding of place value and conventions for writing numerals.

Education ought to incorporate material from a variety of existing cultures to help all children live and work in a multicultural environment locally, nationally and internationally.

(adapted from Nelson *et al.*, 1993)

Talking numbers, making numbers
- Children can learn the names and numerals by pointing to the numerals and saying them together.
- Children can sit or stand in a circle or line each holding a number card and recite as a group, or individually, displaying their number when it comes up.
- You can use table-top number lines, grids or larger versions of these, for example using carpet tiles made into a line or rectangle.
- You can use the 1 to 9 000 000 chart with just the numerals in the 'Silent Way', with the children naming the numbers and building all the numbers from 1 to 9 999 999.

N2

p. 8

Children enjoy brief episodes of reciting together or taking turns in a naming game. For very young children this might involve touching each finger in turn and counting to ten, singing a song such as, 'One, two, three, four, five. Once I caught a fish alive'. For older children and adults it might involve 'Silent Way' naming of very large numbers or even using a different number system.

We can use other languages to help us notice the logic in our own system and seek out the logic in the systems of other cultures past and present.

THE ORIGINS OF SOME IDEAS

Some number systems have remained stable for thousands of years, so we can play at detecting the origins of ideas, listening for similarities and differences. Even though we have ten fingers and ten toes, there is evidence for number systems based on 2, 4, 5, 8, 10, 12, 20 and 60. The Babylonians, for example, regarded 60 as spiritually important. And we still use their 360 degrees in a circle – the most important big 'circular space' being, of course, the Earth – and the number of days in a year being approximately 360. We use a seven-day cycle for the week.

Some children and adults are fascinated by the way languages have developed. Consider September, October, November and December, where 'septem' means 7, 'octo' 8, 'novem' 9 and 'decem' 10. What about expressions such as the span of our life on Earth as 'three score and ten' years, when compared to 'quatre vingt dix'? Would we want to live to 90? Why are there 60 seconds in a minute, 60 minutes in an hour, and 24 hours in a day? Why have 7 days in a week? Doesn't everyone?

It is useful to teach the meanings of the following prefixes:

milli-   a thousandth, related to *mille*, a thousand (when a Roman soldier marched a mile he marched a thousand paces);

centi-   a hundredth, related to *centuum*, a hundred (the centigrade scale is from 0 to 100 divided up into a hundred parts – each is a hundredth; a cent is a hundredth part of a euro; a century is a hundred years or a hundred runs; a centurion had control over approximately a hundred men);

deci-   a tenth, related to *decem*, ten (to decimate means to kill or maim every tenth person, a technique used by the Romans to subdue those who would not submit to Roman rule; the decimal system is a system of tenths);

kilo-   is the old Greek word for a thousand.

These prefixes can be applied to every unit in the metric system. Normally micro- means a millionth, milli- a thousandth, kilo- a thousand and mega- a million; these are the most important ones used in scientific work.

Compare different number systems on the following pages and at the end of 'Saying and making numbers'. Look at the words, numbers and symbols in a range of languages. 'Say what you see' as you read them compare the symbols. How could you remember any of them? What patterns are there?

N2

p. 16

millimetre	pentagon			megawatt
			kilogram	
				millennium
duet	hexagon	triangle		
				heptagon

EXPLORING NUMBER SYSTEMS

Encourage children to talk about what they notice about the symbols and then transfer attention to the rhythms and patterns – ignoring the fact that you might not know the language! Which rhythms and patterns stand out? Which would you like to learn? Try to write 2004 – or your age, or any number – in any number system.

Can you find out when and in which country or continent these systems started? Are they still in use? Try an encyclopaedia such as Encarta, or try the Internet. Involve teachers and children in your school who have knowledge of other number systems and languages.

How do you think the symbols were made originally? With pebbles, sticks or shells; by making marks in the dust or sand; with a pen on paper; by scratching wax; or by pressing an object into soft clay? Can you find out about the significance of any of these symbols, and their original meanings. Use these tables or old documents, photographs, artefacts or pictures to study number systems.

Look at the table of words and numbers for five European languages (see p. 16). Say the words. Can you hear similarities and differences? Look across all the columns for one number such as 3 or 8. Study the table for the Korean number system (shown below). Notice how the horizontal lines are used. Can you see how the Korean system works? The pattern of rods is also used for the 8 compass points and 8 elements.

Can you find out how the symbols are written in the Arabic and Asian languages? Did you know that the Indian symbols were adopted and modified by the Arabs? They have been used unchanged for over a thousand years in the Arabic world. The West and Europe resisted using these new symbols in the 1500s. Some traders and merchants clung onto the awkward Roman numeral system. Now we all use the system developed in India centuries ago, adopted and adapted by the Arabic world and adopted by the West eventually in the sixteenth century. Some other systems worth studying are the Babylonian and Mayan systems.

	Korean	Binary	Force Pa Kua	Direction	Name
0	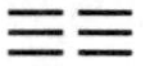 ☷	000	earth	north	kun
1	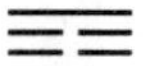 ☶	001	mountain	north west	ken
2	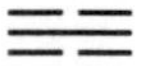 ☵	010	water	west	kan
3	 ☴	011	wind	south east	tui
4	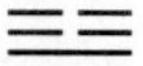 ☳	100	thunder	north east	chen
5	 ☲	101	fire	east	li
6	 ☱	110	steam	south west	sun
7	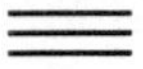 ☰	111	heaven	south	ch'ien
8	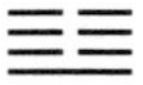	1000			
9		1001			
10	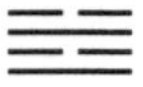	1010			

A CHINESE NUMBER SYSTEM

一	十一	二十一	三十一	四十一	五十一	六十一	七十一	八十一	九十一
二	十二	二十二	三十二	四十二	五十二	六十二	七十二	八十二	九十二
三	十三	二十三	三十三	四十三	五十三	六十三	七十三	八十三	九十三
四	十四	二十四	三十四	四十四	五十四	六十四	七十四	八十四	九十四
五	十五	二十五	三十五	四十五	五十五	六十五	七十五	八十五	九十五
六	十六	二十六	三十六	四十六	五十六	六十六	七十六	八十六	九十六
七	十七	二十七	三十七	四十七	五十七	六十七	七十七	八十七	九十七
八	十八	二十八	三十八	四十八	五十八	六十八	七十八	八十八	九十八
九	十九	二十九	三十九	四十九	五十九	六十九	七十九	八十九	九十九
十	二十	三十	四十	五十	六十	七十	八十	九十	百

A MAYAN NUMBER SYSTEM

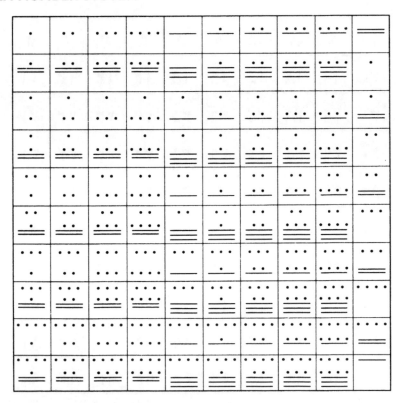

THIS PAGE CAN BE PHOTOCOPIED FOR USE WITH YOUR CLASS

N Numbers and the number system

BENGALI NUMBER SYSTEM

১	২	৩	৪	৫	৬	৭	৮	৯	১০
১১	১২	১৩	১৪	১৫	১৬	১৭	১৮	১৯	২০
২১	২২	২৩	২৪	২৫	২৬	২৭	২৮	২৯	৩০
৩১	৩২	৩৩	৩৪	৩৫	৩৬	৩৭	৩৮	৩৯	৪০
৪১	৪২	৪৩	৪৪	৪৫	৪৬	৪৭	৪৮	৪৯	৫০
৫১	৫২	৫৩	৫৪	৫৫	৫৬	৫৭	৫৮	৫৯	৬০
৬১	৬২	৬৩	৬৪	৬৫	৬৬	৬৭	৬৮	৬৯	৭০
৭১	৭২	৭৩	৭৪	৭৫	৭৬	৭৭	৭৮	৭৯	৮০
৮১	৮২	৮৩	৮৪	৮৫	৮৬	৮৭	৮৮	৮৯	৯০
৯১	৯২	৯৩	৯৪	৯৫	৯৬	৯৭	৯৮	৯৯	১০০

URDU NUMBER SYSTEM

۱۰	۹	۸	۷	۶	۵	۴	۳	۲	۱
۲۰	۱۹	۱۸	۱۷	۱۶	۱۵	۱۴	۱۳	۱۲	۱۱
۳۰	۲۹	۲۸	۲۷	۲۶	۲۵	۲۴	۲۳	۲۲	۲۱
۴۰	۳۹	۳۸	۳۷	۳۶	۳۵	۳۴	۳۳	۳۲	۳۱
۵۰	۴۹	۴۸	۴۷	۴۶	۴۵	۴۴	۴۳	۴۲	۴۱
۶۰	۵۹	۵۸	۵۷	۵۶	۵۵	۵۴	۵۳	۵۲	۵۱
۷۰	۶۹	۶۸	۶۷	۶۶	۶۵	۶۴	۶۳	۶۲	۶۱
۸۰	۷۹	۷۸	۷۷	۷۶	۷۵	۷۴	۷۳	۷۲	۷۱
۹۰	۸۹	۸۸	۸۷	۸۶	۸۵	۸۴	۸۳	۸۲	۸۱
۱۰۰	۹۹	۹۸	۹۷	۹۶	۹۵	۹۴	۹۳	۹۲	۹۱

THIS PAGE CAN BE PHOTOCOPIED FOR USE WITH YOUR CLASS

ARABIC NUMBER SYSTEM

٩	٨	٧	٦	٥	٤	٣	٢	١	٠
١٩	١٨	١٧	١٦	١٥	١٤	١٣	١٢	١١	١٠
٢٩	٢٨	٢٧	٢٦	٢٥	٢٤	٢٣	٢٢	٢١	٢٠
٣٩	٣٨	٣٧	٣٦	٣٥	٣٤	٣٣	٣٢	٣١	٣٠
٤٩	٤٨	٤٧	٤٦	٤٥	٤٤	٤٣	٤٢	٤١	٤٠
٥٩	٥٨	٥٧	٥٦	٥٥	٥٤	٥٣	٥٢	٥١	٥٠
٦٩	٦٨	٦٧	٦٦	٦٥	٦٤	٦٣	٦٢	٦١	٦٠
٧٩	٧٨	٧٧	٧٦	٧٥	٧٤	٧٣	٧٢	٧١	٧٠
٨٩	٨٨	٨٧	٨٦	٨٥	٨٤	٨٣	٨٢	٨١	٨٠
٩٩	٩٨	٩٧	٩٦	٩٥	٩٤	٩٣	٩٢	٩١	٩٠

INTERNATIONAL NUMBER SYSTEM

90	91	92	93	94	95	96	97	98	99
80	81	82	83	84	85	86	87	88	89
70	71	72	73	74	75	76	77	78	79
60	61	62	63	64	65	66	67	68	69
50	51	52	53	54	55	56	57	58	59
40	41	42	43	44	45	46	47	48	49
30	31	32	33	3	35	36	37	38	39
20	21	22	23	24	25	26	27	28	29
10	11	12	13	14	15	16	17	18	19
0	1	2	3	4	5	6	7	8	9

THIS PAGE CAN BE PHOTOCOPIED FOR USE WITH YOUR CLASS

N4 Working with grids

CLOUDS, INK BLOTS AND PAINT SPLASHES

Some teachers use ink blots, paint splashes or blank shapes to explain why some numbers on a number line, number grid or sum cannot be read. The task is to work out what is hidden.

N9, S1

pp. 51, 97

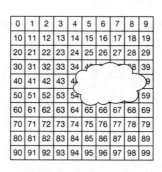

$7 \times \blacksquare = 21$

For the school fair each class has ● tables. Seven classes. Fourteen tables

Ink blots can be added to number lines, calculations, operations and word problems

- What's your guess?
- How do you know?
- Can you be sure?
- What else could the number be?
- What rules are you using?
- What was the key to unlocking the hidden number?

Clouds and blobs (or blots) can be used on number lines and number grids. They can also be used to obscure parts of calculations and word problems. Clouds and blobs can be as large or small as liked, but should, initially at least, obscure only a small part of the grid. The initial teaching point is to look at the visible parts of the grid and read the grid together with the children. Show them how to use what we know about the structure of the grid to work out the numbers that have been obscured. You can create opportunities in group follow-up work for the children to tackle different levels of difficulty, and give a different focus to different groups of children. One group could uncover blots on a number grid while others could look at numbers relating to operations, or specific numbers in written algorithms or in word problems.

Try using an overhead transparency (OHT) of a grid with paper clouds or an interactive white board with these facilities built into the software. You could also try a wall poster of a number grid and cardboard clouds. Posters can keep children's interest over several lessons.

Try an unconventional grid, for example a spiral grid. What size of cloud makes things easy or difficult to work out? Does it matter where you put the cloud?

72	73	74	75	76	77	78	79	80	81
71	42	43	44	45	46	47	48	49	83
70	41	20	21	22	23	24	25	50	83
69	40	19	6	7	8	?6	51	84
68	39	18	5	0	?		52	85
67	38	17	4	3	2	11	28	53	86
66	37	16	15	14	13	12	29	54	87
65	36	35	34	33	32	31	30	55	88
64	63	62	61	60	59	58	57	56	89
99	98	97	96	95	94	93	92	91	90

Children really enjoy whole class activities where they try to guess what is hidden. Ask them to write down the hidden numbers on their individual wipe boards. Encourage them to talk about their guesses and their reasoning. Your task is to learn from them which strategies they are using, and whether they have effective strategies to draw upon. Do their strategies work for all situations and all grids?

SNAKES AND WORMS

Because snakes have a head and a tail the children can think about the way the snake will move across a grid and the order in which it will cover or 'eat' the numbers. A straight snake moving over a conventional grid might eat a row or column of numbers such as: 14, 15, 16, 17, 18; or 14, 24, 34, 44, 54. The children have to predict which number it will eat next. Wiggly snakes can make the problem of predicting even more interesting.

Try making a spiral number line by curling a grid around a suitable cardboard cylinder so that you can keep going in a spiral from 1 to 100 or 0 to 99.

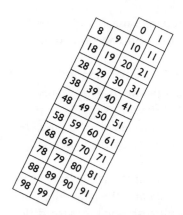

0	1	2	3	4	5	6	7	8	9
10	11	12	13	14	15	16	17	18	19
20	21	22	23	24	25	26	27	28	29
30	31	32	33	34	35	36	37	38	39
40	41	42	43	44	45	46	47	48	49
50	51	52	53	54	55	56	57	58	59
60	61	62	63	64	65	66	67	68	69
70	71	72	73	74	75	76	77	78	79
80	81	82	83	84	85	86	87	88	89
90	91	92	93	94	95	96	97	98	99

- What numbers would the snake eat if it didn't start from 14 but from a different point? What if this was: one number different? Five more? Ten less?
- What would the numbers be for a snake twice as long?
- Where could the snake go if it got to the end of a row or column?

Try making an unusual grid wrapped round a cylinder. Try snakes that follow wiggly paths across a grid

Arrange the children around the OHP or interactive whiteboard and show them a conventional 0 to 99 or 1 to 100 grid briefly for, say, 5 seconds. Count down 'Five, four, three, two, one, zero!' then cover the numbers with a mask containing a single square hole. Ask the children:

Where was the number 1? Where was 20? What about 55? Do you remember where 99 was? How do we see the numbers change as we look from top to bottom? Close your eyes and try to imagine the grid inside your head. Slide the large mask slowly across the grid. Only one number shows each time. If I keep moving in this direction what's the next number we are going to see?

The children offer predictions. If they have individual wipe boards you can ask them to write the number they expect to see next. 'Ready, steady, show!' You can see from their written answers who is guessing wildly and who understands the logic of the grid structure. They can work from your OHT, or move to using their own grids and masks from resources you have prepared beforehand.

MASKS AND HOLES

0	1	2	3	4	5	6	7	8	9
10									19
20									29
30							37		39
40									49
50		52							59
60		62							69
70		72	73						79
80									89
90	91	92	93	94	95	96	97	98	99

> • What kind of grid is this?
> • What number is above 37?
> • What number is below, to the right, to the left?
> • Write down the eight numbers which surround 37. How do you know you are right?

Masks can have a single hole, an 'L' shape that reveals a few numbers, or a hole with flaps around it that can be folded back

What are all the numbers around the revealed section? Prepare a mask with flaps that open around the single revealed number. How much of the grid can you complete? Later, try this using different number grids.

A further and harder step is to learn how to generalise what happens. 'What happens when I move the mask to the right?' (. . . left, up, down, diagonally . . .). You could also try this at the same time as introducing a different grid.

With children who can confidently navigate around a grid showing our Arabic numerals, you could explore alternatives using Chinese, Urdu or Bengali, or Mayan numerals.

N3

pp. 21–23

Ask the children which way to move the mask so that the number will change by 1.

Which way should the mask be moved to change the number by 10?

If you are brave, make up a suitable noise for:

(+1, right, forward) (−1, left, back)

such as a click, tap or step;

(+10, down) (−10, up)

such as a longer sounding horn, hum or buzz.

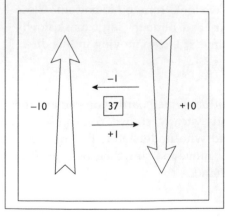

Use a large arrow on a visible part of the OHP to clearly indicate the direction and demonstrate this kinaesthetically. Use different colours for large horizontal and large vertical arrows. Remember that if you are facing the children, your left appears as their right. If you are facing the screen then the orientation is the same for everyone. Get the children to move their hands in the direction of the arrow. They may not know left from right linguistically. Some dyslexic children may find this work difficult because of the spatial/language combination. You can reinforce or even start this work using numbered floor tiles to make a huge grid on the floor before moving onto a poster number grid on the wall or board. Children can use their own versions in pairs on the table. Be careful when you move between the vertical plane of the wall or screen and the horizontal plane of the table or floor.

+	1	2	3	4	5	6	7	8	9	10
1	2	3	4	5	6	7	8	9	10	11
2	3	4	5	6	7	8	9	10	11	12
3	4	5	6	7	8	9	10	11	12	13
4	5	6	7	8	9	10	11	12	13	14
5	6	7	8	9	10	11	12	13	14	15
6	7	8	9	10	11	12	13	14	15	16
7	8	9	10	11	12	13	14	15	16	17
8	9	10	11	12	13	14	15	16	17	18
9	10	11	12	13	14	15	16	17	18	19
10	11	12	13	14	15	16	17	18	19	20

١٠	٩	٨	٧	٦	٥	٤	٣	٢	١
٢٠	١٩	١٨	١٧	١٦	١٥	١٤	١٣	١٢	١١
٣٠	٢٩	٢٨	٢٧	٢٦	٢٥	٢٤	٢٣	٢٢	٢١
٤٠	٣٩	٣٨	٣٧	٣٦	٣٥	٣٤	٣٣	٣٢	٣١
٥٠	٤٩	٤٨	٤٧	٤٦	٤٥	٤٤	٤٣	٤٢	٤١
٦٠	٥٩	٥٨	٥٧	٥٦	٥٥	٥٤	٥٣	٥٢	٥١
٧٠	٦٩	٦٨	٦٧	٦٦	٦٥	٦٤	٦٣	٦٢	٦١
٨٠	٧٩	٧٨	٧٧	٧٦	٧٥	٧٤	٧٣	٧٢	٧١
٩٠	٨٩	٨٨	٨٧	٨٦	٨٥	٨٤	٨٣	٨٢	٨١
١٠٠	٩٩	٩٨	٩٧	٩٦	٩٥	٩٤	٩٣	٩٢	٩١

- What happens if you change the type of grid?
- On an addition grid most numbers occur more than once in diagonals.
- Try a different number system.
- In an Arabic or Urdu number grid the numbers increase from right to left.

Make a variety of masks from paper to cover your OHT grids. Which shapes provide the best challenges? Try a hole of just one square, 2 × 2 (four squares), 1 × 4 (a line of four), 3, 4 or 5 (in an 'L' shape), 3 × 3 (in a cross) covering just five squares, or a strip of ten (horizontally or vertically). The more you give away the easier it is to work out the surrounding numbers. Most interactive white boards allow you a searchlight facility which works like a mask.

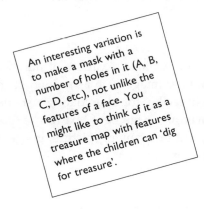

An interesting variation is to make a mask with a number of holes in it (A, B, C, D, etc.), not unlike the features of a face. You might like to think of it as a treasure map with features where the children can 'dig for treasure'.

0	1	2	3	4	5	6	7	8	9
10									19
20									29
30			A			B			39
40			□			47			49
50			C			D			59
60			64			67			69
70									79
80									89
90	91	92	93	94	95	96	97	98	99

Open and close the flaps one at a time after discussing what lies underneath. Start by revealing A.

What might lie under B?
How do you know?
Is it more or less than A?
What is the difference between A and B?
What happens if I move the mask? Let us try.
What is under D do you think?

Were you right?
What is the number between A and D?
What is the difference between A and D?
How do you know?
What happens if I move the mask down 2 places?
What is under A now?

Encourage the children to try and work out the underlying algebra – the rules for predicting the results of the movement. Can they say, for example: 'D is more than A'; 'D is the largest'; 'A is 3 places to the left of B so it must be B count back 3'; 'C is 2 places below A so it must be 2 lots of 10 more than A'.

Try moving to a new place on the grid.

SOME EXTENSION ACTIVITIES

Jigsaws

Make your own jigsaws by copying the number grids, then paste them on to different coloured card before cutting them up into irregular shapes. Store the pieces in separate labelled envelopes. How quickly can a child, pair or group put the pieces together? What strategies did they use? Which grids were easy to piece together? Why? (Change the number of pieces, the type of grid, the shapes of the pieces.)

Dominoes

N3

pp. 21–23

Children can make a set of dominoes for a different number systems, for example Chinese. Try putting one number system on one side with the equivalent symbols of a second on the reverse side? How many dominoes do you need for a double one to double six set?

Board games

'Snakes and Ladders' and other board games could be made using any number system grid. What special games do the children from the countries who use these number systems play?

Other hidden things

N4

pp. 29–31

Interactive white boards provide the facility to download a variety of number grids and to obscure a part of any page or place another image such as a cloud or ink blot over an existing page. There is also a searchlight facility for illuminating just one small part of a page. These facilities can be used over any page be it text (prose, poetry, a recipe, knitting pattern, a different language, . . .) or graphics (picture, image, graph, number line, number grid, diagram, geometric figures, . . .).

Try using a multiplication grid

O5

p. 86

On a multiplication grid, numbers with more than two factors occur more than once. Exposing the number 24 on a 12 × 12 multiplication grid provides a significant challenge. Is it 12 × 2, 3 × 8, 4 × 6, 6 × 4, 8 × 3 or 2 × 12? Each time the purpose is to reveal the algebra lying hidden within the grid. When teaching this at an early stage, *highlight* relevant numbers. When revising secure knowledge, use masks and blobs to hide numbers.

ZERO TO 99 GRID

0	1	2	3	4	5	6	7	8	9
10	11	12	13	14	15	16	17	18	19
20	21	22	23	24	25	26	27	28	29
30	31	32	33	34	35	36	37	38	39
40	41	42	43	44	45	46	47	48	49
50	51	52	53	54	55	56	57	58	59
60	61	62	63	64	65	66	67	68	69
70	71	72	73	74	75	76	77	78	79
80	81	82	83	84	85	86	87	88	89
90	91	92	93	94	95	96	97	98	99

SPIRAL GRID

73	74	75	76	77	78	79	80	81	82
72	43	44	45	46	47	48	49	50	83
71	42	21	22	23	24	25	26	51	84
70	41	20	7	8	9	10	27	52	85
69	40	19	6	1	2	11	28	53	86
68	39	18	5	4	3	12	29	54	87
67	38	17	16	15	14	13	30	55	88
66	37	36	35	34	33	32	31	56	89
65	64	63	62	61	60	59	58	57	90
100	99	98	97	96	95	94	93	92	91

ZIG-ZAG GRID

0	1	2	3	4	5	6	7	8	9
19	18	17	16	15	14	13	12	11	10
20	21	22	23	24	25	26	27	28	29
39	38	37	36	35	34	33	32	31	30
40	41	42	43	44	45	46	47	48	49
59	58	57	56	55	54	53	52	51	50
60	61	62	63	64	65	66	67	68	69
79	78	77	76	75	74	73	72	71	70
80	81	82	83	84	85	86	87	88	89
99	98	97	96	95	94	93	92	91	90

ADDITION GRID

+	1	2	3	4	5	6	7	8	9	10
1	2	3	4	5	6	7	8	9	10	11
2	3	4	5	6	7	8	9	10	11	12
3	4	5	6	7	8	9	10	11	12	13
4	5	6	7	8	9	10	11	12	13	14
5	6	7	8	9	10	11	12	13	14	15
6	7	8	9	10	11	12	13	14	15	16
7	8	9	10	11	12	13	14	15	16	17
8	9	10	11	12	13	14	15	16	17	18
9	10	11	12	13	14	15	16	17	18	19
10	11	12	13	14	15	16	17	18	19	20

MULTIPLICATION GRIDS

×	1	2	3	4	5	6	7	8	9	10	11	12
1	1	2	3	4	5	6	7	8	9	10	11	12
2	2	4	6	8	10	12	14	16	18	20	22	24
3	3	6	9	12	15	18	21	24	27	30	33	36
4	4	8	12	16	20	24	28	32	36	40	44	48
5	5	10	15	20	25	30	35	40	45	50	55	60
6	6	12	18	24	30	36	42	48	54	60	66	72
7	7	14	21	28	35	42	49	56	63	70	77	84
8	8	16	24	32	40	48	56	64	72	80	88	96
9	9	18	27	36	45	54	63	72	81	90	99	108
10	10	20	30	40	50	60	70	80	90	100	110	120
11	11	22	33	44	55	66	77	88	99	110	121	132
12	12	24	36	48	60	72	84	96	108	120	132	144

×	1	2	3	4	5	6	7	8	9	10
1	1	2	3	4	5	6	7	8	9	10
2	2	4	6	8	10	12	14	16	18	20
3	3	6	9	12	15	18	21	24	27	30
4	4	8	12	16	20	24	28	32	36	40
5	5	10	15	20	25	30	35	40	45	50
6	6	12	18	24	30	36	42	48	54	60
7	7	14	21	28	35	42	49	56	63	70
8	8	16	24	32	40	48	56	64	72	80
9	9	18	27	36	45	54	63	72	81	90
10	10	20	30	40	50	60	70	80	90	100

N Numbers and the number system

THIS PAGE CAN BE PHOTOCOPIED FOR USE WITH YOUR CLASS

N5 Working with target boards

TARGET AND MYSTERY NUMBERS

A 'target board' is simply a rectangular grid with a set of numbers on it. The skill is to provide a set of numbers which suit the current topic. Numbers can be large or small, integers, fractions or decimals, in fact anything you might think of connected to mathematics. The grid can be on a flip chart, paper, card, OHT, Excel spreadsheet or an interactive whiteboard. It can be used with children of all ages, and is simple to make, adapt and use.

Numbers can be pointed to with a pen or arrow, and covered with counters or coins as they are selected.

25	41	34	17	9
3	44	30	52	37
45	36	7	43	8
54	31	27	38	28

- Can you make 100 using any numbers on the board?
- Can you use more than 4 numbers?
- Can you make an answer of 1, 2, 3, 4, . . .?
- What strategies did you use?
- Explain your ideas to others.
- Find three linked numbers.

SI

p. 94

4	19	6	14	5
11	3	7	18	17
10	9	16	1	8
13	15	20	12	2

- An odd prime number < 20?
- Three numbers totalling 20?
- Half of one less than 3 × 7?
- How many prime numbers can you find on the board?
- Can you find any square numbers?

The boards can be used with a whole class, group or pairs of children. Using a target board with the whole class generates lots of opportunities for open and closed questions to the whole class, group or individual. This is a good way to work on your questioning techniques.

Here are a few activities that you might try out and then modify to make your own.

'Target Number'

This is similar to 'Countdown'. Carefully select a target number. The children have to work out how to get to that target using only numbers from the board. Each number can only be used once. Try specifying the number of steps to reach the target. For example, to make 100 how about (52 + 45 + 3) or (25 × 3 + 34 − 9) or ((7 − 3) × 25).

You could give points for each operation used, perhaps more for multiplication and division than addition and subtraction. Some targets are easy and others much harder. This work benefits from the use of wipe boards. Encourage children to use their jottings to explain their reasoning and how they reached the target.

Use a timer to put them under pressure. What makes a good target? What makes a good target board for this game?

'Mystery Number'

This is a game where clues are given. For example, which number on the target board is a multiple of 4, has a digit sum of 7 and is a square number? (16)

- Make up a set of boards with a simple two-step compound question and others with a more complex three-step question (differentiation by task). You could design a single board with two different sets of questions.

- Two children can play with a set of cards. Each card has a number and a list of properties. They take it in turns for one to describe the properties of the number shown and the other to guess the number.
- An alternative is to work on all the numbers and then swap boards with another group: first group to finish each stage is the winner. Have spare sets prepared and ready – and expect a noisy session!

COVER UP AND PAIRS

Cover up

Working with a single board and the whole class, ask for a number property such as, for example, *odd*. Children call out the odd numbers on the target board and you cover them up as fast as you can. This might keep you too busy, so let one of the children do the covering up. When you ask for multiples of 3 you are testing the children's knowledge of tables facts and the divisibility rule for 3.

It is useful to ask compound questions, where two bits of information are needed to find the answer. Asking for numbers >50 that are also prime numbers, or for numbers that are square and odd, requires children to combine their knowledge of more than one area of mathematics. Using compound questions is helpful for differentiating tasks for children with different levels of understanding.

This game can also be made into a Bingo-type game. Or another way of playing is for the children to suggest number properties, which will get rid of lots of numbers. They need to look for efficient strategies and find ways of forcing you to cover a number without saying what it is. You have to hang on to the numbers for as long as possible; they have to get rid of them by describing them without actually naming them. Making up the rules for this version will be fun.

It is an easy game to use with groups and pairs after teaching it to the whole class. You will find it easy to provide differentiated boards based around the same concepts.

Pairs

Typically this is for complements to 10 (9+1, 8+2, . . .), complements to 20 (19+1, 18+2, . . .) and complements to 100. It is also good for fractions and measures. So children can learn complements such as $7 + 3 = 10$, $8 + 2 = 10$, $19 + 1 = 20$, $15 + 5 = 20$. Complements to 100 look and feel harder ($43 + 57 = 100$) but it is useful to focus either on giving change from £1 or on the fact that the units figures will always be complements to 10 while the tens will always be complements to 9 (so for $43 + 57$, in the units we have 3 plus 7 making 10 and in the tens we have 4 and 5 making 9).

Children quickly learn 100s complements if you suggest that they think of a 100 pence making up a pound. Therefore $0.43 + 0.57$ is easier if thought of as money or percentages.

15%	99%	75%	90%	5%
45%	30%	70%	85%	40%
35%	60%	95%	10%	50%
25%	55%	20%	65%	80%

- Find pairs that total 100%.
- Which pairs are closest in value?
- How many are <50%?
- What would a better board look like?

25 cm	0.5 m	36 cm	75 cm	45 cm
$\frac{4}{5}$ m	3 m	$\frac{1}{5}$ m	50 cm	$\frac{3}{4}$ m
1 m	55 cm	0.64 m	0.1 m	$\frac{1}{4}$ m
1.05 m	2 m	90 cm	$\frac{1}{2}$ m	95 cm

- Find pairs of numbers with the same value.
- Are there three numbers with the same value?
- Combine numbers to make a whole metre.
- Rewrite the board using only one type of unit.

'DIFFERENCES', 'GUSINTER', DOUBLING AND HALVING

The pairs activity is fine for work on doubles and halves. Double 10 → 20 or halve 4 → 2. Here there is a simple mapping between the first and second number. This can also be applied usefully to algebraic expressions such as $(3x + 5) → (6x + 10)$. The target boards need to be designed so that all the pairs work out. *Any* relationship between two numbers or expressions can make them a pair.

'Differences'

This is an unusual game we invented when looking for ways to use target boards. The game works well for mixed numbers, i.e. a whole number and a fraction, money or measures. The first activity could be to look for a difference of 2: $(2¼ − ¼)$, $(3½ − 1½)$ and so on. What is the biggest difference you can make on the board? The activity forces children to look at the range of numbers on the board from smallest to largest. What is the smallest difference? This makes children look at the proximity of the numbers to one another. What is the largest sum you can make with any two numbers? (Quickly gets boring once they know the strategy.) What is the smallest sum you can make with any two numbers? (Also soon becomes too easy.) Which will produce the smallest odd difference? Which pairs produce a difference that is in the 3 times table? This is harder, but could be frustrating. Why not let the children devise the questions: if they can, then they really understand the mathematical ideas.

£1.25	£2.75	£0.75	£2.25	£3.75
£1.50	£0.50	£2.00	£1.00	£3.00
£2.50	£1.75	£0.25	£2.80	£4.00
£0.20	£1.30	£1.25	£3.25	£3.30

- Find pairs of values which differ by £1, £2.
- Make up a similar board of your own.
- Design boards for use with seconds, litres and grams.

2	51	4	12	9
15	3	30	52	17
45	24	6	34	8
5	13	27	8	5

- Look for the smallest numbers.
- Which numbers do they go into?
- Which numbers are left?
- Are they prime numbers?
- Are they factors of other numbers left over?
- Can you be sure?

'Gusinter'

The Yorkshire version of division sums or 'goes into'! Actually it is really factors and multiples: 3 → 6; 12 → 24. It is interesting to create a board with two or more strings of multiples which perhaps cross. You can put a clean OHT on top and draw the links from one multiple to the next – but it does get messy.

Doubling and halving

This is just a special case of strings of pairs, but doubling and halving are well worth working at. Children can use different colours to show each string, sometimes starting with the largest number to practise halving, sometimes starting with the smallest to practise doubling: 16 → 8 → 4 → 2 → 1 or 7 → 14 → 28 → 56 → 112 → 224 → 448 → 896.

WHO IS IN CONTROL?

Guess what this board is designed for

Here is a meta-cognitive game where you look at a new board and try to work out what games you can use it for. Why is it designed this way? This is a subtle way of asking the children: 'What have we been doing recently that I might want to quiz you on?'

A good opening gambit for risk-takers is to ask: 'What game would be good to play with this board?'

Or you could try: 'I've found this new game, but there are no rules! So, please look at the board for a minute then talk to your maths partner about what you think we could do with this board. What might the rules be? Swap ideas on your table then pick out the best ones to report back to the whole class.'

You will find out some of what they know about the numbers on the board and the relationships between them, as well as what games and rules they favour.

72	739	277	386	736
201	185	687	281	284
614	425	241	333	109
390	462	318	538	891

0.25	0.5	10%	half	$^1/_{10}$
I	$^1/_4$	100%	75%	50%
60%	$^1/_2$	25%	0.45	55%
0.75	0.1	$^3/_4$	I in 4	0.6

The dynamics of the lesson are very different once you move the locus of control towards the class and away from you, the teacher. With this 'teacher who doesn't know the rules or the game' gambit, control is firmly with the children. Let them give you ideas, genuinely teach you and offer their suggestions.

EXTENSIONS

- You do not need a grid, the numbers could be loose cards, random numbers on a page, cards on a line, or tiles on the floor.

- Give children blank grids to re-work an existing grid. Round up or down, change units, convert fractions to decimals or decimals to percentages, etc.

- Try any of the above ideas, but with a time limit. Get the children to work silently, writing their responses on a wipe board or on paper. Then check and discuss.

- Turn the above ideas into 'people maths' activities where each child has a number pinned to them. You give them instructions about what to look for and they move around the playground or hall looking for their complement, or the smallest difference, or their equivalent (0.5 with ½), and so on. Depending on the rules you set, they can hold hands to make long strings or chains of linked numbers.

N1

p. 2

A further source of ideas is Roger Bird (2001) *Target Boards*, on which we have based some of these activities.

A RANGE OF TARGET BOARDS

4	19	6	14	5
11	3	7	18	17
10	9	16	1	8
13	15	20	12	2

Complements (20)

4	16	32	6	3
2	0.5	128	64	12
10	24	16	1	8
1.5	192	48	12	96

Doubling and halving

25	41	34	17	9
3	44	30	52	37
45	36	7	43	8
54	31	27	38	28

Mystery number; Triads

2	51	4	12	9
15	3	30	52	17
45	24	6	34	8
5	13	27	8	5

Multiples of 3

25 cm	0.5 m	36 cm	75 cm	45 cm
$\frac{4}{5}$ m	3 m	$\frac{1}{5}$ m	50 cm	$\frac{3}{4}$ m
1 m	55 cm	0.64 m	0.1 m	$\frac{1}{4}$ m
1.05 m	2 m	90 cm	$\frac{1}{2}$ m	95 cm

Equivalents and complements (lengths)

£1.25	£2.75	£0.75	£2.25	£3.75
£1.50	£0.50	£2.00	£1.00	£3.00
£2.50	£1.75	£0.25	£2.80	£4.00
£0.20	£1.30	£1.25	£3.25	£3.30

Differences and complements (£)

15%	99%	75%	90%	5%
45%	30%	70%	85%	40%
35%	60%	95%	10%	50%
25%	55%	20%	65%	80%

Pairs; complements

72	739	277	386	736
201	185	687	281	284
614	425	241	333	109
390	462	318	538	891

Differences and complements

0.25	0.5	10%	half	$\frac{1}{10}$
1	$\frac{1}{4}$	100%	75%	50%
60%	$\frac{1}{2}$	25%	0.45	55%
0.75	0.1	$\frac{3}{4}$	1 in 4	0.6

Equivalents and complements

2	51	4	12	9
15	3	30	52	17
45	24	6	34	8
5	13	27	8	5

'Gusinter'

THIS PAGE CAN BE PHOTOCOPIED FOR USE WITH YOUR CLASS

GUESS MY NUMBER

Twenty questions but six would be better! This activity is useful for developing children's ability to question effectively. The teacher needs to provide sufficient but necessary scaffolding to help the children to find the number and also to understand why it can be deduced. The target is to try to guess the number with only six questions.

Write down the number secretly somewhere, on the back of the flip chart or on a slip of paper. Encourage the children to consider what makes a good question, and to explain their deductions. Ask for or use alternative language.

Here are some suggestions for different ways of doing this activity:

- purely mentally;
- mentally but writing down logical deductions;
- mentally, but writing down the questions and answers;
- mentally with the questions, answers and deductions all written down.

The children ask the questions, the teacher scribes. A number line or grid can also be used.

No.	Children's questions	Answers	Deductions. Children's words?	
I	Is it even?	No	It must be odd. (An integer I hope?)	
2	Is it >50?	No	It is in the range 0 to 50.	
3	Is it <25?	No	It must lie between 25 and 50.	
4	Is it divisible by 3?	No	It is not 27, 33, 39, 45 (can't be even).	
5	Is it a square number?	Yes	It could be 25, not 36; could be 49.	
6	Is it 49?	Yes	HOORAY!	

Additional aids could be:

- a number line, number grid, Base 10 apparatus, Cuisenaire Rods;
- crossing off, or covering up the numbers that have been excluded (try colours);
- a target board with the mystery number somewhere on the board;
- money.

Or you could play the game with different ranges of numbers:

- try 0 to 9 or 1 to 10; 0 to 99 or 1 to 100; 0 to 1000; and so on;
- 0 to $^-$99; $^-$99 to $^+$99; and so on;
- Use percentages, decimals, fractions ... 0 to 1 with decimals or fractions.

Encourage the children to find alternative ways of asking questions, for example:

- Is it more than 50? Is it greater than 50?
- Is it less than or equal to 50? Is it in the range 51 to 99?
- Is it even? Is it divisible by 2? Does it end in 0, 2, 4, 6 or 8?

Collect and compare elegant questions and strategies. Could they be of use elsewhere in mathematics? Might they be useful in other curriculum areas? Can we use what we have learned outside school?

N6 Working with sets

MAKING MATHEMATICS REAL FOR YOUNG CHILDREN

Zoë Evans (1985) describes how to use toys, boxes, exciting objects and cloths to stimulate and engage young children. She relates her activities, which often involve working with a group of children on the bare floor or mats, to problem-solving and logic in mathematics.

For example, we can take a set of creatures to explore mathematical ideas or issues such as friendship. What could you discuss, given a small group of two hedgehogs, two moles (one huge, the other tiny), or two rats (one plastic or rubber, and one furry)? (You could use, for example, a teasel for one hedgehog and a stone for the other; and make similar substitutions for the other creatures.) With this smaller set, issues such as friendship, feeding, homes, sizes, partners can be approached imaginatively. Are mole and hedgehog friends? What will they eat at dinner time? Put the six animals into two groups of friends. Explain why you have grouped them like this. Can you make a playground for them, a house or room for them to live in?

Other examples, which can be logic sets, include the following.

> The *Number Crew*, the *Tweenies* and similar TV programmes work on children's real hopes and fears and open up a whole range of issues relevant to children as well as maths. Some of this work encourages children to use puppets or toys to stand in their place, unleashing the power for the child to be 'self' in role as well as 'other' in role.

'Presents'

This activity uses a set of boxes/parcels wrapped in interesting wrapping paper. The boxes are different shapes (cube, cuboid, triangular prism, tetrahedron, square pyramid, . . .), different sizes and different weights, and they contain things which make a sound when shaken, such as rice, a cat-bell or pebbles. Children can handle the boxes and suggest what might be inside, what kind of present it might be and who it might be for.

So the child is engaged by the appearance of the object and by imagining what it might contain. Children are often surprised that the largest box is not necessarily the

N8
p. 44

S2
p. 102

S4
pp. 114, 116

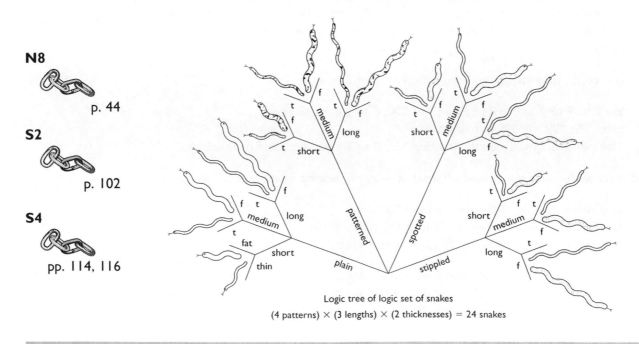

Logic tree of logic set of snakes
(4 patterns) × (3 lengths) × (2 thicknesses) = 24 snakes

heaviest. This attribute is specifically built into the set of boxes to provoke and disturb young children's concept of size and weight (mass).

The set may or may not be a logic set and the covering may or may not have significance. Boxes could be covered in materials that feel very different, such as fur fabric, satin, flannel, corduroy, plastic film or fine sandpaper. This can also lead to work on trying to classify, sort and organise the boxes.

'Snakes'

This uses a set of fabric-covered shapes with different fillings such as kapok, foam rubber, polyester fibre, sand or lentils, giving them all a very different density and feel. The largest are not necessarily the heaviest. They are thin or fat, with forked or straight tongues. Their eyes can be different shapes and colours. Fabrics can be selected for their patterns and/or texture. Children can sort, match and order the snakes in many different ways, even suggesting why particular snakes wish to be together. Fundamental work on measurement is easy with 'Snakes'.

'Teddies'

This activity allows each child to bring his or her own teddy to the group. List and sort the teddies' names. Sort and order the teddies. Use them in a simulated picnic where children plan what to do, and then gather and make place mats, sandwiches, cakes, drinks and hats for the teddies.

'Dogs'

This activity uses a set of six dogs of different sizes, each with their own lead, bed, bowl and bone. The teacher can explore size differences and can set up a range of situations with some or all the dogs and their equipment. Children discuss and decide which lead, bed, bowl and bone goes with which dog. What happens if the largest dog ends up with the shortest lead or smallest bone, bowl or bed? Is this a better situation than the reverse where the smallest dog ends up with a big bed, bowl, bone and long heavy lead? What happens if not all the sizes of leads, beds, bowls and bones are available? What are the limits to functionality? Whose lead is missing? Which dog is missing? How many bones should each dog have and what sizes should they be?

> My model for place value, dreamt up as a student working in a chocolate factory, is as follows:
>
> 10 sweets in a bag or tube or ten pieces of chocolate in the bar
> 10 bags, tubes or bars in a box
> 10 boxes in a carton
> 10 cartons on a palette
> 10 palettes in a lorry
> 10 lorryloads on a train
> 10 trainloads into the hold of a ship
>
> How many sweets is that then?

'Chickens and Eggs in Their Nests'

This activity uses a set that offers great potential for all four rules! Each chicken has a nest into which children can put a number of eggs. Eggs can be collected into egg boxes. Boxes of ten are now available. You can use pebbles for eggs and small bamboo baskets as nests. Buy or make toy chickens and chicks.

'Trains, Carriages and People'

This activity is similar to 'Chickens and Eggs in Their Nests'. Here you can have quite large numbers of Play People in a carriage and join carriages to make a train.

A logic set for possible football strips with 4 different shirts, 3 different shorts and 2 different pairs of socks?

Shirts (4)

Shorts (3)

Socks (2)

$2 \times 3 \times 4 = 24$ different strips

N7 Working with square numbers

SQUARE NUMBERS

The square numbers are positive integers produced by multiplying each number by itself. The pattern of square numbers can be represented using a pegboard.

×	1	2	3	4	5
1	1	2	3	4	5
2	2	4	6	8	10
3	3	6	9	12	15
4	4	8	12	16	20
5	5	10	15	20	25

Pegboards and multiplication tables create strong visual images with the square numbers following a diagonal pattern.

Number	1	2	3	4	5	6	?	?
Square	1	4	9	16	?	?	?	?

- How many pegs are needed to fill a one-by-one square; a two-by-two square; etc.?
- Where can you find the 'square numbers' in a multiplication table?
- Continue the pattern: 1, 1; 2, 4; 3, 9; 4, 16; . . .
- How many factors do the square numbers have?

The teacher could start by providing a very different looking table, such as the one shown above. This emphasises the relationship between each counting number and its square. Children who respond well to visual patterns will find it relatively easy to read and predict the next numbers in the sequence.

Children can go on to find the differences between successive square numbers (the difference between 1 and 4 is 3, the difference between 4 and 9 is 5, . . .). This can be created visually using coloured Click Cubes.

Someone who is comfortable with algebraic expressions will know that it is possible to read $y = x^2$ as if it was a recipe or a set of instructions. Think of any number you like, and imagine the expression rewritten with your number in place of the x, for example, $y = 3.5^2$. Now carry out the calculation by squaring 3.5 and the result will be the value of y when $x = 3.5$. Put these in a table of results so that the patterns are easier to find.

O5

p. 87

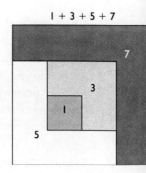

1 + 3 + 5 + 7

y	12.25	16	20.25		
x	3.5	4.0	4.5	5.0	

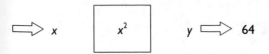

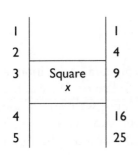

It is important to get a dynamic sense of what is happening as the two sets of numbers change. If we can do this, we are more likely to get a feel for the mathematics involved. Kinaesthetic awareness can come from using a calculator which has a square function. The key pressings form a routine and each set of pressings can be associated with the visual read-out. Some people respond very well to diagrams that incorporate a sense of movement. Both the *function machine* and the *mapping* encourage a left to right reading.

> Think of a positive whole number (x). Put your number into the squaring machine and see what comes out (y).

We can also read the function machine and the mapping from right to left and 'undo' or reverse the squaring process.

> If 64 comes out of the function machine, what number was put in? What happens to fractions, decimals and negative numbers?

D

p. 185

We need to provide different types of representations and find a way to bridge the connections between algebraic, geometric and arithmetic representations of the same mathematical ideas. We can explore the arithmetic of square numbers by collecting and listing them. The algebraic relationships emerge when we look at growth patterns, reversibility and differences between successive square numbers. We also need a knowledge of negative numbers and their squares when using graphical methods. Making lists and tables of findings helps with spotting patterns.

For $y = x^2$ a value of 0 for x produces a value of 0 for y. When x is given the value 1 then y becomes 1. When we substitute -1 for x the corresponding value for y is still positive $(+)1$. If we make $x = 10$ then y becomes 100. The resulting graph has a pleasing shape and symmetry.

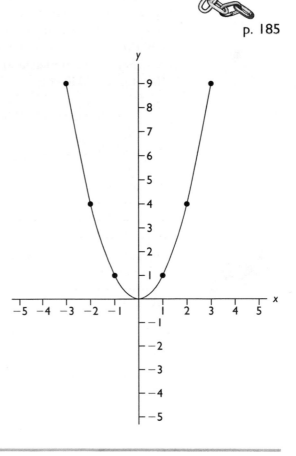

N8 **Exploring algebra**

ALGEBRA RULES AND PATTERNS

We can think about algebra as the study of rules. There is an algebra of addition, an algebra of multiplication, an algebra of co-ordinate geometry, and so on. We can look at 5 × 6 arithmetically and recall the answer as 30. However, once we begin to look at the calculation in more general terms as the product of an even and an odd number, we are beginning to think algebraically. All of a sudden the rules of multiplication in different situations become important. We can ask whether an odd number times an even number always results in an even number product. To answer this we need to know the rules of the situation.

The early versions of the National Curriculum emphasised links between algebra and pattern-making activities, and pattern-making is a good place for teachers to begin. Can young children detect the rules of a repeating pattern? One way of checking is to see if they can predict the next item. Red, green, red, green, red, green, . . . ? The child who consistently gives the correct answer to, 'What comes next?' is reading the situation algebraically. All the work we do with the laws of arithmetic can be developed algebraically by getting the children to use arithmetic to answer the question 'What comes next?'.

The algebra curriculum in primary schools can begin with pattern recognition of objects and then develop to include the study of simple rules of arithmetic, before moving on to more complex work with number sentences and equations. In this way algebra extends from the Foundation Stage through into Key Stage 1 and Key Stage 2. A further benefit is the potential for unification that algebra brings. Children's understanding of mathematics is developed more effectively when we teach algebraic understanding alongside numbers. Algebra provides opportunities to develop the skills of:

- logic, reasoning and proof, through activities such as prediction and creating inverse operations such as 'undoing' subtraction with addition;
- finding equivalence, disproving by counter-example, proving by induction, solving problems with an unknown (what goes in the box if 5 + □ = 12?);
- writing and solving equations.

Algebraic understanding can be supported, for example, by investigating odd and even numbers using Click Cubes. A stick of eight cubes can be broken into two equal towers, but can we do the same with nine? What about ten? Suppose we say that eight makes two *even* towers (four high) and nine makes two *odd* towers (a four and a five). Can we find some more even numbers? Can we guess which numbers will be odd before we break the stick into two pieces? Can we predict for 999, 1000 and 1001 without using cubes but just by imagining and using what we've just learned from the algebra of the situation?

O5

p. 82

SOME ALGEBRAIC GAMES

Patterns can be created using word games or through the use of familiar objects, for example by drawing a sequence of shapes such as square, triangle, square, triangle, . . .

Children can be encouraged to make their own repeating patterns using print media in art sessions. Sequences can be made with threaded beads and repeated movements can form dance sequences in Physical Education (PE). All these activities offer opportunities for pattern recognition, stating the rule, inventing your own rule, and using the rule to predict what comes next.

It is useful to do plenty of work with activities that emphasise rule-keeping, structure and pattern but which do not involve counting numbers. These activities can also be used to encourage a search for pattern and structure.

My Granny likes apples but she doesn't like pears.
My Granny likes ambulances but she doesn't like fire engines.
My Granny likes apricots but she doesn't like pineapples.
Guess something else that my granny likes!

A stick of Click Cubes can be lifted slowly from a feely bag, or brought out slowly from behind a flip chart. This activity is very much enhanced by using a glove puppet and asking the puppet to predict what the next colour is likely to be. When the children start calling out the correct prediction, the puppet can become puzzled and unsure, or start to get things wrong. The teacher asks the children to help the puppet by explaining their prediction.

Teacher: 'Yellow, red, orange, orange, yellow, red, orange, orange. What's going to be next?'

Children: 'Yellow!'

Puppet: 'I'm not sure. I really want a blue one to be there next time. I like blue, it's my favourite.'

Teacher: 'Can anyone explain why it's not going to be blue next?'

Play People, toy trains with carriages, plastic shapes, can all be pulled slowly from a tunnel or from behind a cloth where they've been hidden. These activities emphasise the internal structure that applies to each set of objects. Knowledge of the structure and the ability to apply the rule(s) allows us to predict what comes next.

These early activities can lead directly to number work: for example looking at the number patterns produced when we add 5 to a starting number such as 3. Alternatively it can lead to more sophisticated work with cubes on growth patterns. The children can make simple growth patterns that follow a rule. The teacher asks everyone: 'Say what you see.'

GROWTH PATTERNS

I can see 3 up each side and then 4 up each side then 5 up each side. The tops change by 2 each time.

I can see the sides go up by 1 each time and the tops go up by 2 each time.

I can see that the growth is 4 each time, 9, 13, 17, so 4 times the position plus 5 will tell you how many you need to build the next shape. So it's a $4p+5$ pattern.

The National Curriculum for Key Stage 1 requires that children are taught to 'create and describe number patterns', and at Key Stage 2 they are taught to 'understand and investigate general statements' and 'search for patterns in their results, develop logical thinking and explain their reasoning'. If we combine the use of Click Cubes with these National Curriculum requirements, we can create some interesting activities that support algebraic work.

Useful resources include graphs, grids and mappings, number squares, multiplication tables, Cuisenaire Rods and function machines. Children enjoy making physical 'function machines' and the activity lends itself to cross curriculum work.

Function machines and mapping activities are useful activities for practising arithmetic and for using and applying known number facts. Increasingly complex machines can be designed and their operations can be reversed – supporting an important algebraic idea (e.g. that multiplication can be 'reversed' by division).

A starting point can be through the use of shapes. By making up rules about what a function machine will do to a shape pushed into it, children can apply the rules and predict what the function machine will produce as an output.

N3

pp. 21–23

N4

pp. 29–31

O5

p. 80

N6

p. 38

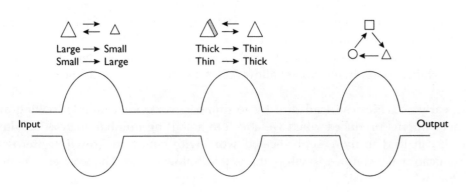

FUNCTION MACHINES

If we put a large shape in, it will be shrunk and a small shape will be enlarged. A thick shape will be made thin and a thin shape will be made thick. Squares will be become triangles, triangles will become circles and circles will become squares. Tell me what will happen to a small red thin circle?

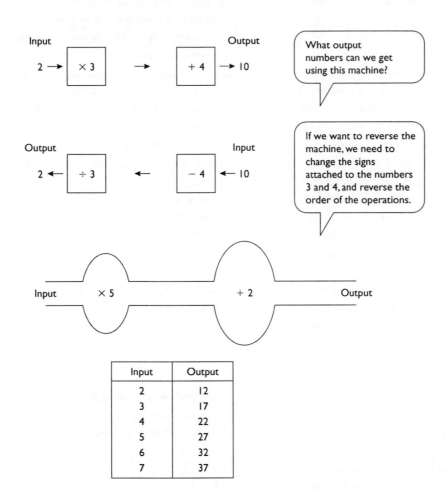

Children learn that the four rules of number (addition, subtraction, multiplication and division) can be thought of as operations that are carried out using a machine: there is an input, an operation and a result or output. A similar activity can be set up using a calculator with a function key, or using a computer. A useful teaching resource is the Teacher Training Agency (TTA) booklet *Using ICT to Meet Teaching Objectives in Mathematics.*

O3

p. 66

Progression for developing algebraic thinking and skills – an example

Sorting and grouping common objects by different criteria, both given and chosen.

Responding to teacher's questions with simple explanations and reasons.

Grouping all the seashells and separating them from the conkers.

Putting all the jigsaws in the correct cupboard, putting other games elsewhere.

All these words are names of animals, . . .

Games such as 'My Granny Likes' . . . apples but she doesn't like pears . . .

Recognising patterns in a collection of objects, words, music, dance etc. being able to follow them, and then invent your own examples.

Working to improve different memory types: pattern, spatial, recognition and semantic – facts, definitions, classifications and episodic – filmic, narrative, procedural.

Offering and inviting explanations of the rules, explaining why a rule has been broken, and what is needed to put things right again.

Red lorry, yellow lorry, red lorry, yellow lorry, . . .

Apple, plum, peach, cherry, apple, plum, peach, cherry, . . .

Loud, soft, soft, loud, soft, soft, . . .

Jump, crouch, hop, hop, step, jump, crouch, hop, hop, step, . . .

Pellmanism, Snap, Kim's game, Happy Families (but beware the stereotypes, e.g. all white, all married – Mr and Mrs, etc.)

Predicting the next item in the sequence.

Providing reasoned arguments for your predictions: 'I think the next one's got to be 3 because . . .'

Square, triangle, square, triangle, . . .

1, 2, 3, 4, 5, . . .

7, 6, 5, . . .

1, 2, 1, 2, 1, 2, . . .

2, 4, 6, 8, . . .

1, 1, 2, 3, 5, 8, 13, . . .

And then, what about: apple, elephant, tie, egg, . . . buffalo, orange, . . . (could it possibly be a sequence? How will you ever know?)

Using symbols and boxes to represent possible solutions to simple number sentences.

Forming equalities and inequalities in written number sentences. Finding solutions in a variety of contexts.

Learning to write and read number sentences and interpret their meaning.

$5 > \square$

$5 + 2 = \square + \square$

$7 + 3 \neq \square$

$3 \square 2 = \triangle$ (no operator given)

Working on inverse. If I double 6 – how can you undo what I've done? (I can get back again by halving 12.)

Introduce division as 'undoing' mutiplication

$54 \div 6 = \square$ Let's try $6 \times \square = 54$

Playing computer games like 'Blocks' which can also be played as a table-top game with three dice, paper-and-pencil, Number Cards or Fans.

$\square + \square = 24$

$\square \bigcirc \square \bigcirc \square = 24$ ($\bigcirc$ means any operator)

Interpreting and solving number problems. Offering explanations and reasons.	'I'm thinking of a rod that is as long as two red rods plus a white rod. Which rod am I thinking of?' 'I'm thinking of a whole number that's one less then half of 26. Tell me my number.' 'I tried taking one away from 26 but that didn't really help.' 'Try doing the halving first.' 'Let's play there and back again. I start at 11, add 3 multiply by 2 and arrive at 28. Can you take me back again by undoing what I did?'
Verbally expressing relationships.	We found out that every minute, the temperature went down by 4 degrees.
Writing problems and solutions to number problems in words and pictures. Identifying and following written rules of procedure.	'I'm going to invent a rule then write it out in steps for my partner to try.' (1) Think of a number. (2) Halve it. (3) Then add one.
Distinguishing between discrete counts and continuous measures.	Measures such as temperature, height and weight are continuous. They are never exact and measurement is only ever an approximation. Shoe sizes, dress sizes, days of the week and months are discrete. You can't have 'Wednesday and a tenth'.
Writing algebraic sentences accompanied by evidence of reasoning and explanation.	'If everyone in my family kissed each other once, we'd all get 5 kisses and there'd be 15 kisses all together. Guess how many there are in my family. I think it's $f(f-1)/2 = 15$ so $f = 6$ I think you've got 6 people in your family and everyone gets 5 kisses because they don't kiss themselves!
Developing logical thinking that makes it possible to argue the value of the 100th term in the series, without generating all 100 terms.	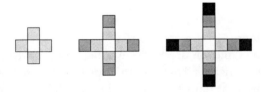

FOUR SIMILAR INVESTIGATIONS WITH DIFFERENT CONTEXTS

Traffic lights

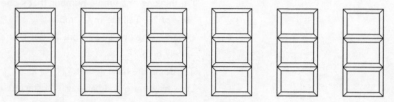

Use linking cubes (Multilink) to make all the different combinations for one red, one green and one orange (amber) cube. The children can start with the traffic light colours in order. How else could these three cubes be arranged? Be systematic and start with one colour then two then the three traffic light colours.

This shows the 3! = $3 \times 2 \times 1$ (three factorial) aspect well.

Extend this activity to bell or chime bar ringing. What could happen with four colours, four chime bars.

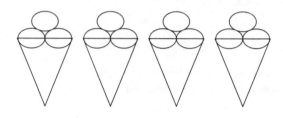

Ice creams

Ask the children what their favourite ice cream flavours are? (Write them in a list with appropriate coloured blobs alongside.) The children can choose up to three different flavours from this list, and they can have up to three balls/scoops of ice cream: all the same flavour; two the same and one different; or all three different. (Give the children a prepared sheet with blank dishes or cones with space for three scoops.) Colour in their favourite combinations. (The results make a great display and generate much discussion.) Change the rules.

C

p. 175

Number plates

There is a small fantasy island where the authorities wish to register everyone's scooters. The registration plates only have room for three symbols. What could go on the plates if only one symbol was allowed? How many different plates could they have? What if two symbols; then what if three? (Restrict the investigation to numbers only to start with.)

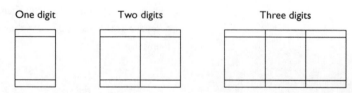

Flags

The children are to design flags with up to three colours in bands either horizontally or vertically. They can then pick their three favourite colours and work out how many different flags they could design. Make a sheet with blank flags to copy or get the children to sketch the flags on the computer, or ruled paper. Make the task possible by making rules. (Good links to national flags and symmetry.)

SIX PEBBLES AND ONE EGG BOX

How many ways can you arrange 0, 1, 2, 3, 4, 5 and 6 identical pebbles, eggs or counters in an egg box?

- What rules will you make? Assume that the position and orientation of the box for half a dozen eggs is fixed.
- Try with 0, then 1, then 6. This is 'thinking to extremes'; looking at the opposite ends of a problem.
- Talk to one another. Let *everyone* explain, demonstrate and experiment with their ideas; note them down.
- Try to record the different arrangements in some systematic way. Look at patterns. Look *for* patterns.
- Try drawing a simple graph of the number of different arrangements for 0, 1, 2, 3, 4, 5 and 6 pebbles.
- Negotiate with other groups to exchange information. What have you to offer? What do you need?
- Write up and display your findings.
- Try to see the problem. Say what you see. With 3 eggs is it half full or half empty?
- You will need to be both flexible yet stick to your ideas. Don't be afraid to push and justify your own viewpoint but listen to the views of others. Be prepared to 'have a go' and yet to 'let go'.
- This is an investigation where you *must* actually do it physically and practically. It helps if someone starts to record the possible combinations as soon as possible. Remember to keep the orientation of the egg box fixed and assume that all the eggs/pebbles are identical.
- Solve 0–6 for one type of bottle or pebble or egg. Is empty a possible case? Come to see that you have in fact solved other problems e.g. full/empty, half full/half empty.

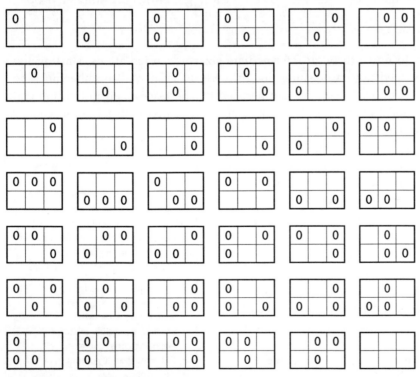

Solutions for 0, 1, 2 and 3 eggs

N9 Taking ideas from 'floor to head'

STARTING WITH LARGE OBJECTS ON THE FLOOR

'Floor to head' is a simple model to help you think about using a variety of resources to enable children to internalise mathematical concepts and make these concepts both meaningful and available.

Especially with younger children, you might start with large-scale objects such as number tiles on the floor or with the children each holding a different number card. Get the children to associate physical movements with problem-solving and decision-making.

> Which two children have cards with numbers that add up to make 7?
> Come and stand together.
> 3 and 4? Yes, 3 and 4 make 7.
> 6 and 1? Yes, well done!
> Stand inside the set ring if you are wearing trousers. Everyone else stand outside.
> Where should Seema stand?
> Who is holding a number that is less than the number on my card? Wave your card in the air!
> Even number people, take your even number card and put it on the floor tile that is one more than your number. Ready, steady go. Now odd number people . . .

S3

p. 112

The activities could move through intermediate sizes and orientations, starting with large numbers pegged onto a washing line, moving to large wall number lines and grids. These large physical resources can be used by the teacher, an individual child or a group to demonstrate an idea that can then be repeated with table-top versions of the same or similar resources.

This model is not just arguing that large resources are good because they can be seen by everyone in the classroom. Nor is it arguing that the move from floor to table top to head, should take place over weeks – they could all be part of the same lesson!

A

p. 148

From:	Washing lines, floor tiles, Brio, Duplo, Action Mats, hopscotch, skipping ropes as Venn diagrams, playground 100 squares, interactive whiteboards
To:	Cuisenaire, Play People, Multilink, dominoes, jigsaws, personal computers and laptops
To:	Paper grids and 100 squares pasted into books, 30 cm rulers, angle measurers, compasses, hand-held calculators

Thinking about floor to head
Children learn best by being involved in activity within a language-rich environment.
The most successful learning is achieved when activities are firmly associated with higher-order language skills, where children are:

- explaining their reasoning
- applying logical arguments
- questioning each other
- predicting possible events
- exploring consequences
- elaborating an argument
- interpreting ideas.

Large floor resources offer a different kinaesthetic experience that is valuable in its own right and demands particular types of responses to questions. The move to table-top resources models the mathematics in a different way and allows different interactions between children and between children and teacher.

The teacher's main role throughout is to provoke and sustain the higher-order language and thinking skills that children may find difficult to sustain without adult support.

FINDING HIDDEN NUMBERS AND PATTERNS

The skilled teacher also helps the children to bridge the thinking space between large floor resources and smaller table-top resources, by asking sophisticated questions about what remains the same and what is different about these two ways of exploring and representing the mathematics.

Children will develop internal images of these resources through modelling mathematical problems with them. They benefit from working with a whole host of resources using the various sizes of number cards, lines and grids. They are more likely to construct and generalise relationships and the rules governing number systems if the teacher tells them to put the ideas into their head and provides regular opportunities for the children to return to the different types of resource.

N4

p. 24

Missing and hidden numbers provide the opportunity for children to visualise and guess what is missing or hidden and build a model of the resource in their heads. The power of this mental image must not be underestimated and children should be given challenging tasks both with and without the resource. Blank number cards, lines and grids are also useful. Number lines and grids with one or two numbers missing, covered with a blot or cloud, or perhaps in the wrong place, force children to notice patterns and predict what should be there. Using lines or grids with only one or two numbers showing through a mask requires a greater understanding of the algebra of the unseen numbers. Is it an addition grid? A cut-up number line?

Use singing, clapping, a drum or other instrument or just your voice to reinforce a number pattern such as odds and evens, or the 3 times table; or use cards held by children, tied or stuck on their backs, or hung on a line.

- Get children and parents to make different sorts of number lines.

- Get some large carpet tiles and paint or stick numerals on. Carpet and floor tiles are very easy to use. Put them down in different ways or use them as a grid.

- Masking tape is cheap and easy to apply to floors without causing damage.

- Make sets of A4 laminated number cards with ties or Velcro. Use them on the floor with programmable toys such as Roamer – make FD 1 the length of the A4 sheet.

- Make wall and table lines with various sets of numbers, 0 to 10, 0 to 100, some with marked lines and others blank.

- Metre rulers can be made from canes or broom handles, marked on one side, blank on the other.

- Make number grids and multiplication grids using Roman numerals, or use numerals in Chinese or one of the many Indian scripts.

- Make Urdu and Arabic grids and look at the similarities with the script we use.

- Think about teaching counting in French, German, Spanish or Welsh to unearth their internal number structure and hear how different or similar they are to English.

N3

pp. 21–23

KINAESTHETIC EXPERIENCE

Use a variety of resources to enable children to internalise mathematical concepts from different starting points and different representations. Children develop greater resilience when they see the same mathematics represented in surprising and different ways. Helping them to describe and explain the differences and the difficulties in using very different representations will help them to internalise the mathematical concepts. Children who get this wider experience are more likely to use mathematics in a broader range of situations.

Although this is a very oversimplified view of building mental models it has the advantage of being easy to put into practice.

When you design and make resources, think about the same mathematics being represented in different ways. Think about:

- the size of the resource
- how many children can work with it and see it at once
- how it can be used in conjunction with the child's own movements
- resources that are designed to be used in the horizontal plane and others in the vertical plane
- making some 2D and some 3D resources.

For many reasons it is often preferable to 'start big', using a child-sized (or larger) resource that will make a big visual impact on the children. Larger resources encourage gross motor movement, extending children's kinaesthetic experience. Large wall-based images, now available through the interactive whiteboard, can be used at any age or stage.

Computers help flexibility and provide almost limitless options for what and how mathematics is displayed, hidden and revealed. Actions on the screen can be saved, replayed and played backwards (undone). A variety of resources can be prepared in advance or developed with the class.

Most adults and children benefit from walking out shapes, especially when using programming languages such as LOGO. Often there is a quite sudden wish to be more in control as an individual, for example when programming a screen turtle, although only a few weeks before the floor turtle was moving at the same speed as the learner's thinking processes.

The body movements across the floor or playground walked out in the horizontal plane need to be translated at a later stage to the vertical plane where they become small head movements or finger twisting as problems are thought about in relation to a vertical monitor screen.

Toy turtles are useful objects to aid thinking (pencil sharpener with a circular protractor stuck to the base), stuck to the screen with Blutack for the early stages of transition from floor to screen or wall. Even some very high-powered professors of mathematics readily made their cardboard 3D turtles when I introduced 3D turtle graphics to them. They either flew them through the air or swam them through imaginary water, 'Finding Nemo'.

FROM 'FLOOR TO HEAD'

It is interesting to note that with guidance in lesson time children can make better use of playground resources. If encouraged to experiment they will make up new games. Some schools take playground resources seriously by including children in design and construction. Jigsaw and other puzzles, dominoes and card games can be used during wet playtimes.

Floor

- Use carpet tiles, A4 cards, or playground chalk to make number lines from 0 to 10 or higher, number grids from 1 to 100 or 0 to 99.
- Encourage whole body movement with help if necessary, hold hands and count numbers aloud as you step from one number to the next. Represent with drawings and diagrams later.
- Walk on the number line or grid. Walk out shapes. Play at being a robotic toy, a Dalek, a Turtle. Watch others move, predict where they will go next.
- Create interesting moves (chessboard knight) on a playground number grid.
- Make sequence cards with each card holding a single instruction for a move. Use them to instruct others to move.
- Then use the cards to program a robotic such as a turtle or a Roamer, to plan movements and to work out the result in advance.

Wall

- Using whole class and large lines or grids, the teacher demonstrates and models, using long blank lines, or OHP.
- The whole class can work on lines and grids: use missing, covered or muddled numbers, or 'masks, blots and clouds' to develop visualising skills; work on 'Silent Way'; use software and interactive whiteboards.
- Explain and show moves to others. Predict the results. Which questions are efficient?
- Make up your own moves and work with the class. Sketch out the moves.

Table and group

- Group work with teacher's help: could be ICT-based.
- Group work with table-top version of the apparatus; record on large sheets; report to the class.
- Children work in pairs or individually in book or on sheets of A4 paper: for example, use large 100 cm table-top number lines, later move to 300 mm ruler (which each child should have).

Head

Visualisation:
- Use 'feely' bags to describe hidden shapes, or counting objects under the blanket without seeing them.
- Close eyes and imagine number lines and 100 squares, describe what you can see.
- Imagine walking out shapes in LOGO.

S1

p. 98

S3

p. 113

N Numbers and the number system

O1 Number lines

EMPTY NUMBER LINES

When they are doing mental calculation as a first resort, children will need to make jottings to support their thinking. The empty number line is ideal for supporting mental calculation because the relevant numbers can be drawn quickly.

One of the significant features of mental calculation procedures is that they are idiosyncratic – we choose a method to suit *our* thinking *and* the particular numbers we are using. For example, sometimes we count on, sometimes we use subtraction, and sometimes we think about difference. It is this flexibility of approach that we are seeking to develop in children. We can represent the different calculation strategies on the number line and children need to be taught to apply these. When they are fluent in their use, children can make choices about which one to use to solve a particular problem.

Vertical pencil-and-paper addition and subtraction 'sums' focus on a narrow range of strategies, and this restricts the choice of strategies that children think are available to them. Faced with a vertical 'take away' sum most children think that the use of mental methods such as counting on and difference are not allowed. Empty number lines encourage a more flexible approach. We may choose to use a take away strategy but it is less likely to be seen as an imperative.

Obviously, people's thinking varies and there is not a one-to-one match between a number story and the chosen strategy. What we are looking for, with the use of number lines, is to find the most appropriate (i.e. accurate, simple, swift, error-free) calculation method.

As teachers, we can help children achieve this by:

- teaching children a selection of strategies, but not expecting them to remember the strategies initially;
- teaching children explicitly, through demonstration and modelling, how to write numbers on a number line;
- matching talk and action, by talking out loud to children to share our own thinking and calculation strategies;
- providing children with frequent opportunities to practise all the strategies;
- encouraging children to internalise the strategies and then call them up from memory as required.

Strategies that can be used on the number line include:

- counting on or back
- bridging through a decade number
- finding the difference
- partitioning
- shopkeeper's method.

Counting on is useful for numbers which have a small difference, for example 432 − 425:

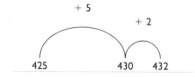

NUMBER LINE STRATEGIES

Counting back

For example, 37 − 4:

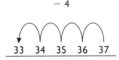

Counting back is a useful strategy for solving subtractions with large differences, particularly where one number is small. It requires a search for the shortest fragment of number line necessary to solve the problem. In number line work, you can teach a routine of visualisation followed by action:

> Imagine the pen working by itself. Think about thirty-seven minus four. Now show me with your finger where the pen will go. Now draw on your wipe board where it went.

Some children will start by finding 37 and then visualising the counting back as jumping back in four single steps. Reward them for this, but ask: 'Can you imagine one big jump?' If they can, then encourage them to visualise a single jump *whenever possible*. If they cannot, then model the single jump with a variety of small numbers, avoiding the need to cross a decade, for example 86 − 5, 34 − 2, 69 − 8. As this becomes secure, allow them to watch you work with another child who can visualise a single jump. Later you can look at the case where the decade has to be crossed and the name of the tens changes, for example in 34 − 7.

Bridging through a decade

For example, 34 − 7:

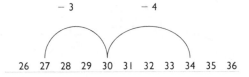

As a support technique, bridging through a decade is likely to be needed for a while, but may disappear later except in tricky situations, such as 604 − 27 where it may be invoked again to bridge the 600. Bridging demands very easy access to the results of partition and it requires immediate recall of triads of numbers, such as 7, 4 and 3, and how they relate to each other. It also demands that we move easily from one triad to another: 4 and 3, 6 and 1, and 5 and 2 go with 7. Which triad is the one needed right now?

The expression 34 − 7 can be thought of as 34 − (4 + 3) but we also need to know that the decade (30) is 4 away from 34 in order to be able to choose the triad 4, 7, 3. For the calculation 34 − 9 we would need to think immediately of the triad 4, 9, 5.

Finding the difference

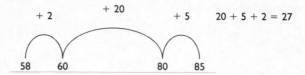

Finding the difference is a useful method where counting on can be done smoothly, as, for example, with 85 − 58. The difference is the distance on the number line that separates the two numbers. Most people find counting on easier than counting back. Starting with 58 we count to 85 with the minimum number of jumps. Initially a child may need to include several jumps, for example by automatically going to the next decade (60) and then to the decade before 85 (80) before finishing at 85.

Partitioning

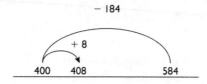

Partitioning is a frequently used strategy. It appeared above in the example of 34 − 7 where the 4 in 34 can be matched by a 4 obtained by partitioning 7 into 4 and 3. In an example such as 584 − 176 a more sophisticated partitioning can be applied by trying to match the 84 in 584 by imagining the partition of 176 into 184 and −8. The resulting calculation becomes: start with 584 and subtract 184 to give 400 then add 8 to compensate for the fact that initially the 176 was increased by 8 to 184.

Shopkeeper's method

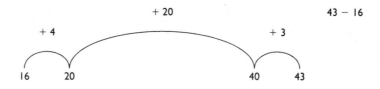

This is associated with the tendency, prior to the advent of the automatic checkout, to give coins of small value first when giving change. So offering a £5 note for goods worth 93 pence was likely to result in the shopkeeper giving change in a particular order, while keeping count of the addition from 93 pence to £5:

> Ninety-three and 2p makes ninety-five and 5p makes a pound, and
> four pounds makes £5 altogether.

Counting on along the number line is a modification of the shopkeeper's method of subtraction, modified because the smallest steps are not necessarily the first to be made, as in: 43 − 16.

WORKING WITH EMPTY NUMBER LINES

Start with an empty line chalked on the blackboard with the children sitting in a circle. Make a mark on the left-hand side and talk about writing conventions for Arabic, Urdu and other numeral systems. Some systems go from left to right, others from right to left; some from top to bottom, others from bottom to top; and scripts such as Tifinar, a Tuareg language, can be written in any direction.

Make a mark and ask for suggestions. What could it be? 0? 1? Take a quick vote. Ask for any other suggestions.

'25.'
'Why?'
'Well it could start anywhere.'

Put in the 0, following a general consensus. If you are brave, ask what is to the left of the mark. Try putting marks, but no numbers, from 0 to 20. With a stick or pointer, in 'Silent Way' mode, point, gesture, and wait for a response. Once the children are off, you should hear 0 1 2 3 4 5 6 7 8 9 10 20.

If you go from 0 in twos, the children may get ahead. You can slow them down. Point backwards in twos from 20; then forward in threes, back in threes; forward in fives, back in fives. Re-mark the fives. Then discuss the importance of anchor points.

Now start at 0 again. Point to the next mark but say 'ten'. Wait and proceed: 20, 30, 40 . . . they're off again. Steady them. Move backwards and forwards in twenties. Then you can try some fifties.

The pace, resting, waiting, anticipating, being 'with it' are all in your mind.

Start again at 0, wait, point to the next mark and say 'one hundred'. To the next and wait, and off they go. There may be some struggle with one thousand. Try again. 'One thousand one hundred' may cause difficulties, some might say 'two thousand'.

Remember to praise and confirm: 'Well done. We can use this blank number line with any set of numbers.'

Chalk in the numbers 0 to 20 with their help. Use objects as markers and try to make up stories for 'jumping teddies', using teddy bear counters. Draw some loops to show the jumps. Ask in how many ways they can make 10? How many ways can they get 'Green Gertie' from 0 to 10? Try different suggestions and consider different strategies.

Put up another teddy, 'Yellow Jasmin'. Discuss difference while Green Gertie sits on 2 and Yellow Jasmin sits on 9. The children could decide that age is a good reason for difference. Gertie could be 2 years old while Jasmin could be 9. What would be the difference in their ages? How do they know? Show the class. Field a few suggestions: counting on, counting back, in ones, in twos, a little jump, a big jump. Ask which way is best? You can explain one of the suggestions: 'the difference will not change as they get older'. In one year's time Gertie's and Jasmin's ages will be 3 and 10. This will make the difference seem easier to find.

Put the two teddy bears on a metre plastic ruler with Blutack. Show them the constant difference, sliding the ruler along the board number line.

Set them the task of making 12 or 24 in different ways. $\square - \square = 12$

Suggest 'Hop, step and jump' as a new puzzle for those who finish: find three different numbers which, when added, make 12 (or 24)! The three numbers increase in size and must all be different: *hop* the smallest, *step* the middle number, and *jump* the largest. Ask if there are numbers the children cannot make? Look at $1 + 2 + 3 = 6$. Stipulate that the numbers must be positive, but ask if they need to be whole numbers? Suggest that they are whole numbers this time. (Y3/Y4 class lesson notes.)

N2

p. 8

O2 The story of 24

DEVELOPING THE TEACHING OF PRACTICAL TASKS

Start with a simple number, for example, 9, or a secret number.

> 'I'm thinking of an odd number in the 3 times table, it's one less than the first two-digit number. What's my number?'
>
> 'Nine.'
>
> 'How did you know?'
>
> 'Because nine is odd . . . because nine is one less than ten . . . because three times three is nine.'
>
> 'Right. You know a lot about nine. Let's write all this down and see if we know any more about this number.'

A

p. 149

Collect and extend the range of information about a small number used as an example. Then introduce 24. Encourage the discussion of lots of different ways of recording the properties of 24. Then demonstrate by recording the properties, for example, in words, symbols, pictures, diagrams, graphs, and show how the information can be displayed in an exciting and communicative way over a week.

The story of 24

What can we get from working with the number 24?

- opportunities to work with operators and the properties of numbers
- more varied ways of recording
- opportunities for doing, talking, recording, sketching, drawing, constructing and deconstructing, brainstorming, linking
- studying number patterns
- links and relationships between different areas of maths
- work with area, perimeter, algebra and data handling
- opportunities to develop children's flexibility, creativity, imagination, perseverance.

Activities with 24

Where do we see and hear about 24? Brainstorm the relevance and incidence of 24 in our lives. For example:

- we have 24 hours in a day
- we use a 24-hour international time clock, which never shows 24.00
- we still buy eggs in dozens, and
- two dozen is still a familiar phrase in English despite the decimal system.

Use simpler, familiar numbers with younger children. Produce a poster of all the ideas linking the number and refer to it over the week.

O6

p. 92

Saying what you know about 24

Encourage children to finish statements about the properties of 24.

Twenty-four is/has/can/cannot/is not/. . .

Begin some statements about 24 and invite children to finish them.

24 is an even number	24 has the following factors . . .
24 is a multiple of . . .	24 can be divided by . . .
24 is the product of . . .	24 is the sum of . . .
24 is greater than . . .	24 is less than . . .
24 is not equal to . . .	24 is not a prime/odd number
24 cannot be divided by . . .	24 is not a multiple of . . .

DEVELOPING AND EXTENDING MATHEMATICAL STATEMENTS

Use thinking boxes when writing mathematical statements. Usually □ represents a missing number whilst ○ represents any operator. Even the simplest equations are hard to read and children need to be taught explicitly to read them in lots of different ways with a variety of language.

Read the following equation:

$$\square \, \bigcirc \, \square = 24$$

This could be read as:

'Number, operator, number, equals twenty-four.'

Does twenty add four equal twenty-four?

The following equation is much harder for children:

$$\square \, \bigcirc \, \square \, \bigcirc \, \square = 24$$

This can be read as:

'Number operator number operator number equals twenty-four.'

So, could this be two times four times three? Let's write it!

$$2 \times 4 \times 3 = 24$$

Is that correct?

Teach children how to read and say number sentences in lots of different ways

I'm thinking of two numbers. I do something with them, such as add, subtract, multiply or divide, and the answer is twenty-four. What could my two numbers be if I'm thinking about addition? Something add something makes 24.

$$\square \, \bigcirc \, \square = 24$$

Watch while I point to each part of the equation. Read it with me. This time we'll read from right to left. Think of 24 as the answer to a problem. Think of the equals sign as a balance. Think of a number, think of an operation, now think of another number. We need to operate on the two numbers on the left-hand side and the answer needs to be 24. These equations are difficult to read. Let's try reading it again, but in a different way.

Consider the following possible statements using whole numbers. For each of the four operators:

$$\square + \square = 24 \qquad \square - \square = 24 \qquad \square \times \square = 24 \qquad 24/\square = \square$$

finite   infinite   finite   finite

- What happens when you change the position of the 24?
- What happens if the equality sign = is replaced with an inequality such as < , >, ≠, ≤ or ≥?
  For example, $\square \, \bigcirc \, \square > 24$
- Write down as many statements as you can about the number 24. (In the version with the most freedom the target number must appear at least once in the statement.)

You may use time limits, restrictions on which operations to use, and reward the use of some operations more than others. You may restrict the number of solutions which appear similar, this is particularly true for the infinite number of answers possible with subtraction.

SOME NOVEL STATEMENTS FOR 24

Do allow one or two days during which children can try to produce an almost infinite number of solutions before you restrict them. I remember one pupil filling a complete exercise book in one evening and proudly showing me his systematic work the next morning. He needed to do this once, but never repeated the exercise. He had felt the power and limitless creativity of infinity.

You can give 'star points' for a completely novel solution. This might include the use of decimals, fractions or index notation.

Once they become aware of other operators such as $\sqrt{}$ and ! (factorial where $4! = 4 \times 3 \times 2 \times 1 = 24$) some children will explore this new freedom with enthusiasm.

$$5^2 - 1 = 24$$

$$10 \times 4.8 \times 0.5 = 24$$

If $\sqrt{16} = 4$ and $\sqrt{9} = 3$, then $\sqrt{16} \times \sqrt{9} \times 2 = 24$

If we look at different ways of giving verbal instructions, we discover that some have written equivalents, for example: 'Add twenty and four.' This instruction matches the prefix notation of

$$\bigcirc \, \square \, \square = 24$$

and the finished instruction can be written like this (+ 20 4 = 24).

Despite a certain amount of confusion that adults may experience, many children like to play with *prefix, infix* and *postfix* notation as a further relaxation or change of the rules about how statements can be made.

Infix looks like this:

$$\square \, \bigcirc \, \square = 24$$

It is what we are used to saying: 'Twenty add four is twenty-four.' Unsurprisingly this becomes (20 + 4 = 24).

Postfix looks like this:

$$\square \, \square \, \bigcirc = 24$$

'Take twenty and four then add them.' This is represented by 'Reverse Polish' notation (20 4 + = 24), which was used on some early electronic calculators and is how computers perform internally.

You could place the problem in a real-life context by using money or sports scores, though initially this will only use addition. For example:

Coins making up 24p, e.g. 10p + 5p + 5p + 2p + 2p

'How can you make 24p?'

'What about £24?'

'Can you work out how a cricketer might have made 24 runs?'

MAKING STATEMENTS ABOUT 24

Give the children 1, 2 or 3 minutes to write down as many statements as they can linking the numbers 3, 8 and 24. Use either of the figures below as an aid. Make up rules to encourage risk-taking.

Try to use only symbols such as + − × / and the numerals 0 to 9.

$3 \times 8 = 24$ $24 = 3 \times 8$
$8 \times 3 = 24$ $24 = 8 \times 3$
$3 (8) = 24$ $24 = 3 (8)$
$3 . 8 = 24$ $24 = 3 . 8$
$^{24}/_3 = 8$ $8 = {}^{24}/_3$
$^{24}/_8 = 3$ $3 = {}^{24}/_8$
$24 \div 8 = 3$ $3 = 24 \div 8$
$24 \div 3 = 8$ $8 = 24 \div 3$

 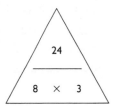

Use numerals for the numbers but replace the operations by words rather than symbols:

3 times 8 makes 24   3 multiplied by 8 is 24   3 lots of 8 equals 24

Use words only for the numbers:

three × eight = twenty-four   twenty-four / eight = three

Use only words:

Three times eight makes twenty-four   twenty-four divided by eight gives three

Find all the factors of 24.

- Use the ladder method to extract all the prime factors.
- Combine these prime factors to produce a complete set of pairs of factors and triads of factors.

2	24
2	12
2	6
3	3
	1

$2 \times 2 \times 2 \times 3 = 24$
$2 \times (2 \times 2 \times 3) = 24$
$(2 \times 2) \times (2 \times 3) = 24$
$(2 \times 2 \times 2) \times 3 = 24$
$1 \times (2 \times 2 \times 2 \times 3) = 24$

$2 \times 12 = 24$
$4 \times 6 = 24$
$8 \times 3 = 24$
$1 \times 24 = 24$

$2^3 \times 3 = 24$
$12 \times 2 = 24$
$6 \times 4 = 24$
$3 \times 8 = 24$
$24 \times 1 = 24$

The 8 pairs of factors can be presented as ordered pairs:

(1, 24) (2, 12) (3, 8) (4, 6) (6, 4) (8, 3) (12, 2) (24, 1)

These pairs can be graphed as (x, y) (see p. 64).

FACTORS OF 24

Triads of factors

$$1 \times 1 \times (2 \times 2 \times 2 \times 3) = 24 \qquad 1 \times 1 \times 24$$
$$1 \times 2 \times (2 \times 2 \times 3) = 24 \qquad 1 \times 2 \times 12$$
$$1 \times (2 \times 2) \times (2 \times 3) = 24 \qquad 1 \times 4 \times 6$$
$$(1 \times 2) \times 2 \times (2 \times 3) = 24 \qquad 2 \times 2 \times 6$$
$$(1 \times 2) \times (2 \times 2) \times 3 = 24 \qquad 2 \times 4 \times 3$$
$$1 \times (2 \times 2 \times 2) \times 3 = 24 \qquad 1 \times 8 \times 3$$

Represent the factors of 24 on the number line. Draw curved lines to join all the same multiples.

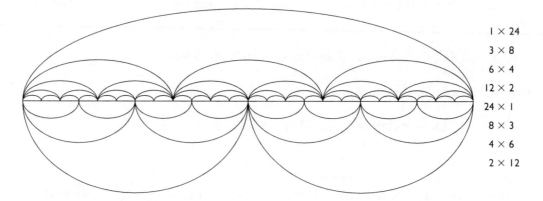

	1 × 24
	3 × 8
	6 × 4
	12 × 2
	24 × 1
	8 × 3
	4 × 6
	2 × 12

Use colours to suggest common factors as in Color Factor rods which are coloured with shades of red for 2-ness and shades of blue for 3-ness or put the coloured rods on the number line.

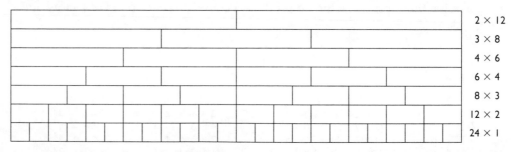

	2 × 12
	3 × 8
	4 × 6
	6 × 4
	8 × 3
	12 × 2
	24 × 1

Factor wall with Color Factor or Cuisenaire Rods

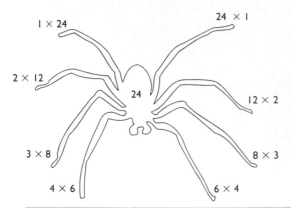

Try drawing diagrams or mappings to show relationships between some of your statements.

Try, for example, insects with 6 legs, spiders with 8 legs or crabs with 10 legs with the target number on the body. Ask for statements to be written on the ends of the legs.

Make a network of the factors for 24. Ask the children to draw their own. Copy the complete network but leave out the factors. Copy but leave out the central number. Copy the network but leave out all the numbers. A pupil did this to challenge me!

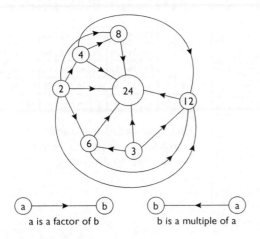

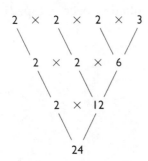

a is a factor of b   b is a multiple of a

Factor network for 24

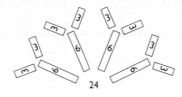

These additive factor trees could be made
using Color Factor or Cuisenaire Rods

Draw a factor tree showing the way 24 breaks down into its factors.

Factor trees

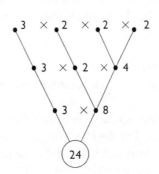

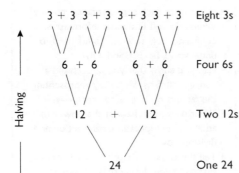

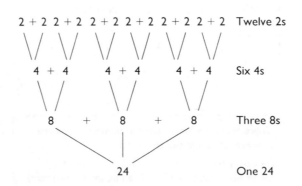

O Operations and calculations

O Operations and calculations

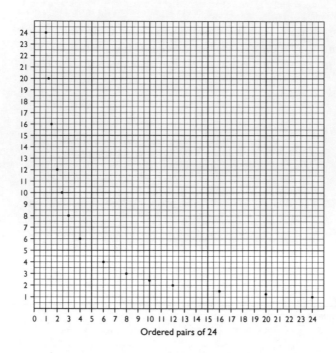

Ordered pairs of 24

×	1	2	3	4	5	6	7	8	9	10
1	1	2	3	4	5	6	7	8	9	10
2	2	4	6	8	10	12	14	16	18	20
3	3	6	9	12	15	18	21	⑳24	27	30
4	4	8	12	16	20	㉔24	28	32	36	40
5	5	10	15	20	25	30	35	40	45	50
6	6	12	18	㉔24	30	36	42	48	54	60
7	7	14	21	28	35	42	49	56	63	70
8	8	16	㉔24	32	40	48	56	64	72	80
9	9	18	27	36	45	54	63	72	81	90
10	10	20	30	40	50	60	70	80	90	100

Find a multiplication grid and then search for all the places where 24 appears. Explain the pattern

ASSESSMENT AND EXTENSION ACTIVITIES

Opportunities for assessment and review
Get the children to produce a display of their 'Story of 24'. Discuss the different representations of 24. How have the opportunities for differentiation been grasped? Can they be improved?

Extension activities
Encourage the use of calculators and tabulate results.

A

p. 155

- Do you have to use whole numbers (integers)?
- What if *not*: 24? Base 10? English?
  A positive number? A number with lots of factors?
- Repeat these activities with a different number?
- Which numbers might prove interesting? Why?
- Which numbers would you *not* select? Why?
- Try numbers such as 36, 23, 8, 0, 1, or infinity.

- What does each representation convey?
- Which do you find most informative, confusing, easy to understand, hard to understand, boring, and why?
- Can you show that you understand a concept such as 'factor' by representing the factors of 24 in a different way?
- What do you feel about the power of addition, multiplication, subtraction and division now?
- Tell the class or write about what has surprised you during these activities/ problems/investigations.

MI

p. 128

There are three longer investigations with 'real-life' contexts shown at the end of MI.

24 paving tiles	(fixed area problem)
24 sheep hurdles	(fixed perimeter problem)
24 accommodation units	(fixed volume problem)

FACTORS OF 24 AND TEMPLATES FOR NUMBER SENTENCES

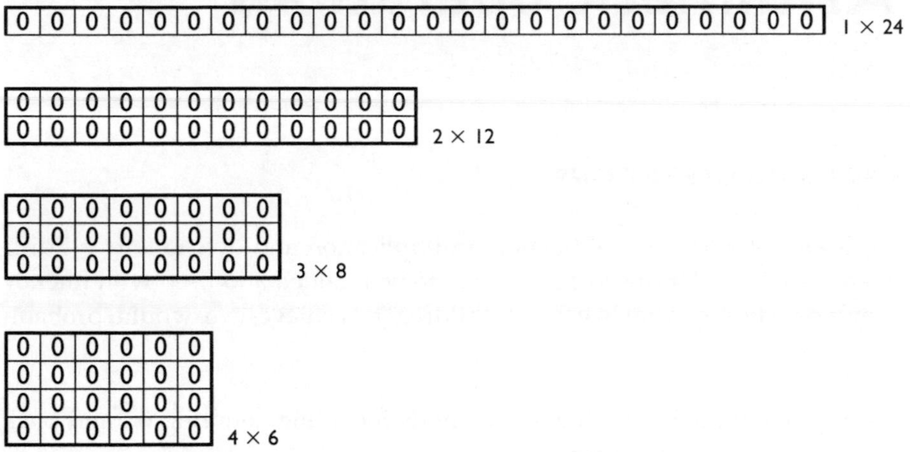

|0|0|0|0|0|0|0|0|0|0|0|0|0|0|0|0|0|0|0|0|0|0|0|0| 1 × 24

2 × 12

3 × 8

4 × 6

Egg box factors of 24

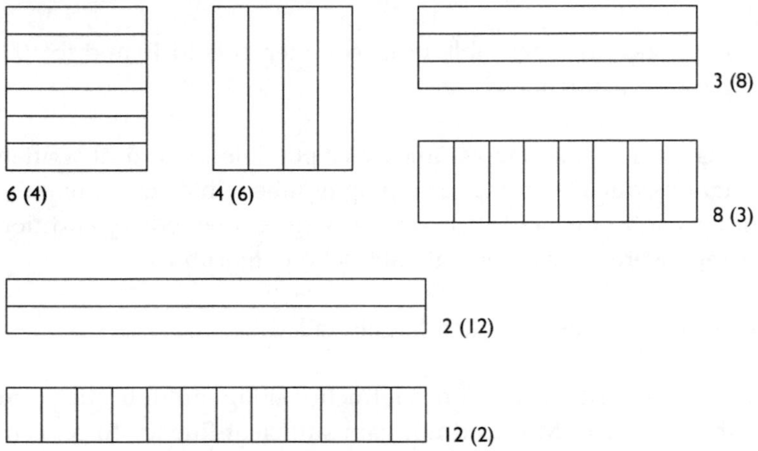

3 (8)

6 (4)   4 (6)

8 (3)

2 (12)

12 (2)

Factors of 24 with Cuisenaire Rods

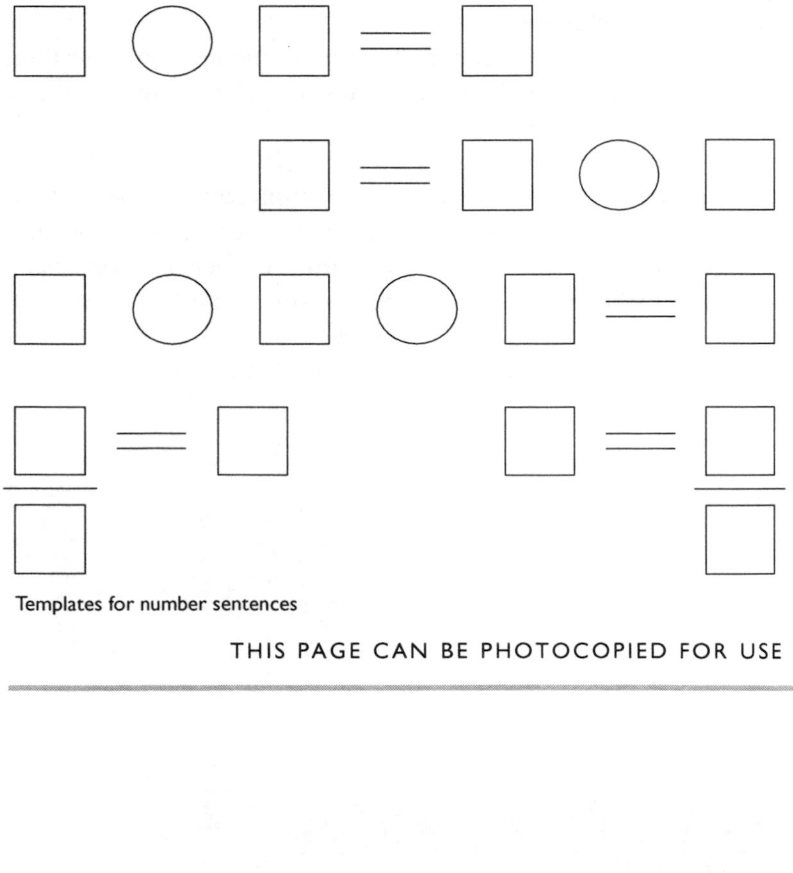

Templates for number sentences

THIS PAGE CAN BE PHOTOCOPIED FOR USE WITH YOUR CLASS

O3 Arithmetic operations

FLUENCY IN USING OPERATIONS

The four operations of addition, subtraction, multiplication and division are all difficult to learn and need regular practice if they are to be retained and used with fluency. If we start by considering what we want children to achieve, we would probably argue for:

- access to a range of mental arithmetic methods including counting on and back, rounding, approximating, estimating;
- technical fluency, meaning easy access to some techniques such as using fingers, a number line, a calculator, and some written algorithms (for example, Gelosia and long multiplication);
- easy recall of knowledge such as times table facts, complements to 10 and to 100, and addition of simple vulgar fractions.

E/F

p. 188

Traditionally the focus has been on moving as quickly as possible to vertical written sums. Children were taught cardinal counting, grouping numbers into sets of ten, the addition of sets to form tens and units and then vertical written methods of addition of tens and units. Later they were shown vertical subtraction algorithms.

There are three main reasons why this approach largely failed:

1   Children failed to learn how written addition, subtraction, long multiplication and long division algorithms worked. Most did not gain sufficient fluency to concentrate on the big picture – they spent most of their time struggling to make the sums work.
2   Children generally failed to do mental arithmetic swiftly and accurately, since they were not taught appropriate techniques.
3   Children had very little awareness of 'number'. They had little idea whether their answer was reasonable or whether they had made a mistake. They were very likely to ask: 'Are these adds or take aways?'

D
p. 177

The key to fluency in arithmetic is to teach mental calculation *strategies* rather than written algorithms. This approach demands that operations such as addition and subtraction are taught together rather than separately, with the teacher emphasising how they relate to each other. Alternatives to subtraction, for example counting on and finding the difference, become much more important.

The final point to make is that the choice of mental arithmetic methods is partly determined by the actual numbers involved and partly by personal preference, so children need to be taught to make choices about the methods they will use.

Consider the particular choices children might make based on problems they are working on. For example:

- Naomi is six years old and her sister Molly is one. I could ask Naomi how much older she is than Molly.
- If she has strong impressions of being very different from her sister, she might enjoy using a method that is called finding the difference. She might have a strong affinity with the 'babyness' of her sister and want to count back to when she was that small.
- Or she might want her sister to grow up a bit and be old enough to play with her, so she might think about counting on.

Typically, we are all subtly influenced about the mental arithmetic method to choose. From a teacher's perspective, we are not much interested or likely to know which particular thoughts prompt Naomi's choice of method; our job is to make sure she *has* a choice – by systematically and explicitly teaching a range of mental calculation strategies and encouraging her to make a choice about which one to use.

We need to regularly introduce new methods to solve old problems. For example we could represent Naomi's age with a dark green Cuisenaire Rod to represent 6 and a white rod to represent 1?

> Put them side by side and notice the difference in length. Now find the rod that fits in the gap. Ah! It is a yellow (5) rod.

Particular structured apparatus supports particular ways of thinking. Which resource(s) would you use at Key Stage 1 or Key Stage 2 for each of the operations shown below?

Operation	Meaning	Model	Resource
Addition	Combining	3 brown eggs and 2 white eggs	
	Union	Tie a 3 m rope to a 2 m rope	
	Adding on	3 eggs, then I found 2 more	
	Comparison	I have £3. Tony has £2 more	
	Complementary – subtraction	Tim gives £2 to Rich. He has £3 left	
Subtraction	Difference	Ben is 4 and Molly is 1	
	Comparison	Ben Nevis and Mont Blanc	
	Take away	15 cakes, 7 get eaten	
Multiplication	Multiplying factor	I have £3, Tig has 4 times as much	
	Rate	4 girls each with 3 dogs	
	Repeated addition	4 snakes each 3 m long	
	Cartesian product	4 flavours and 3 sizes	
	Partnering	4 shapes in 3 colours	
Division	Grouping	18 eggs, 6 in a box	
	Repeated subtraction	How many boxes?	
	Sharing	18 marbles in 3 bags	
	Partition	How many in each bag?	

Possible resources to choose from
- Number line or track
- Time line
- Blank number line
- Number grid
- Fingers
- Number cards
- Cuisenaire Rods
- Multilink or Cubes
- Teddy counters
- Base 10 equipment
- Money
- Bundles of straws, etc.

Because mental calculation methods emphasise the relationships between the four operations, children need to understand how the rules of arithmetic apply, although they don't need to know the names of the laws, such as associative, commutative and distributive.

O Operations and calculations

NUMBER OPERATIONS

The order in which we do operations matters. For example, children need to know that addition and multiplication obey the commutative law, but neither subtraction nor division do.

2 + 3 = 3 + 2	2 − 3 ≠ 3 − 2
2 × 3 = 3 × 2	2 ÷ 3 ≠ 3 ÷ 2

Doing and undoing

$$2 \xrightarrow[-3]{+3} 5 \qquad 2 \xrightarrow[\div 3]{\times 3} 6$$

• How do we reverse an operation?
• How do we get back?
• What is the inverse operation?

There and back again

Give the children a starting number and a finishing number. They then have to get from the start to the finish, and back again. Target boards, function machines, number grids and number lines can all be used to present and support the activity. You could also devise a sheet for children to record their work.

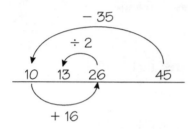

As an individual activity, a child can choose two numbers on their target board. For example, if they were to choose 13 and 45, they could decide to start from 45, get to 13, and then come back again. Perhaps they could use a dice as well, which could determine how many operations they have to use. If the dice showed 3, they would circle the words 'add', 'take', 'divide' on the record sheet, to show the operations they have chosen to use.

They can write out their working as a number sentence. A capable child might write:

To get there	45 − 35 + 16 ÷ 2 = 13
and back again	13 × 2 − 16 + 35 = 45

This could be hard to read for both you and other children. What is the child's thinking? Have they written down every part of the calculation? How did they get there? How can they get back? What happens when they go back the way they came?

We can read the number sentence 45 − 35 + 16 ÷ 2 in several ways and get different results. If we want to show clearly that the answer is 13, we can use brackets. Brackets signify, do this first, with inner brackets calculated before outer brackets. The expression

$$(((45 − 35) + 16) ÷ 2) = 13$$

is read as follows:

• Do the 45 − 35 first.
• Find the answer and use it to complete what is in the second set of brackets, '(10 + 16)'.
• Finally calculate what is inside the third, outer set of brackets, which is '(26 ÷ 2)'.

We might ask for a written sentence:

To get from 45 to 13

• I start with 45, which is my first target number.
• I take away 35, which makes 10, which I keep in my head.
• 10 plus 16 makes 26, which I keep in my head.
• 26 divided by 2 makes 13, which is my second target number.

To get back again

• 13 'times-ed' by 2 makes 26.
• 26 take away 16 leaves 10.
• 10 and 35 make 45.

RULE FOR BPODMAS

If the brackets are positioned differently the results will be different.

- The expression (45   35) ׀ (16 : 2) is read as: calculate (45 − 35) and (16 ÷ 2) separately and add the two results. 45 − 35 = 10 and 16 ÷ 2 = 8. So 10 + 8 = 18.
- We read 45 − (35 + 16) ÷ 2 = as: prepare the calculation in the brackets, then follow the BPODMAS rules, by completing the division before the subtraction. The expression then reads 45 − 51 ÷ 2, with the division to be done before the subtraction: 45 − 25.5 = 19.5.
- The expression ((45 − 35) + 16 ÷ 2) = is read as: calculate 45 − 35 first, which produces (10 + 16 ÷ 2). Do the division next to produce 10 + 8 = 18.
- Without brackets, the calculation is division first, addition second, subtraction third, so 45 − 35 + 8 = 45 − 43 = 2.

In some ways addition and subtraction can be thought of as 'undoing' each other. The same is true for multiplication and division. In these activities we develop the use of the four rules as operations, that is, we encourage children to think about addition, subtraction, multiplication and division as *actions* carried out on numbers. These actions produce certain other numbers as a result.

Children need to know that adding and subtracting zero does not change a number. In the same way, multiplying and dividing by 1 leaves numbers unchanged. Zero is known as the *identity* for addition and subtraction and 1 is the *identity* for multiplication and division.

Look for games and activities that help children combine the four basic operations of addition, subtraction, multiplication and division.

> BPODMAS is a mnemonic for the agreed order of tackling operations in a number sentence:
>
> - Brackets
> - Powers
> - Of (as in 2/3 of 64)
> - Division
> - Multiplication
> - Addition
> - Subtraction.

Board games for two people or two teams

Version 1

The children select a target number on the board and try to make that number using four dice.

I	2	3	4	5	6
7	8	9	10	11	12
13	14	15	16	17	18
19	20	21	22	23	24
25	26	27	28	29	30
31	32	33	34	35	36

Version 2

Use only three dice and any operators you know but use each number once and only once. So 2, 3 and 5 could be $2 \times 3 \times 5 = 30$, $2 \times (3 + 5) = 16$, $(5 + 2) \times 3 = 21$, $3 \wedge 2 + 5 = 14$ ... Each player tries to make 'four in a row' on the grid. Encourage the use of a wider range of operations such as ! (factorial), √ (square root) and ∧ (to the power of).

Version 3

Using only two dice, which numbers cannot be made? Which can be made lots of ways?

Extensions

Change the number of dice. Use different dice with more/fewer faces. Select a target number and try to get as close as possible in the same way as 'Countdown'. Play a game on the computer such as Blocks (MEP, 1986).

> - Child A throws four dice, 3, 3, 4, 6, and claims 35 by writing 36 − 4 + 3.
> - Child B throws 1, 1, 2, 5, and claims 36 by writing, 25 + 11.
> - Child A throws 1, 1, 1, 4, and claims 1 by writing 4 − 1 − 1 − 1.
> - Child B throws 1, 1, 2, 4, and claims 24 by writing 24 * 1/1.
> - Miss a turn if you cannot go. First player with 'four in a row' wins.
>
> **Change the rules.**

EXAMPLES OF VARIOUS ALGORITHMS

Addition

Stepping stones can break down the process.

Mentally, with no written working:

- 359 + 126 is the same as 360 + 125 (take 1 off 126 and add it to 359)
- 360 + 100 make 460 then 460 + 20 makes 480, and lastly 480 + 5 gives 485

- How might this problem be worked out on a number line?
- What would it look and feel like with Base 10 apparatus?
- Place value arrow cards fit well with some methods.

$$359 \longrightarrow 300 + 50 + 9$$
$$+ 126 \longrightarrow 100 + 20 + 6$$
$$\boxed{485} \longleftarrow \boxed{400 + 70 + 15}$$

	359		
+	126		
	400	300 + 100	→ 400
	70	50 + 20	→ 70
	15	9 + 6	→ 15
	485	400 + 70 + 15	→ 485
	Written down	Mentally	

Subtraction

- How were you taught to subtract?
- Which method do you use now?
- Which method do you teach? Why?

$$\begin{array}{r} {}^{5}\cancel{6}\,{}^{11}\cancel{7}\,{}^{1}5 \\ -\ 1\ 4\ 7 \\ \hline 4\ 7\ 8 \end{array} \qquad \begin{array}{r} {}^{5}\cancel{6}\,{}^{9}2\,{}^{1}5 \\ -\ 1\ 4\ 7 \\ \hline 4\ 7\ 8 \end{array} \qquad \begin{array}{r} 6\ 2\ 5 \\ -\ 1^{1}\,4^{1}\,7 \\ \hline 4\ 7\ 8 \end{array}$$

How were you taught?

stress place value (round up units) (round up tens)

$$625 \longrightarrow 600 + 20 + 5 \qquad 625 + 3 \xrightarrow{\text{round up}} 628 + 50 \rightarrow 678$$
$$-147 \longrightarrow -100 - 40 - 7 \;\boxed{\text{or}}\; -147 + 3 \longrightarrow -150 + 50 \rightarrow -200$$
$$478 \longleftarrow +500 - 20 - 2 \qquad 478 \longleftarrow 478$$
mentally

'Stepping stones' methods break down the steps and encourage mental methods leading to an efficient and effective algorithm

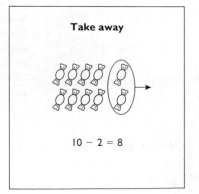

Take away

10 − 2 = 8

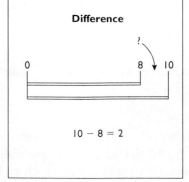

Difference

10 − 8 = 2

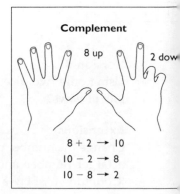

Complement

8 up   2 down

8 + 2 → 10
10 − 2 → 8
10 − 8 → 2

Counting on

Here is a number line method. Counting on from 147 to 625

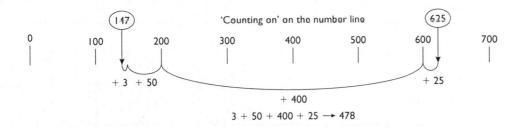

'Counting on' on the number line

$$3 + 50 + 400 + 25 \rightarrow 478$$

Multiplication

Book-keeping method

X	50	2	
30	1500	60	1560
8	400	16	416
	1900	76	1976

Area method

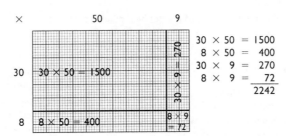

30×50	=	1500
8×50	=	400
30×9	=	270
8×9	=	72
		2242

Can you work out how these multiplications have been done? What skills, facts and understanding do they need?

Egyptian method

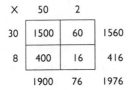

1	52	
2	104	2×52
4	208	4×52
8	416	
16	832	
32	1664	32×52
38	1976	38×52

Keep doubling the larger number until you have nearly enough. Pick out what you need to make up the other number:

$$38 = 32 + 4 + 2.$$

Ancient Egyptian method which links to binary.

Gelosia method

$$478 \times 319 = 152\,482$$

The Gelosia method was one of many used by Arab mathematicians over 800 years ago. It was introduced into Italy 500 years ago.

Method used by Russian peasants until the twentieth century

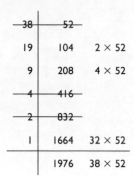

~~38~~	~~52~~	
19	104	2 × 52
9	208	4 × 52
~~4~~	~~416~~	
~~2~~	~~832~~	
1	1664	32 × 52
	1976	38 × 52

- Keep doubling the larger number.
- Keep halving and rounding down the smaller number.
- Cross out all the lines where this smaller number is even.
- Add up what is left of the doubled numbers.

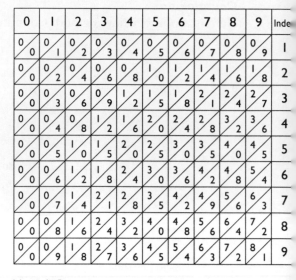

Napier's Bones

What if you cannot do it?

- Make it simpler.
- Use a calculator.
- Make a sensible guess.
- Use some apparatus.
- Use small-squared paper.
- Draw a picture to represent the problem.

In 1617 John Napier, a Scot, devised a multiplication system called Napier's Bones based on the Arabic Gelosia method. Cut up the columns. How do they work?

A traditional UK method

$$52 \longrightarrow 50 + 2$$
$$\times\, 38 \longrightarrow 30 + 8$$
$$416 \longleftarrow (50 + 2) \times 8$$
$$1560 \longleftarrow (50 + 2) \times 30$$
$$1976$$

Ruth Merttens (1996) advocates stories and role-play, similar to Steiner's, to help teach subtraction. The sum 22 − 18 might be a 'Mind the Gap' problem, where you try to find the missing piece. Whereas 22 − 4 might be a 'Robber Sum': here a child plays the robber role and removes 4 bricks from the line of 22 bricks on a number line. What stories do you know or tell?

Addition +	Subtraction −	Multiplication ×	Division ÷	Equals =
add	subtract	multiply	divide	means
sum of	difference	product	quotient	will be
plus	minus	'times'	'share'	answer is
increase	decrease		split	is same as
more than	less (fewer)		group	is
and (union)	take away			makes
combine	compare			equivalent to
total				gives
positive	negative			

NUMBER AND PLACE VALUE ACTIVITIES

Work in a group of four, choose one activity, make it, play it then extend it.

'Card Game'

You need a pack of cards marked either 0 to 100, 0.01 to 0.99 or 1.00 to 1.99 and a paper strip. Make the paper strip with ten sections, each large enough for a playing card. To play the game shuffle and deal ten cards to each player. Players take it in turns to place as many cards as possible in ascending order in the sections of the board, turning over one card at a time and placing it in an appropriate space. The winner is the person who places the most cards. Remember ... cards can only be placed in ascending order.

'Calculator Game'

You need a calculator, a set of Base 10 (Dienes Blocks), a dice marked 1 to 6 and another with two faces marked 't' (tenths), two faces marked 'h' (hundredths) and two faces marked 'th' (thousandths). For this game the blocks are valued as follows: largest block 1, flat 0.1, rod 0.01, single cube 0.001. Each player starts with a large block (worth 1). Players take it in turns to throw the two dice. Players subtract the value given by the two dice from the blocks. For example, the two dice show 'th' (thousandths) and 5, so the player subtracts 5 thousandths from the blocks. Another player checks the result with a calculator. First player to zero is the winner.

'Highs and Lows'

A game for two players or two teams. You need a set of cards 0 to 9 twice (so two 0s, two 1s, etc.). Each player needs a board that is large enough to place a playing card in each of the appropriate boxes. Make a decimal point symbol and place that in an agreed position on each board. Shuffle the cards and place face down. The first player turns the top card over and places it in one of the three boxes. Player two takes the next card and so on. The winner is the player (or team) that forms the highest number. (Variations: play making the lowest number win; play with the winner being the one nearest to an agreed number.)

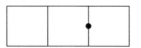

'Dice Game'

You need two dice, one marked from 1 to 6, the other with two faces marked tenths, two faces marked hundredths, two faces marked thousandths. You need two paper meters, one for each player. Set the meters to zero (0.000). Players take it in turns to throw the two dice and add the result to their meter. The other player checks the result with a calculator. The first to 1.000 is the winner.

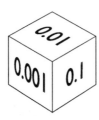

'Decimal Patterns'

You need a number line marked from 0 to 1. Find a decimal value for the family of fractions from 1/7 to 7/7 or 1/17 to 17/17 and mark each on the number line. Investigate the patterns of decimal numbers formed by the set of fractions. Use a calculator.

ALL THE FOURS INVESTIGATION

All the fours

Make the values 0 to 10 using only the numeral 4 and any operations you like. Put the values 0 to 10, double-spaced, down the left-hand side of the page. Start anywhere you like, putting in mathematical statements which evaluate to that number, but only use 4 and any operator you know such as +, −, ×, ÷, ! and √, e.g. for 5, 4 + (4/4) = 5 *or* 4 + (4÷4) = 5.

If you can make 1 then surely you can make any number.

$$2 = 1 + 1 \text{ and } 3 = 1 + 1 + 1$$

Try to find solutions for all the values from 0 to 10.
See if you can find alternatives. Is there a right way to do this?

C

p. 175

This can be a five-minute activity or can be developed as a larger task. Start with pencil-and-paper or wipe boards. Extend by using an interactive whiteboard or calculator.

'All you need is the magic number 4. With this number you can make all other numbers.' – Can this be true?

Or start as a broken calculator activity:

If the only buttons that worked were the function buttons and the 4 button, could you make all the values 0 to 10 appear on the display?

Children should be encouraged to record all their workings as they work on this.

Write down what you are thinking, as well as the mathematical equations and statements.
　　Once you have got answers for all the values 0 to 10, talk to someone else who has also finished, and compare answers and methods.
　　Discuss which ways are most elegant, are easiest, are most obscure.
　　Can you see any patterns?
　　For this work you will need to persevere and co-operate with others. You might get stuck over some values and need help, so you must ask for it.
　　You should annotate your work, make a neat copy or collaborate to produce a group version.
　　Start with what you know; build up the solutions in a systematic way; look for alternative solutions.

- What if *not* 4 or 0 to 10 or integers?
- Will it work with other numbers?
- You must use exactly four 4s.
- Can you find solutions from 10 to 20?
- Or −10 to −20?
- Use a spreadsheet to generate patterns.
- Which numbers are missing?

REAL MONEY INVESTIGATION

Real money

Start with a bag of 1p and 2p coins. Use real bronze money because it is cheaper than plastic play money and the real thing looks and feels much better.

- How much money was in the bag?
- How can you keep it safe and not lose any?
- How many ways can you make up 1p, 2p, 3p, . . ., 10p?
- Does the order matter?
- Play and make patterns with real coins on a big piece of white paper, so that the coins stand out.
- Write on the paper to help label the patterns for 1p, 2p, 3p . . .
- Arrange the coins clearly to demonstrate the patterns that you can see.
- How many patterns are there? How do you know? Do the patterns repeat?
- How can you record this work? Use plain or squared paper – or a camera.

This seemingly simple investigation provides opportunities for:

- using mathematical methods and ideas to solve practical problems;
- working on number bonds and combinations;
- free play and looking for patterns;
- problem-solving: finding a technique for checking the coins;
- working systematically, checking and monitoring your own work.

Value	Ways of making up the value with 1p and 2p coins			Alternatives
1p	1			
2p	1 + 1	2		
3p	1 + 1 + 1	1 + 2		2 + 1?
4p	1 + 1 + 1 + 1	1 + 1 + 2	2 + 2	2 + 1 + 1?
5p	1 + 1 + 1 + 1 + 1	1 + 1 + 1 + 2	1 + 2 + 2	2 + 1 + 2?

A

p. 158

Assessment opportunities

- Cognitive style from observing play.
- Knowledge and creativity in problem-solving – do they use what they already know?
- Ability to see pattern.
- Ability to record pattern and method of recording used.

Extensions to the activity

- Add different coins?
- What would happen with postage stamps?
- Can you model the same number patterns with different apparatus, such as Cuisenaire Rods?
- The patterns are essentially the same but they will look and feel very different.
- How do chemists count pills?

O4 **Arithmogons**

ARITHMOGONS AND PYRAMIDS

'Arithmogons' are mathematical templates for practising calculations, such as addition, difference and multiplication.

Addition
- Put single digit numbers in each of the circles. The children can then calculate the numbers in the squares.
- Put numbers in two of the circles and in one of the squares: ask children to complete the arithmogon.
- Put numbers in two of the squares and in one of the circles.
- Put numbers in the three squares – can the arithmogon be completed?

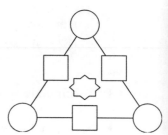

Subtraction
Subtraction is more difficult. The number in the square is the difference rather than the sum of the two numbers in the circles either side. To increase difficulty use two-digit numbers, fractions, percentages or decimals.

Multiplication
Try again using multiplication and find the number in the square by *multiplying* the two numbers in the circles. Put a number in the central star as a target number and provide just one other number somewhere.

Provide a completed arithmogon and ask children to find the rule. Devise square, pentagonal and hexagonal arithmogons.

Bracelets and necklaces can be completed by putting operations such as +4, ×2 or −7 in the ovals and a starting number. Children then calculate numbers for the squares. A bracelet could have fewer than 14 beads. Necklaces are longer. Try working both clockwise and anticlockwise on the same bracelet.

CHAINS, DARTBOARDS AND PYRAMIDS

Chains

Chains can be started by applying a rule. Keep going and see when, where, and if, it stops. Start with the number 9 and the following rule. 'If the number is even – halve it and add 1. If it is odd, double it.'

The number 9 is odd so double to make 18 . . .

$$9 \to 18 \to 10 \to 6 \to 4 \to 3 \to 6$$

- What will happen next?
- Try other numbers in the range 1 to 9. Make a mapping of all the possibilities.
- Can you do this algebraically?
- Odd $\to$ Even $\to$? It depends! Could be odd or even. Why?
- What other rules might prove interesting?
- How else can you represent the chains?

Dartboards

Dartboards can be considered as mathematical objects with single, double and treble zones. Play a game such as 501 (or use a smaller number to start with for a shorter game). Divide the class into 2, 3 or 4 groups (it gets a bit tedious with 6 groups). Each team can pick 3 numbers each turn.

Obviously treble 20 will give 60 which is more than a bull's-eye of 50. You can make whatever rules you or they like. Each space can only be used once in each game.

Make it a quiz where 'doubles' and 'trebles' give harder questions: if you get it wrong you miss the board. Use wipe boards as scorecards for everyone, but check their answers each round by putting the score on the class black/whiteboard.

Make simpler dartboards with only a few numbers on, such as 1 to 9. Use a different number system, even Korean tri-graphs for 8 compass points. Be creative.

N3

p. 20

Pyramids

Addition pyramids may seem trivial until you try them for yourself and perhaps do them algebraically to prove to yourself what is really happening.

Start with a small four-brick base pyramid and numbers from 1 to the number of bricks in the base, in any order. Put the sum of the adjacent bricks into the brick above. Work systematically across each row of bricks starting at the base. 'What number do you get at the top?' Act surprised when not all answers are the same.

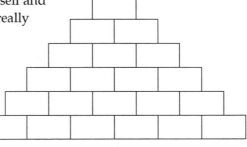

Who can get the largest number at the top of the pyramid?
How do you know it is the largest?
How do you get the smallest?
Are you sure?

ARITHMOGONS

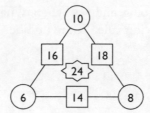

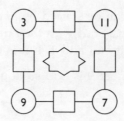

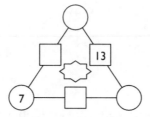

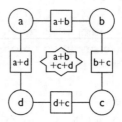

PYRAMIDS

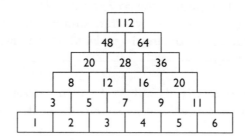

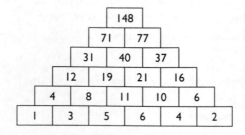

BLANK ARITHMOGONS

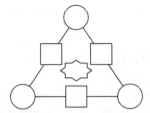
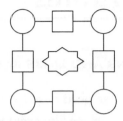

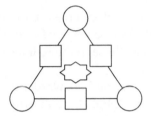
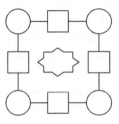

BLANK PYRAMIDS

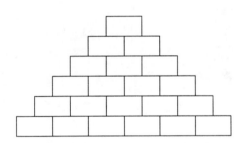

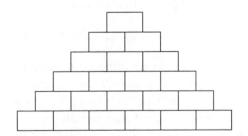

THIS PAGE CAN BE PHOTOCOPIED FOR USE WITH YOUR CLASS

O5 Teaching multiplication tables

PATTERNS AND LINKS IN MULTIPLICATION TABLES

Many children need to go through several learning stages over a period of some years, before they can commit complex lists such as the 7 times table to memory. Their learning of number patterns begins at the Foundation Stage with a realisation that numbers possess special qualities or properties. They could be telephone numbers, shoe sizes or birthdays, for example. Some number properties such as even and odd can be explored from Foundation or Year 1 onwards.

At a later stage children can pick out those numbers that have a particular property. *Twenty, fifty and seventy are in the 10 times table because they end in a 0.* Later on comes the ability to remember a list of numbers such as those in the 5 times table. This is a significant feat that we teachers tend to overlook.

Just to check, try saying your favourite nursery rhyme backwards, or recite the alphabet from Z to A. Difficult? But we know our alphabet don't we? Are there different kinds of knowing?

Storing a sequence in memory takes some doing. The best way is to work towards it gradually, working on small chunks of information at a time. Effective teachers really help children to see and make connections between different types of knowing and different ways of working. We help children to make new knowledge more secure when we provide visual, auditory and kinaesthetic (VAK) learning, or rhythmic experiences, as part of the learning process.

S4

p. 118

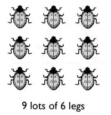

9 lots of 6 legs

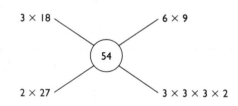

Look for examples in everyday life that children can associate with the numbers they are learning. Show them examples of pairs, dozens, sevens (such as days of the week). Get children to use familiar images such as an octopus or spider's legs, four-wheeled vehicles or four-legged animals, tricycles, six-legged insects.

N8

p. 44

Look out for links and patterns. Instead of teaching the 6 times table from scratch:

* colour 6 and its multiples on a conventional hundred square;
* find the multiples on a 10 × 10 multiplication grid;
* make the number with Cuisenaire Rods using only one colour at a time;
* take a multiple of 6 such as 54 and find out all you can about it;
* work on one multiple of 6 a day during a lesson introduction;
* at the end of each daily session add the multiple to a number line on the wall.

LEARNING THE MULTIPLICATION TABLES

Here is a suggested order for learning the multiplication tables. The order assumes that we can get the children to link new ideas with previous knowledge. Children do not make links by chance, the teacher has to draw their attention to the important connections between known facts and facts that can be deduced, to mediate the links.

$$2, 0, 1, 10, 5, 4, 8, 9, 3, 6, 7, \ldots$$

Children need to know how to *double* and how to *halve* numbers. Teaching them the 1, 2, 10 and 5 tables emphasises how useful doubling and halving can be and gives them power over the even tables for a start.

Consider teaching the divisibility rules alongside these multiplication tables facts.

O6

p. 90

Learn twos, fours and eights using doubling
• Use real and invented animals' legs to help model this.
• Sing 'The animals went in two by two'.
• The children can make a memorable display of different animals with 2, 4, 6, 8, and 10 legs.

Zero and one
It is important to teach the 0 (zero) and 1 (one) times tables:

   $n \times 0 = 0$ is only one fact to remember.

Any 0 anywhere in a sequence of multiplication reduces the answer to 0.

Identity
$n \times 1 = n$ means that you always get what you started with if you multiply any number by 1.

This is called the *identity* for multiplication, it leaves things unchanged. You always know where you are with 1.

Tens and fives
With whole numbers multiplying by 10 is easy:
• Write a 0 on the end.
• For 5 times, halve the number and make an educated guess.
• If it was even, then write a 0.
• If odd move the decimal point 1 place to the right:

   $8 \times 5 =$ half of 8 is 4 so it must be 40;
   $7 \times 5 =$ half of 7 is 3.5 so it must be 35.

• If this appears too complex then if the number is odd, round it down to the nearest even number, halve it and affix a 5.
• Or halve 10 times the number.

Try teaching 100 times and 50 times tables. Children love the power over numbers that this gives.

Nines
Teach the finger method, which involves looking for nines complements:
• Spread out your 10 fingers on the table in front of you, palms up.
• Counting from left to right, curl your 3rd finger up, to denote *3 lots of 9*.
• There should now be 2 digits (a thumb and finger) to the left of the bent finger. These are the tens of the answer.
• There should also be 7 digits to the right of the bent finger. These are the units of the answer.
• Reading the fingers correctly denotes that $3 \times 9 = 20 + 7 = 27$.
• Try it with other fingers from 1 to 10.
• For 8×9 bend back the 8th finger from the left.
• Look at the pattern in the answers: 9, 18, 27, 36, 45, 54, 63, 72, 81, 90.
• In each case the digit sum is 9.

Threes and then sixes
• Use triangles for counting in 3s and insect legs for 6s.
• Egg boxes help us to visualise half a dozen.

Sevens
Sevens often prove hard to remember. Look at calendar patterns for February and March.
Make use of the 7 days in a week.

MULTIPLYING ODDS AND EVENS

Children need to know about *odd* and *even* and the power of evenness in multiplication. It is always surprising to discover that only an *odd number multiplied by an odd number* results in an *odd* number answer when working with whole numbers. This knowledge gives children predictive power over the multiples, even if they do not know the exact answer. Knowing if the answer is going to be odd or even lets children practise prediction and allows them to gain control over what they are doing.

- Use the interactive whiteboard or an OHT of a 12 by 12 multiplication grid.
- Have a clear space where children can move about the classroom.
- Have two labels ODD and EVEN pinned or held up clearly in different places in the classroom.
- Let every child have a wipe board and pen.
- Show children the multiplication grid on the OHT.
- Point to several children in turn and ask them to choose and read out any number from the grid and write it on their wipe board.

> - Look at a multiplication table from 1 times 1 up to 12 times 12.
> - How many odd multiples are there?
> - How many even multiples?
> - Count them. 25% are odd and 75% are even.
> - 1 in every 4 is odd and 3 in every 4 are even.

×	1	2	3	4	5	6	7	8	9	10	11	12
1	1	2	3	4	5	6	7	8	9	10	11	12
2	2	4	6	8	10	12	14	16	18	20	22	24
3	3	6	9	12	15	18	21	24	27	30	33	36
4	4	8	12	16	20	24	28	32	36	40	44	48
5	5	10	15	20	25	30	35	40	45	50	55	60
6	6	12	18	24	30	36	42	48	54	60	66	72
7	7	14	21	28	35	42	49	56	63	70	77	84
8	8	16	24	32	40	48	56	64	72	80	88	96
9	9	18	27	36	45	54	63	72	81	90	99	108
10	10	20	30	40	50	60	70	80	90	100	110	120
11	11	22	33	44	55	66	77	88	99	110	121	132
12	12	24	36	48	60	72	84	96	108	120	132	144

- Ask the children to take their wipe boards and stand beside the correct label, ODD or EVEN, depending on the number they have chosen.
- Stop after ten children or so have come out.
- Ask them about the sizes of the two groups of children.
- Are the groups the same size?
- What seems to be happening?
- Ask a few more children to come out.
- Use all the children and then sit the children down.
- Send the odd numbers back one by one.
- Each child shows their wipe board.
- They give you their number and you prompt them for the multiplication fact.

> 'Read me your number please'.
> *Fifty-five.*
> 'What makes fifty-five?'
> *Five elevens!*

N8

p. 42

What do we notice about all these numbers? Where do they appear on the OHT (make sure it is still visible to the children)? Do the same quickly with the children who have an even number.

Gradually all the children return to their seats, to work on a small paper version of the multiplication grid. They can scrutinise the grid for a few minutes. They can colour or circle the odd numbers. They can count how many times different numbers appear – try an odd number, e.g. 11, and an even number e.g. 24. They can count the actual number of odd and even numbers on their paper grid and calculate the proportion of even to odd. Use a 10 × 10 grid if you wish.

> even × even = even
>
> even × odd = even
>
> odd × even = even
>
> odd × odd = odd

You can now teach them explicitly to read the grid as a look-up table.

At the close of the lesson you can ask the children how many odd numbers and even numbers there are in a number line from 1 to 100. Emphasise the proportion. 'Fifty per cent are even and fifty per cent are odd.'

> When we are counting along a number line, we go odd, even, odd, even, odd, even, . . . Try it. 17, 18, 19, 20, 21, . . . , 75, 76, 77, 78, 79. So half the counting numbers are even and half are odd. What is the surprise about the multiplication grid?
>
> I'm going to ask you a trick question and unless you're very careful, you'll get the wrong answer – like I did when I first thought about it!
>
> Does the multiplication grid have half even and half odd numbers?

Hopefully the children will be able to give you the correct but surprising result. They will also have learned to recognise quite a few of the multiples that they will need to eventually learn, and they should be able to use the multiplication grid as a look-up table.

Loop Cards

Loop Cards are a popular and simple activity to use in a variety of maths lessons. The best tactile experience is with blank playing cards. Manufacturers used to give them away free, until they discovered that teachers created lots of different activities with them! The card is divided into two parts. At the top of card 1, write a question in words, numbers or symbols. Then write the answer to the question on the bottom part of card 2. Think of a second question for card 2 and put the answer on card 3.

To make sure you only have a single loop of questions and answers, prepare a separate answer sheet that lists the problems you want to set. Write different Loop Card sets in different colours (for example, all times tables in blue, all fraction problems in orange, all decimal problems in green), so children and you can store and find them easily. Write a small code in one corner to denote the set and how many in the complete set (e.g. A/30) so a child can collect them, check none have been lost, and store them away without bothering you.

B

p. 164

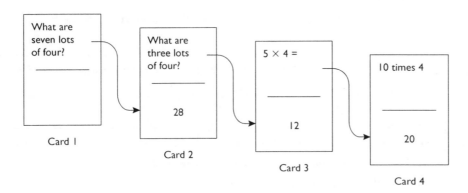

STRATEGIES FOR MULTIPLICATION USING DOUBLING AND HALVING

× 0	Multiplying by zero produces zero. There is only one possible answer: 0, nothing, zilch, zero. $n \times 0 = 0$
× 1	The answer is the same as the question. The number remains unchanged. 1 is known as the identity for multiplication.
× 2	Double the number. For big numbers or decimals check the answer is reasonable. $\quad$ $2.1 \times 2 = 4.2$ $\qquad$ $21\,000 \times 2 = 42\,000$ $\quad$ $2010 \times 2 = 4020$ $\qquad$ $2.001 \times 2 = 4.002$
× 3	Either double the number and then add the number to the double, or use your 3 times table.
× 4	Double and double again.
× 5	5 is half of 10 and multiplying by 10 is easy. You halve the number and then write a zero (if the number was even) or adjust the decimal point (if the number was odd). $\quad$ $82 \times 5 = 41 \times 10 = 410$ $\qquad$ $81 \times 5 = 40.5 \times 10 = 405$ $\quad$ $4680 \times 5 = 2340 \times 10 = 23\,400$ $\quad$ $4670 \times 5 = 2335 \times 10 = 23\,350$
× 6	Double, double again and add the two results. Twice the number and 4 times the number make 6 times the number. $\quad$ $2n + 4n = 6n$ $\quad$ $53 \times 6 = 318$ $\quad$ $106 + 212 = 318$ Or double 3 times the number.
× 7	Try 6 times the number plus the number or 8 times the number minus the number. $\quad$ $6 + 1 = 7$ $\:$ and $\:$ $8 - 1 = 7$ Now you know why ×7 is so hard.
× 8	Double, double, double: $2 \times 2 \times 2 = 8$ You might prefer to multiply the number by 10 and then subtract twice the number. $\quad$ $10n - 2n = 8n$
× 9	Use the finger method, or subtract the number from ten times the number. $\quad$ $10n - 1n = 9n$ $\qquad$ $8n + 1n = 9n$ $\quad$ $n \times 3 \times 3 = 9n$
× 10	Write a zero at the end of a whole number. If it is a decimal then move the decimal point one place to the right. Or move the number one place to the left! $\quad$ $539\,856 \times 10 = 5\,398\,560$ $\quad$ $12.456 \times 10 = 124.56$ For multiplication by 100, affix two zeros or move the decimal point two places to the right or move the number two places to the left. For 1000 go three, for 10 000 go four and so on.

MAKING A LOOK-UP TABLE FOR DIVISION

This is a good way to make a look-up table for long division. Children enjoy the power of generating tables of facts that you do not know, for example the 17 times table.

Can you break numbers down? I might say, for example:

> 'I don't know my 200 times table, but I know my 2 times. I know how to double, and how to multiply by 100. So $200 = 2 \times 100$.'

Multiple	Product	Notes
1×17	17	Easy, write it down
2×17	34	Double 17
3×17	51	Add 1×17 and 2×17
4×17	68	Double twice 17
5×17	85	Half of 10 times 17
6×17	102	Double 3 times 17
7×17	119	Add 6×17 and 1×17
8×17	136	Double 4×17
9×17	153	8×17 plus 1×17; or 10×17 minus 1×17 – take your pick
10×17	170	Easy, write a zero on the end

What is $653 \div 17$?		comment
653		Try 10×17
170	10×17	
483		Lots left so
340	20×17	try 20×17
143		That is more than
136	8×17	8×17 but $< 9 \times 17$
7	**38×17 remainder 7**	

Doubling and halving is a simple but powerful strategy that can be used to generate simple multiples.

- Can the children derive these for themselves?
- Are there alternatives?

Make copies of the tables grid readily available. For example, make sure the children have them pasted into the back of their books, then they have to turn to the back of the book each time they need a multiplication fact. Eventually they don't bother unless they are unsure or really do not know. Learn and apply it. Use it or lose it.

> Do you imagine the decimal point fixed in space with the numerals moving past it?
> Try looking at the decimal point on a calculator when you multiply or divide by 10s.
> Technically, when multiplying or dividing by 10, it is the relative position of the digits which is altered and not the decimal point!

LOOKING FOR PATTERNS ON THE MULTIPLICATION GRID

Find the row or column that begins with 3. Notice that the *differences* between successive numbers are also the *name* of that set of multiples. So, for the 3 times row, the numbers are 3, 6, 9, 12, ... and they increase by 3 each time as we read from left to right and decrease by 3 as we read from right to left.

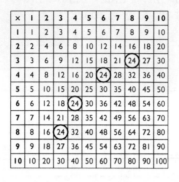

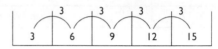

Looking at 9, we can see that 9 + 3 = 12 and 9 − 3 = 6. Read in this way, the multiplication grid emphasises multiplication in terms of successive or repeated addition (and repeated subtraction if you go from right to left).

Another way of reading the grid is to see the grid as providing *trios* of numbers. To show this to the children, we can find '3' by looking along the top row and '4' by looking down the left column of the grid. Where they meet we find '12'.

By emphasising the connections between this trio of numbers we can link multiplication with division and get children to think about these two operations as 'complementary' – we can think of one 'undoing' the effect of the other. We need to use lots of different visual ways of emphasising the links between each trio of numbers and give children plenty of practice in reading the symbols.

$$3 \times 4 = 12 \qquad 12 \, / \, 4 = 3 \qquad 12 \, / \, 3 = 4$$

- Twelve is three lots of four.
- Four times three gives twelve.
- If I multiply three and four I get twelve.
- Three into twelve goes four.
- Twelve divided by three equals four.
- Three and four are factors of twelve.
- Twelve is a multiple of three and it's also a multiple of four.
- Twelve is in the 3 and the 4 times table.
- Twelve is where the 3 times table and the 4 times table bump into each other.

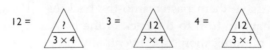

Three triangles for 3 × 4 = 12

MORE PATTERNS ON THE MULTIPLICATION GRID

Different rectangles on the multiplication grid can be highlighted when children use an interactive whiteboard and when they are working with paper grids. They need to notice that, in every case, the bottom right-hand number in any rectangle gives the multiple and the area of the rectangle in squares.

×	1	2	3	4	5	6	7	8	9	10	11	12
1	1	2	3	4	5	6	7	8	9	10	11	12
2	2	4	6	8	10	12	14	16	18	20	22	24
3	3	6	9	12	15	18	21	24	27	30	33	36
4	4	8	12	16	20	24	28	32	36	40	44	48
5	5	10	15	20	25	30	35	40	45	50	55	60
6	6	12	18	24	30	36	42	48	54	60	66	72
7	7	14	21	28	35	42	49	56	63	70	77	84
8	8	16	24	32	40	48	56	64	72	80	88	96
9	9	18	27	36	45	54	63	72	81	90	99	108
10	10	20	30	40	50	60	70	80	90	100	110	120
11	11	22	33	44	55	66	77	88	99	110	121	132
12	12	24	36	48	60	72	84	96	108	120	132	144

The diagonal spine of squares

×	1	2	3	4	5	6	7	8	9	10
1	1	2	3	4	5	6	7	8	9	10
2	2	4	6	8	10	12	14	16	18	20
3	3	6	9	12	15	18	21	24	27	30
4	4	8	12	16	20	24	28	32	36	40
5	5	10	15	20	25	30	35	40	45	50
6	6	12	18	24	30	36	42	48	54	60
7	7	14	21	28	35	42	49	56	63	70
8	8	16	24	32	40	48	56	64	72	80
9	9	18	27	36	45	54	63	72	81	90
10	10	20	30	40	50	60	70	80	90	100

Different ways of making 20

There is *a mirror line of symmetry* either side of the spine of squares: $5 \times 7 = 35$ and also $7 \times 5 = 35$, so perhaps it is not that surprising. An awareness of this should almost halve the number of facts you need to learn. This is also true for addition but not for division and subtraction.

On the tables grid, the square numbers form an axis of reflective symmetry. Fold the grid along the square numbers and see that the multiples match on each side. *Prick* the grid anywhere to prove this, by unfolding and comparing the two pin holes.

Some square numbers occur only once. Which? Most numbers occur twice.

The spine of squares

Look down the diagonal from top left to bottom right to find the square numbers 1, 4, 9, 16, 25, 36, 49, 64, 81, 100, 121, 144. Notice the alternating pattern of an odd square number followed by an even. What is the difference between successive numbers? From 1 to 4 is a difference of 3. The other differences are 5, 7, 9, 11.

Notice how the units digits of the square numbers form a pattern that stops at 5 and then reverses.

0, 1, 4, 9, 16, 25, 36, 49, 64, 91, 100

What happens after 100?

N7

p. 40

O Operations and calculations

UNDERSTANDING AND MAKING THE LINKS

Some numbers occur more than twice, for example 12 and 24, because they have more than one pair of factors on the grid, e.g. 2 × 12, 3 × 8, 4 × 6, 6 × 4, 8 × 3, 12 × 2 for 24. Mark them and observe the curved pattern. Extending the grid to 30 × 30 will show this better. Try using Excel to make the grid.

There is still disagreement about the need for rote learning rather then learning for understanding. Children need a fluent knowledge of number facts: number bonds to 10, number bonds to 20, 9s complements and so on, including multiplication facts up to 10 × 10 = 100 or if you prefer 12 × 12 = 144, and maybe even further.

Without this fluent, accessible and almost automatic knowledge, children cannot demonstrate enough facility with numbers to enable them to solve problems without focusing solely on number facts. What is needed is a whole range of strategies to apply to numbers and number problems. Children also need a richly interconnected conceptual network or structure where the numbers belong not just to a family of, say, multiples of 6, but much more. So, for example, it may be useful to think of 36 as a square number, and all that this brings with it, or as an even number, or as having the factors 1, 2, 3, 4, 6, 9, 12, 18, 36. We might need to think of the factors grouped in pairs, (1 × 36), (2 × 18), (3 × 12), (4 × 9), (6 × 6), (9 × 4), (12 × 3), (18 × 2), (36 × 1).

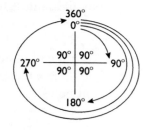

All 12s and 24s

Making new from old

Making new from old by constructing previously unknown number facts from currently known number facts. This can be thought of as extending our knowledge using a small set of specific strategies.

You can use the knowledge that 9 × 4 = 36 to help you realise that 4 × 90 = 360. There are four right angles in one complete rotation or revolution. Knowing that 9 × 0 = 0, 9 × 1 = 9, 9 × 2 = 18, 9 × 3 = 27 and 9 × 4 = 36 can help you derive the four angles as 90, 180, 270 and 360, and then back to 0 again.

Thinking about any one fact can lead you to other facts. You can also derive new facts based on the ones you already know.

So 9 × 0.4 = 3.6 and 0.9 × 0.4 = 0.36

Four lots of 9p make 36p, which is the same as £0.36;

9000 × 0.04 = 360 and so on.

£3.6 million shared between 400 people must have a 9 in the answer!

3 600 000/400= 36 000/4, halved gives £18 000, and halved again gives £9000.

The secret is to use what you know. To change things into a form that you are happier to work with and to check that your answer is sensible.

FURTHER MULTIPLICATION GRID ACTIVITIES

A hidden magic square?
This was discovered by a Year 5 class thirty years ago.

Look at the units digits in any *even* times table, i.e. 2, 4, 6, 8, 10, 12.

Write down the patterns and try to find further patterns.

2 4 6 8 0 2 4 6 8 0 2 4 6 8 0 in the 2s?

4 8 2 6 0 4 8 2 6 0 4 8 2 6 0 in the 4s?

6 2 8 4 0 6 2 8 4 0 6 2 8 4 0 in the 6s?

8 6 4 2 0 8 6 4 2 0 8 6 4 2 0 in the 8s?

0 0 0 0 0 0 0 0 0 0 0 0 0 0 0 in the 10s?

2	4	6	8	0
4	8	2	6	0
6	2	8	4	0
8	6	4	2	0
0	0	0	0	0

Look for patterns in this grid of units digits for even tables. Is it a magic square?

Equivalent fractions

Look at the *equivalent fractions* for ½ that appear in the 1 and 2 times rows.

1	2	3	4	5	6	7	8	9	10
2	4	6	8	10	12	14	16	18	20

If you cut up a tables grid into strips of rows, then you can make sets of equivalent fractions for any numerator or denominator up to 10: for example, 3/7.

3	6	9	12	15	18	21	24	27	30
7	14	21	28	35	42	49	56	63	70

One less than the square

- You can make many different patterns from the multiplication grid.
- Try odds and evens, then multiples of one number, for example 7.
- Find routes from one multiple to the next; which is the most efficient route?
- Compare patterns for 2s, 4s, 6s, and 8s, or 1s, 3s, 5s, and 7s.
- Try writing down the digits 0 to 9 in a circle and joining them to make the different cyclic patterns that you have found.
- Calculate the digital root of each multiple and put it in place of the multiple.

One less than the square? What do you notice about products one less than the square such as 35, one less than 36, or 3, 8, 15, 24, 35, 48, 63, 80, 99, 120, 143, 168?

$$n^2 - 1 = (n + 1)(n - 1)$$

or

$$36 - 1 = (6 + 1)(6 - 1) = 7 \times 5$$

So if you know that $8 \times 8 = 64$, then you know that $(8 + 1)(8 - 1) = 63$. True!

O6 Divisibility rules

RULES FOR DIVISIBILITY

Divisibility rules give children and adults power over numbers and ease the feelings of helplessness which some of us experience when confronted with a large unknown number. Building up a knowledge of divisibility develops children's knowledge of the properties of numbers and improves their mental calculation strategies.

Using the rules of divisibility allows us to check if one number can be divided by another number, such as 2 or 3 or 5, without having to do the whole division. Some of these rules date back more than a thousand years and were devised by Arabic mathematicians. They started using them before they developed and passed on Indian and Chinese methods of calculation such as those we use today. Inspecting the last one or two digits is usually enough. Sometimes it is necessary to add up all the digits. These rules are also useful for checking the results of multiplication.

p. 172

One way to introduce this work is to plan a focused series of lessons over a three-week period. In week 1, introduce those rules which demand inspection of the last digit, the units digit, to see if it is odd or even. This is also useful revision for Year 3 children who should know about odd and even numbers.

As mental oral starters, you can ask the children for any very large number they know, for example their telephone number, or the ISBN number from a book. Get each group to write their number on a piece of card, which they can flash at you for only a few seconds. Make it appear magical that you can quickly tell them if the number can be divided by 2, 5 or 10. Place the cards under pre-prepared headings on a flip chart 'Can be'/'Can't be' divided by 2, etc. Then get the groups to check your claim by any method they like. *Then* point out how long it takes them. Offer to show them how to do it at your speed. Review your strategies with them.

Some younger children and those with orientation difficulties associated with some forms of dyslexia will need to be shown very clearly exactly where to look to locate the right-hand end digit. Divisibility by 2 is an easy starting place for this work. If you can halve a number without a remainder, then it is divisible by 2, but it is much quicker just to check to see if the end digit is even.

What numbers will divide into 2538 without a remainder?

- 2, because it ends in an even number
- 3 and 9, because the digital root is 9
- 6, because it is even and the digital root is 9. What else?

- To find the digital root just keep adding the digits:

    $2 + 5 + 3 + 8 = 18,$
    $1 + 8 = 9$

Divisibility rules

- If the last digit of a number is:

    0, 2, 4, 6 or 8, it is divisible by 2
    0 or 5, it is divisible by 5
    0, it is divisible by 10.

- If the last two digits make a number divisible by 4 then the whole number is divisible by 4.

- If the last three digits make a number divisible by 8 then the whole number is divisible by 8.

- If the digital root (digit sum) is 3, 6 or 9, then the number is divisible by 3.

- If the digital root (digit sum) of an *even* number is 3, 6 or 9, then the number is divisible by 6.

- If the digital root (digit sum) of a number is 9, then the number is divisible by 9.

- Add digits to get the digit sum.

- Repeat the process for the digital root.

Plan a series of lessons over a three-week period. You could include a few lessons on digital roots.

- Week 1, start with rules about the units digit, to see if it is odd or even.
- Week 2, teach the ideas of digit sum and digital root. Use the rules for 3, 6 and 9.
- Week 3, use a mix of: simple starters; invented numbers for the children to play detective, working as fast as they can; then consolidation with practice using target boards. See N5.

Offer calculators and paper for children to check that your claims for 2, 5 and 10 are really true for all integers. Can they do the necessary mental calculations quickly and accurately, or do they need some practice? Can they use a calculator to divide? Older children should be able to use short division or a calculator to find factors, but you may need to revise this at the start of the week. Give them the chance to try out these new skills over the next few days.

Show or call out a number. The children are to write it down and then quickly write down as many factors as they can using divisibility rules and tables facts they know. What numbers can 2538 be divided by? When you ask, they show the answers so far. Which did they get and which did they miss? Use target boards and ask for numbers that can be divided by say 2, or 5, or 10, then all they need to do is inspect the unit digit and write down or call out these numbers.

> **457 920**
> Can this number be divided by 5? By 10? By 2?
>
> **34 825**
> Is this number a multiple of 5, of 2, of 10?

'Number Detective'

'Number Detective' provides more practice with divisibility rules for 2, 5 and 10, during a lesson introduction or plenary. Use a flip chart and some playing cards 0 to 9. Get a child to write a number at random on their individual wipe board. Copy it on to the class flip chart, but replace the units digit with a '?' or a '*'.

72	739	277	386	736
201	185	687	281	284
614	425	241	333	109
390	462	318	538	891

Where are the multiples of 2, 5 and 10?

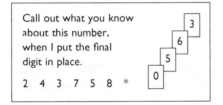

Call out what you know about this number, when I put the final digit in place.

2 4 3 7 5 8 *   3 6 5 0

Take a playing card at random from the pack and place it over the '*' to complete the number. Get the children to call out as fast as possible what they know about the number. Working in pairs, ask them to write on individual wipe boards.

A much more rhythmic pattern, which is very powerful, is to use software such as ATM Counter. Set the count to increment fairly quickly by 1 each time, starting from any number you like. Distribute Number Fans and organise the children into three parts of a choir, one group with 2 on their fans, one group with 5 and one group with 10. As the counter increments, the chanting rhythm will pick up. The children hold up their cards and call out their numbers, starting with the end digit as zero when all three groups will call out and wave their Number Fan vigorously. *Two, Five! Ten!* (1), (2), *Two!* (3), (4), *Two!* (5), *Five!* (6), *Two!* (7), (8), *Two!* (9), (0), *Two! Five! Ten!* Put the liveliest in group 2 and increase the speed of the count to keep them busy!

The serious point is that children who think mathematics is about guessing and barking at numbers, will be astonished to discover the cyclic rhythm of the call-outs, showing there is no randomness at all here.

N2

p. 8

O Operations and calculations

Work with the whole class and an interactive whiteboard or OHP on the first occasion. Children can take it in turns to read and answer questions while you write the answers. If the children do not know some of the rules, such as how to find the digital root of a number by adding all the digits (for example, 1 254 769 380, 1 + 2 + 5 + 4 + 7 + 6 + 9 + 3 + 8 + 0 = 45, 4 + 5 = 9), then deal with this idea in the lesson introduction.

Remember that you can determine the questions beforehand. If you want to take the risk then let them suggest questions to ask. This can involve rephrasing and rewording the rules, which can be useful for some children. Do not try to cover more than three bits of information in this way. Too much new information will overload them. Your questions will evolve into the divisibility rules.

In week 2, teach the ideas of digit sum and digital root. Use the divisibility rules for 3, 6 and 9. Put the 'best' questions from weeks 1 and 2 on a large poster in the classroom and cover it before the start of the lesson. Ask the children to recall the questions. Uncover the questions and let them work on specific numbers.

In week 3 use quick and light-hearted starters. Invent a number on a flip chart and have the children play detective as fast as they can. Use a prepared target board. Use an OHP calculator to confirm predictions or generate numbers. Use the main part of the lesson to try out some of the other ideas from the divisibility rules activities.

> **Add digits to get the digit sum**
>
> • The digit sum of 56 283 is 5 + 6 + 2 + 8 + 3 which is 24.
>
> • Repeat the process for the digital root:
>
> • The digital root is always a single digit, in this case 2 + 4 = 6.

Consolidate one area of factual knowledge, such as combining rules for 6 (2 × 3), 15 (5 × 3), or division by 11. You can then pace the work more slowly so that children who prefer to work more methodically with pencil-and-paper or wipe boards and pen have time to think things through.

Set tasks that allow for differentiation, and then pool findings at the end of the lesson in a plenary where generalisations can be made and further work suggested.

Trying out these ideas on unsuspecting adults at home always promotes excitement, but be prepared for the question: 'But why do they work?'

The essential point is that children should feel empowered, that they have power over numbers and it is not the other way round, where they feel helpless and even fearful when faced with arithmetic. We want children to be able to demystify numbers, to get to know them, to inspect and recognise them by their properties. The most obvious properties are odd and even, whole (integer) and part (fractions or decimals). We want them to gain familiarity with numbers and their properties: to be able to deconstruct numbers by saying them, naming them, writing them, making them, partitioning them into hundreds, tens and units for example, or factorising them.

O2

p. 58

MORE COMPLEX IDEAS AND CHECKING

Combining rules implies that you can work out the rules for any combination of factors for which you already know a divisibility rule.

Division by 12

12 is 4 × 3 or 2 × 2 × 3, so you would expect that if the number was divisible by both 3 and 4 then it must be divisible by 12. Apply the rules for 3 and 4. The digit sum must be 3 and the last two digits must be a multiple of 4, that means 4 must be a factor (the number must be divisible by 4).

Division by 15

Division by 15 is the same as division by 3 and 5. What of 120 or 150?

Division by 11

Division by 11 is fun. Start with the most significant (most important) digit on the left, then take away the next one, add the third, take away the fourth, and so on until the end of the number. If the answer is 11 or 0 then the number is divisible by 11.
Try it with 985 182:

$$985\ 182: \quad 9 - 8 + 5 - 1 + 8 - 2 = 11$$
$$1023: \quad 1 - 0 + 2 - 3 = 0$$

It is not worth doing this with small numbers because they can be inspected, for example, 66, 99, 121, 484, 572. Can you see the 11s?

There are methods for 'casting out' 7s, but checking for divisibility by 7 is probably easiest by short division.

Checking by 'casting out 9s'

For hundreds of years, one of the most important uses for these rules has been to check if an answer is correct. The oldest method for finding the digital root is by 'casting out 9s'. You cross out or ignore 9 or numbers that add up to nine. It's faster but causes one or two new problems. Can you find them? Instead of a digital root of 9 you get 0. Using the digital root, or 'casting out 9s' method, to check is no guarantee, but your answer is *probably* correct. 345, 453, 4530 and 3045 all have a digital root of 3.

Addition and subtraction

To check *addition*, add the digital roots of the numbers you are adding and this should be the same as the digital root of the answer. If the two digital roots are the same, then the sum is *probably* right. If the two digital roots differ, the sum is wrong.

To check *subtraction*, subtract the digital roots of the numbers you are subtracting. If the result is negative then add 9. This should be the same as the digital root of the answer. If you cast out 9s then instead of the digital root 9 you get 0. Also if A − B = C then A = B + C.

Multiplication and division

To check *multiplication*, multiply the digital roots of the numbers you are multiplying and this should be the same as the digital root of the answer (product). If the results are not the same then the answer is definitely wrong.

To check *division*, multiply the digital root of the number you are dividing *by* and the digital root of the answer (quotient): the result should be the same as the digital root of the number you are dividing *into*. If A/B = C then A = B × C.

S1 Visualisation techniques and activities

VISUALISING NUMBERS

Work with the whole class. Tell the children that you are going to help them to improve their mental powers and in particular their mathematical memory! Have individual wipe boards and pens available for all children. A flip chart will be useful to you, because you will need to hide what you write. An electronic whiteboard is an ideal alternative. Ask the children for some of their favourite or special numbers. Ask them why they have favourites. Turn over one page of the flip chart ready to hide the numbers later on. On a clean flip chart page, write down about 10 or 12 of their favourite numbers (probably best to keep most of them to single- or two-digit numbers, first time round). Keep the numbers well separated on the flip chart and place them in a completely random way.

Tell the children they have 10–20 seconds to look at the numbers before you hide them. When the numbers are hidden, invite them to write down as many as they can remember on their own wipe boards. Observe what, how and where they write. Stay neutral. Don't enthuse or criticise. Do they replicate the spatial patterns you originally produced? Do they write a list? Which numbers do they remember, which do they forget? Who remembers them all? Who has difficulty? Are you surprised by who is good at recall? Remind them, this is not a competition to see how many numbers they have remembered. Rather, we want to find out how to *improve* our memories. Wait until most children have stopped writing. Reveal the hidden flip chart page and ask them to check how well they have done. Ask them to use a different colour to write down the ones they missed. Discuss to see if there are any numbers that appear to be easier or harder to remember.

Get them to clear their wipe boards ready for a second attempt. Try again with a new set of numbers that you select, this time based on the earlier discussion. Choose some numbers that form a pattern, for example numbers in the 3 times table, but include others that might be more difficult to remember, for example, some two-digit prime numbers. Let them look carefully at this new collection. Ask a few children to say what they notice. Encourage pattern-spotting and discussion of the physical arrangement. Suggest that they close their eyes or look away and try to 'see' as many numbers as possible inside their heads. Work on strengthening their ability to visualise. Open eyes, look but do not write yet.

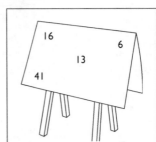

On the first occasion, this activity can take half an hour or more. It would fit with a lesson on looking for number patterns. To be effective, repeat the activity once or twice a week for half a term as part of a lesson introduction or plenary lasting two to three minutes, with you selecting number patterns that you want the children to remember (e.g. multiples of the 6 times table).

Flip chart with collection of favourite numbers

N5

p. 32

RESOURCES

Fibonacci website at www.mcs.surrey.ac.uk/Personal/ R.Knott/Fibonacci/fibnat.html

- How did you try to remember the numbers?
- Did you see patterns, even numbers, sequences, odd ones out?
- Did you make a photo in your head?
- Did you write a list?
- Get the children to suggest to each other different ways of improving their score of remembered numbers.
- Being relaxed improves short-term memory.
- Patterns and sequences are easier to remember than strings of unrelated information, so look for patterns in the numbers on show.

VISUALISING NUMBERS AND THE NUMBER LINE

> Check if any numbers have been overlooked. Close eyes. Try to visualise the whole set. Think about number sequences. Open eyes and check again. Close eyes and strengthen the mental picture. Ready, steady, go!

Now hide the numbers. Let them write on their wipe boards. Compare the results with those of the first try. Congratulate those who have improved. Allow some time for children to report on any change of strategy they have made and discuss the improvement. For maximum effect, repeat twice a week for half a term, spending only five minutes maximum on the activity as part of a lesson introduction or plenary. Avoid creating failure by making it too hard. Strengthening the skills of visualisation is what this is all about. Review progress at the end of a chosen period. Introduce the activity into lessons when children are having difficulty in remembering sets of numbers, e.g. a new 'times table'.

With younger children in Key Stage 1, ask the children to write numerals in the air in response to: 'Show me how we write the number . . .'. They can also 'write' on their own hand, on the hand of the person sitting next to them, on the back of the person sitting in front of them. Their friend has to say whether they recognise the numeral by feel.

A pair of children can play with a few dominoes with dots or numerals. The dominoes are face down. One child picks a domino and without showing it to their partner, 'reads' it out loud. The second child tries to 'see the domino in their head' and then draws what they see on paper or a wipe board. A simplified version involves the two children being given duplicate sets of five or six dominoes. One child picks a domino and reads it without showing it. The second child finds that same domino in their own pile.

- Close your eyes and try to see our number line inside your head.
- Keep your eyes closed while I count slowly.
- Try to see the numeral in your head when I say it. . . . 1!
- Can you see a number 1 inside your head?
- Write me a 1 on the floor with your finger. 2!
- Can you see a number 2?
- Write a big number 2 in the air. 3!
- Can you write a number 3 on your hand . . . 4! . . . 10!

Use a washing line as an *empty number line* with a class or group where large numeral cards can be pegged out in full view. You begin by holding all the numeral cards to peg on the line. Initially, work with the numerals in order from 1 to 10 to consolidate the counting sequence.

What is this number?
Six.
Good. Show me how to write the number six. Write it in the air.
Can you put it on the number line please? Show us where to put it on the number line.

A *muddled number line* is useful with children who are fairly secure with the sequence from 1 to 10. Say, 'Cover your eyes or look at the floor.' The adult then either removes one of the numeral cards from the washing line, or turns it round to hide the numeral, leaving the card in its correct place.

Open your eyes. Which number is missing? The one after the seven?
What's the number that comes after seven?
Eight.
Who wants to put the eight back in the right place for me please?

DEVELOPING THE ABILITY TO VISUALISE

Missing numbers from the line is more challenging because it demands that the sequence is already held securely in memory.

> Close your eyes and think hard about all the numbers on our number line while I count slowly.
> *One, two, three, five, six.*
> What do you mean I've missed out four? I've just read the numbers that are on the line! You think four is missing? Let's see if we can find it in the box. Write four in the air nice and big so I can see what I'm looking for in the number box. Is this it? Who thinks they can put it in the right place on the line?

Remembering and imagining activities strengthen visual memory. These activities can be done with eyes closed or gazing at the floor.

- Imagine walking to the door.
- Imagine walking from your table to the carpet.
- Imagine lining up by the door and walking to the hall.
- Where in the classroom would you see a circle, a square, an oblong?
- Imagine a clock with hands; the long hand is on the 6 and short hand is halfway between the 12 and the 1. What time is it?
- Imagine the number 42; which digit is on the left?
- Imagine a large yellow square; slide a blue right-angled triangle into one of the corners of the square so the right angle of the triangle fits into the corner of the square. How much yellow can you still see?
- Imagine the number 518; which digit is in the middle? Swap this digit for a 9 and say the new number.
- Imagine writing your name; look at the first letter and think of another word that starts with the same letter.
- Imagine looking at a clock in the mirror; does 12 o'clock look the same or different when you see it in the mirror?
- Look in the mirror and imagine a clock showing 9 o'clock; what time is it really?

(For more visualisation activities see *Shape and Space Activities* available at: www. standards.dfee.gov.uk/numeracy/publications/.)

> *Emptying the line* is a useful closing activity.
> Amy, I'm looking for a number that's between four and seven please.
> *Six.*
> Is six between four and seven? (pointing carefully!) Yes six is *in between* the four and the seven. Well done Amy! Take it down and put it in the box please.

> Jared, I need a number that comes *after* eight.
> *Nine.*
> Is Jared right? Yes of course he is!
>
> Close your eyes and imagine this number. I'm thinking of a number that has a straight line across the top and a short straight line going down then a big curved line. Write it in the air if you think you know which one I'm thinking of.

Children can be encouraged to imagine *numeral shapes.* Many children invent visualisation activities for themselves. David, aged five, stated, without prompting, that he took numbers home with him by putting them in his head while he was at school. When he was in his bedroom he 'made them come up on the bedroom wall'. To support this inventiveness, have a pile of numeral cards on your lap. Work with a small group or the class. Make sure the children can't see the numeral cards to begin with.

> I'm going to show you a numeral that has got straight and curved lines. I wonder what it could be?
> *Three? Five? Nine?*
> Show me how we write a five. Write a five in the air in front of you. Do it slowly so we can all watch. Can you all see how we write a five? Let's see if you were right. [Show card.]

Working with *hundred squares* can provide visualisation opportunities for older primary children. Practise reciting small chunks of the numbers in the 100 square as a warm-up.

> Cover your eyes or look away. What number is to the left of 75? To the right of 17? Below 23? Above 92? Slightly harder. What numbers surround 54? What numbers surround 77? What numbers surround 82?
>
> Trick question coming up. What numbers surround 1? What numbers surround 100?
>
> A more difficult question coming up. What numbers surround 41? Have a quick look at the hundred square if you need to, then look away again.
>
> What numbers surround 91?
>
> Relax and look at the 100 square. Which questions did you find it difficult to visualise? Can you say why?
>
> Let's try some more. Watch this time while I do a practice question for you. What number do I land on if I start at 91 and I jump up 1, and right 2? Watch. 91, 81, 82, 83. The answer is 83.
>
> Ready to have another go? Cover your eyes this time.
>
> I'm going to start at number 55. Try to see 55 in your mind. Try to see it clearly. Try to see the numbers that surround 55. Ready? 55 and up 3. Now right 3. Where am I? Think about it. Now write the answer on your wipe board. Write the answer now! Show me your wipe board answer. I'll do it again with you watching and you mark your answer right or wrong.

N4

p. 24

1	2	3	4	5	6	7	8	9	10
11	12	13	14	15	16	17	18	19	20
21	22	23	24	25	26	27	28	29	30
31	32	33	34	35	36	37	38	38	40
41	42	43	44	45	46	47	48	49	50
51	52	53	54	55	56	57	58	59	60
61	62	63	64	65	66	67	68	69	70
71	72	73	74	75	76	77	78	79	80
81	82	83	84	85	86	87	88	89	90
91	92	93	94	95	96	97	98	99	100

Matching pairs

Matching pairs requires a small collection of numeral cards on a table covered with a cloth, some with duplicates, e.g. two 3s but only one 4, two 5s and two 6s, but only one 7 and one 8. Uncover the cards and let the children look for five seconds. Cover them up again.

> Who can tell me a pair that they've noticed?
> *6. There's two 6s!*
> Let's have a look. Yes, you're right! You win the 6s. Who's going next?

You can choose carefully who goes first and last because it gets easier when there are fewer cards left.

VISUALISING SHAPES

Paper folding

Paper folding provides lots of opportunities for work that can range from easy to very difficult. To strengthen the visual memory of non-visual learners, do a few easy activities over several weeks, just taking a couple of minutes each time. Have on hand plenty of scrap A4 paper that can be cut up and discarded. Work with the whole class for a while to establish the activity, then allow opportunities for groups and pairs to work quietly.

You need a piece of A4 paper and a pair of scissors. Fold the paper twice. It will have one completely closed folded edge and several different-looking edges. It is useful to get children to notice these small differences. For now, just draw their attention to your piece and tell them they will be able to fold their own paper in a few minutes. 'Trap' the folded paper with the scissors but do not cut yet. It is possible to trap the paper with the scissors and hold them both up high, so everyone can see exactly where the scissors will cut.

> I'm going to cut this corner off. Then I'll unfold the paper. What will the unfolded paper look like? Will there be a corner missing? Will there be a hole in the middle? Will it be a square hole? A circle? I'll give you a chance to think. I'll put the scissors down and start again. Watch carefully while I unfold the paper.
>
> Now I'll fold it again. Watch – here's the first fold. Now here's the second fold. Look at the different edges. I'm going to cut the corner off where all the closed folds are. What will happen to the piece of paper? Close your eyes. Imagine I snip off the corner. Now imagine me unfolding the paper. Okay. Now let's do it for real.

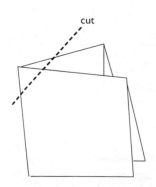

cut

Continue the activity above by getting the children to work with paper and scissors and explore the activity themselves. Suggest they imagine folding their A4 twice, but cutting to create a square or a parallelogram. Is a rectangle possible? A circle or ellipse? Many children have strong visual and kinaesthetic memory but others will find this activity quite difficult.

What is surprising is how quickly many children improve. They will find that working with shapes in this way is very beneficial and enjoyable. Start work with simple shapes and build up the level of difficulty from there. Interestingly, adults' visual memories are not much further developed than children's, though they may be better at spatial awareness through practice at parking cars, loading dishwashers, packing suitcases and tidying things away. Tidying up the classroom by packing things away improves children's spatial awareness as well as making the classroom tidy!

To extend the activity start with a sheet of A4 and fold 4 times. There are 4 ways of cutting a square quarter off the folded shape. What will the result be? Will the 4 ways produce the same pattern when the paper is unfolded?

N9

p. 53

DEVELOPING THE ABILITY TO VISUALISE

Imaginary paper cutting doesn't produce any mess.

> Imagine an equilateral triangle. How many sides has it got? How many vertices? Are all the sides the same length?

Imagine you have a pair of scissors. Cut the corners off the triangle carefully with three neat cuts, which are exactly the same. What shape have you got now?
An upside down triangle.
I've got an octagon – no it's not – it's got 6 sides.
A hexagon then? How did you know it has 6 sides?
There were 3 triangle sides before and then I made 3 cuts, so 3 plus 3 makes 6.
What happened to the bits that got cut off?
They floated away.
What shape were they?
Three little triangles!
Equilateral?
I'm not sure.
Anyone see something else?
I just got an upside down equilateral triangle, straight away!
Well done, that's good. Anyone know why both results are right?
Let's try the whole thing again. This time we can start by imagining a square. Ready?

Work with the whole class, with their eyes closed or, if that is uncomfortable, with hands gently covering eyes to reduce external stimulation and promote stronger mental images. This sequence of activities is designed to strengthen the ability to create and then control visual images. Start by practising making images.

> Imagine a little dot and put it in the middle of your mind so you can move it around. Make it go up and down, left and right, round in a circle or a zigzag. Try making it stop and start. Try changing colour. Try a different background colour. I want you to get as much control as you can. I'll wait while you have a little play. Don't worry if you can't see any pictures in your mind. Just imagine your dot moving and stopping.
>
> Bring it back into the centre of your vision. Make it grow into a circle and then shrink it down again. Make it grow to infinity, then try to get it back. Make it into a little circle and hold it still. Now move the circle around. Shrink it back to a dot – and relax!

Imagining number lines
Imagining number lines can be used to gain greater control over visual images.

I want you to think about the numerals 1, 2, 3, 4, 5. Think hard. Try to see them in your mind. Can you see them all at the same time? What do they look like?
All jumbled and moving around.
Can you stop them from moving?
Numbers all in a line.
Like a piece of a number line?
All jumbled up.
Good. Now concentrate on the 4. What's happened?
My 4 went red and started flashing.
My 4 went bigger and the other ones disappeared.
Now bring them all back so you can see them all at the same time. Very gently try to look closely at the 1 without losing the others. Try again.
Now let's imagine a part of the hundred square. Can you see 86, 87 and 88? Look underneath 86 and what do you see? Now look above 86. Can you see how far it is to 90?

S2 Activities and investigations

This is a rich area with plenty of opportunities for teaching mathematics and for emphasising the human response to environment. Humans are opportunists and technologists, many of whom have an innate desire to decorate themselves and everyday objects such as pottery, walls and floors. Teachers need to cultivate those children who have an ability to visualise, and who can describe what they see with precise detail.

Most children go through phases of spatial exploration, although much of it is done before formal schooling. They get involved in space filling, tidying shelves and cupboards, fitting objects into others (cramming lunch boxes with small toys), connecting large pieces of furniture with adhesive tape or string. Linda Pound gives a good account of these activities as *schema* in her book *Supporting Mathematical Development* (1999). For children with a passion for shape, art and spatial activities, this part of the mathematics curriculum can be crucial in gaining access to the rest of mathematics.

In all cultures there are marvellous examples of the celebration of nature and the appreciation of natural form. There are many starting points for classroom activity. Young children's curiosity about symmetry and asymmetry is easily exploited through play with large construction materials for use on the floor, and also table-top activities with Poleidoblocs, Play People, Duplo, pattern blocks, large cloths and blankets and so on. This provides for a response to the materials, an exploration of inner feelings about form, symmetry, proportion, inside and outside, and the beginnings of notions of aesthetics in relation to architecture, art and technology.

> The NNS has one strand devoted to 'Shape, space and measures'. (See NNS (1999) *Framework*, Section 1: 39–40.)

Visual learners in particular benefit from the shape and space curriculum. Currently the mathematics curriculum overemphasises the importance of numbers. It is important to begin moves to redress this imbalance by restating the importance of shape and space work. Children live in a highly stimulating world of movement, shape and colour, much of it provided by television and computer software. Children do not need to remain passive recipients in a visual electronic world. Both electronic and traditional classroom activities can link art, mathematics and technology in ways that provide opportunities for aesthetic involvement and discrimination.

> Visual learners in your class may have a preference for solving spatial problems, for using their visual abilities to support their intellectual and logico-mathematical reasoning. They may want to draw, doodle or scribble and use other visual and spatial means to support thinking, particularly in number work. They may need to record their knowledge and express their ideas in visual, diagrammatic ways.

An important part of the pedagogy of mathematics is to find ways of working visually with children. Visualisation and imagining are powerful tools for the teacher to develop. The ability to visualise has benefits not only in shape and space work but in all areas of mathematics, including number, particularly in the use of number lines, and in other curriculum areas, encouraging risk-taking, creativity and fast manipulation.

ACTIVITIES FOR SHAPE, LANGUAGE AND VISUALISATION

To develop language and the ability to visualize:

> There's only one shape in the bag today.
> Is it a square shape?
> *No it's not, I think it is a little bit oblong.*
> I've put three shapes in the bag today. Name one before taking it out of the bag.

Find the shape that someone else has named:

> Elspeth thinks there's a cuboid in the bag.
> Can you find it?

Find the shape when only its qualities are described:

> I've lost my shape! It's got a round base, only one edge, two faces, and a point. Can you find it for me please?
> *Here it is, it's like a pointy hat.*
> Find the two shapes that have something in common.
> Can you find the yellow shape? [They know they cannot, but they still try!]

There are various options that develop visualisation, language and discrimination.

For young children especially, guessing what is contained in a bag is an enjoyable task. Put a few shapes in a bag and pass it round.

- What sound do we get when we shake the bag?
- Put your hand in and feel a shape.
- What does the shape feel like?

Back-to-back activities are a variant on the 'bag of bits'. Children sit in pairs back-to-back with four or five Click Cubes each. One of the pair assembles their cubes to make a shape they can describe to their partner. The partner has the same number of cubes and sits waiting for instructions. Sitting back-to-back, the designer describes their design and the builder copies it. This demands the accurate use of positional language, (next, before, on top, underneath, . . .).

Large blankets are very useful – they can be square, rectangular or circular. They can be laid on the floor and, for classes that are difficult to manage, the perimeter can usefully define the edge of the work area. Children like to lie, sit or stand on them. You can fold the cloth in half in different ways and compare how many can lie on it. How many can stand around the perimeter? Fold and fold again. How many bottoms can fit this time? Without using the children, you can simply demonstrate different types of folding: each time discussing what has changed and what has stayed the same.

Action Mats (by Multilink and supplied by E.J. Arnold) are expensive but tremendously durable. They have a series of shape puzzles printed on the surface. The mats can be used on the floor but are also small enough to fit on a table top. The problems range widely in difficulty across several mats.

S3

p. 108

There are many books which show the variety of shapes that can be made using all or some of the pieces. Jigsaw puzzles exist for all ages and providing the level of difficulty is not too great, using jigsaw puzzles improves hand and eye co-ordination as well as matching part to whole, and searching for pattern. Work on the relative areas of the pieces. Which are the same area? Why?

The Chinese tangram has been around for centuries and there are many wooden and plastic versions as well as paper-based and computer versions.

CLASSIFYING QUADRILATERALS

Use Geostrips or Meccano to make a range of quadrilaterals. Either use the table below as a system of classification to show which quadrilaterals are possible using strips of various lengths, or make lots of different shapes, then try to fit them into the table.

Write or draw the shapes you make	All four strips different	One pair of strips same length	Two pairs but different lengths	Three the same length	All four the same length
All angles different					
One right angle					
Opposite sides parallel					
Opposite sides equal length					

N6

p. 38

- Make and sort some paper quadrilaterals using a Venn diagram.

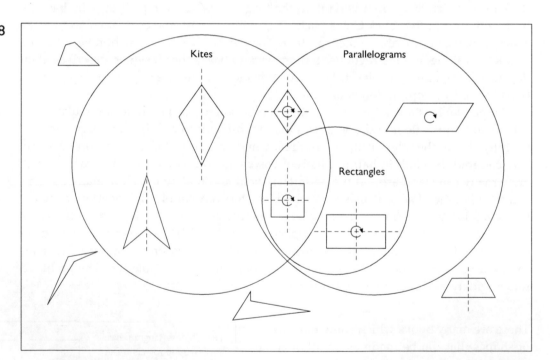

Venn diagram of quadrilaterals

- Or use a Carroll diagram to show the result of your sorting.
- What conclusions can you draw?
- Have you included all your quadrilaterals?
- Does your diagram include all the quadrilaterals that can be made?

SHAPE AND SPACE PRACTICAL TASKS

What can you make from the two halves of a square?
Does the square have to be cut along the diagonal to make two halves?
Try similar activities with a rectangle and a hexagon.

Two dancing triangles

Take a square of paper about 10 × 10 cm and draw in the two diagonals. Carefully cut along both diagonals to make four similar triangles. Use these triangles to make as many different shapes as you can. Invent rules to constrain or free you in the positioning of the triangles and the type of shape allowed.

Use a selection of Poleidoblocs or make some 3D shapes with Polydron and use an OHP to look at shadows. Ask children to bring in a torch. Late in the afternoon in November or December is a good time because of the relatively low natural light levels, so you do not need to worry about curtains or blinds.

Give a collection of shapes to each group and let them use their torches to project images of the various shapes. As a whole class activity, put one of the shapes on the OHP, project shadows onto the screen. After a simple exploration, start to explore the creation of unexpected shadows.

Suggest the children put the torches onto some Blutack (so they do not roll), and rotate the different 3D shapes slowly in the beam. Turn each shape round, turn it over. What shadows can you make?

For you to demonstrate with the OHP, you will need some Blutack. Stick a cube onto the OHP glass plate by a vertex. What image does this project? Balance a tetrahedron on its four different vertices. Balance a thick cylinder on its curved surface (but you will need to keep the Blutack hidden underneath this time). What can you conclude from the shadows and their related shapes?

Try making 2 × 2 tiles with 4 square tiling generators or beer mats. How many different 2 × 2 tiles can you make with 4 of these tiles?

Shape name	Faces	Corners	Faces + corners	Edges

- Use Polydron, Clixi or ATM beer mats to make some 3D shapes.
- Explore how many faces can meet at a corner.
- Make a table of faces, corners and edges to show your results.
- How many shapes have you created?
- What conclusions can you draw from your table?

PASSOLA OR POLYGRAMS

Passola (or polygrams) is a 'people maths' activity where a ball of string is passed from one to another according to a fixed rule which leads to the generating of patterns in circles.

P = number of people in the circle, S = number of steps to next person who will get the ball of string. Demonstrate with one group in front of the rest of the class. Select six people labelled 0 to 5 or 1 to 6. The first is the starter.

> Stand in a circle holding hands, drop hands when you are happy with the shape of the circle. Mark the spot on the floor where you are with a piece of masking tape. If you are good at catching then all stand otherwise all sit on the floor.

A ball of string/wool is passed/unrolled to the next person on your left. This is 1 step with 6 people so it is 'passola (6, 1)'. Stop when you get back to the person who started. Try passola (6, 2), that is, 6 people pass it on to the 2nd person on their left. Notice that some never get to touch the ball of wool. Try to visualise the patterns for passola (6, 3), (6, 4), (6, 5) and (6, 6), sometimes known as polygram {P/S}, e.g. {6/3}.

Next try passola with 7 people and 1 step (7, 1). Repeat the throws until everyone feels confident with the step before unravelling the string/wool starting with the starter. Visualise passola (7, 0) and (7, 7) and try them if you need to. Now roll the string back into a ball and try passola (7, 2) and so on. Encourage the children to say what they think is going on as they work: to 'say what they see'.

Try putting the wool down carefully on the floor, to look at the pattern more closely, trying to keep the shapes as regular as possible. What shapes can you see? Count the triangles, kites and heptagons.

Model the activity with people and string/wool or a ball first before recording the activity on paper. As you work, a group member who is not in the circle could write down the rules in plain English as you uncover them.

(7, 1) (7, 2) (7, 3)

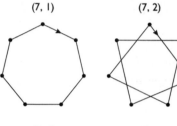
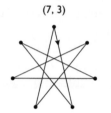

(7, 6) (7, 5) (7, 4)

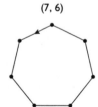
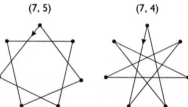

> • Which steps result in the same shape?
> • What happens if you pass right instead of left, will it make any difference?
> • What happens with other odd numbers of people?
> • What happens with prime numbers?
> • What happens with even numbers of people?
> • Which combinations of steps and people produce stars?
> • How could you produce tighter stars?
> • Can you predict most outcomes?

A p. 150

C p. 175

While taking part in the passola activity, notice the difference between doing it, waiting for the ball of wool, wondering where it is going next *and* watching the ball of wool, predicting when it is going to come to you, predicting the pattern and knowing where it is going with confidence. Discuss the rules you were given and those you have found out, before you start to record the patterns on paper.

- Roll a wet or paint-laden tennis ball across a large hoop placed on top of a larger sheet of paper. A high risk strategy!
- Draw on paper using a template. Make your own template.
- Make patterns on card with wool or silk thread.
- Model on the computer using LOGO:
    ```
    TO passola :people :step
      REPEAT :people [FD 100 RT :step * 360 / :people]
    END
    ```

PENTOMINOES INVESTIGATION

Pentominoes explores the different shapes that you can make from 5 square tiles or cubes. The sides must fit together without overlapping. Make the rules early on, use square Clixi, Polydron or beer mats or use Multilink or Centicubes (you may wish to limit the shapes to one layer only at first).

In this investigation you need to look for similarities and differences, share ideas, reject and accept your own ideas and the ideas of others. You need to justify your decisions and understand the rules you have made to limit this investigation.

It is important for you to work on your own within the group. Consider taking on a role such as recorder, sketcher, spy, trader, rule maker or strategist.

A

p. 158

Be systematic by trying 1, 2, then 3, then 4 squares, this might make the problem of predicting how many there will be in a set simpler to solve. If you have found all the shapes for 4, is there a systematic way to look for potential shapes with 5? *Clue* 4 + 1 = 5. Try using colour to help distinguish shapes.

- Work in a group and when you have made a new shape, put it in the centre of your group's workspace. Remove it if someone else has already made that shape.
- When you think that most of the shapes have been made, then stop to discuss carefully what makes the shapes different. Naming them will help identify them.
- Show your work to other groups. You can present the work to the class with small squares on an OHP or cut-up imitation tiled vinyl to show on the floor.
- Concepts of symmetry and isometries (the same shape but with different handedness, like left and right hands) are likely to appear.
- Record or display your work in some way before the next lesson.

Variations and extensions are easy to develop.

- What if not 5? What if not squares? What if cubes? Try Hexiamonds.
- Work on tile patterns and tessellation for any of the pentominoes; 3D pentacubes can be more than one layer deep use Centicubes or Multilink.
- You can make puzzles by trying to fit together all the pentominoes.
- Work on the ways of recording 2D and 3D representations.
- Allow the 2D shapes to be turned around but not turned over.
- Tabulate and to try to generalise from your results.

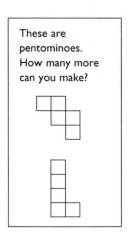

These are pentominoes. How many more can you make?

Pentominoes

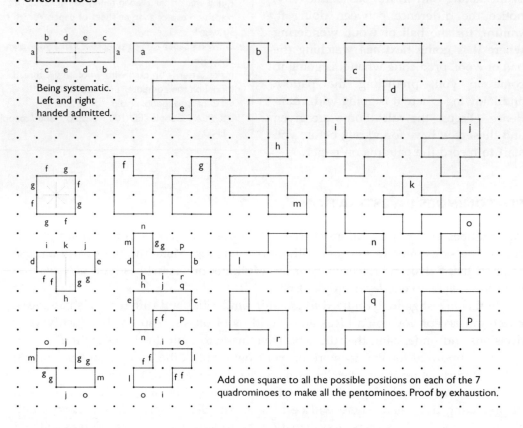

Being systematic.
Left and right
handed admitted.

Add one square to all the possible positions on each of the 7
quadrominoes to make all the pentominoes. Proof by exhaustion.

Hexiamonds

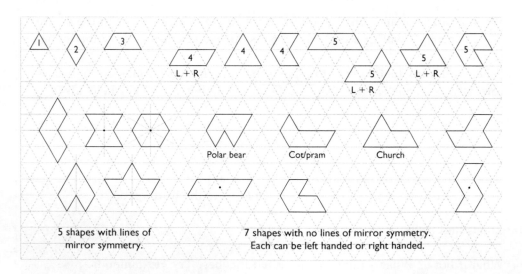

5 shapes with lines of
mirror symmetry.

7 shapes with no lines of mirror symmetry.
Each can be left handed or right handed.

Name the shapes. Can you find the butterfly, plane, rocket and ship? Which shapes have rotational symmetry? How can you be sure you have found all the shapes?

No. of triangles	No. of shapes	No. of shapes + L & R isomers
1	1	1
2	1	1
3	1	1
4	3	4
5	4	6
6	12	19

HEXIAMONDS

Hexiamonds explores the 2D or 3D shapes that you can make from 6 equilateral triangles. Use materials such as Clixi, Polydron, beer mats or card. This should make it easier to produce the alternatives easily and quickly and give you time to sort out which are different and which are the same but perhaps in a different orientation.

- What rules might you make to get the work done in time?
- Work as a group in collaboration or as individuals sitting round a table.
- How can you be sure all the shapes are actually different?
- Clear a space in the middle of the table and put your shape there for others to see. If the shape you have just made is a new shape leave it there. If it is the same as one already there, then try to change it to make it different.
- When you think you have most of the variations, at least one person in each group should record the shapes. [Use triangular paper (sometimes called isometric paper); if none is available then sketch the shapes on plain paper.]
- Another person could tabulate the results. How many for 1 triangle? For 2? 3? 4? 5? And lastly 6?
- Are your results the same as other groups? Send a spy or trade information.
- At the very least offer the number of alternatives and see if everyone agrees.

As teacher, you could record this, and keep updating it during the session. If you make different rules then you may well get different results.

- One way of starting with a simplified activity is to start with only 1 triangle, then with 2 triangles and so on, exhausting all possibilities each time. The solutions for 4 must result in part from one more triangle added to the existing set of 'triamonds'.
- When you have a complete set of hexiamonds, try to classify those shapes that will make a closed 3D shape from the hexiamond.
- Another approach is to start with 6 triangles and make them into any 3D shape. Then unpick this shape and see what the net for it looks like.
- Work such as this can lead to work on design and packaging, making a net for a 3D shape, mats, etc.

> - It is a good idea to name the shapes so that you can talk about them.
> - Try to make a record of the shapes you make. How can you do this easily?
> - Discuss your findings with another group.
> - Try to work systematically, making rules to limit the investigation so you can complete it. Try to avoid an investigation with an infinite number of solutions.

C

p. 175

This can be used as a one-session investigation or, over a period of weeks, with a 'special needs' class to work on the cardinality of 6. It can also be used to explore the relationship between 2D and 3D shapes, to design and make multicoloured patterned mats (hexagonal). Congruence, symmetry and tessellation have also featured as key concepts for extension activities.

S3 **Working with cloths**

This work develops children's knowledge of shape and space through VAK activities using a variety of large cloths. It is based on ideas from de Bono (1974) and Evans (1985). Curtains and sheets are useful but must be pliable and capable of being folded at least three times.

'THE MAGICIAN'S CAPE': A CIRCULAR CLOTH

'The Magician's Cape' is a good activity to use to start with, using a circular cloth folded up. You can gradually reveal its original shape by unfolding slowly. Three different activities follow, which can be used independently or together in the same session, varying the time spent on each. It is important to approach this activity flexibly, paying particular attention to pace, which must be influenced by the age of the children and their responses.

A

p. 155

Start by sitting the children on the floor in the smallest circle possible around the cloth. Ask children: 'What is this?' Briefly accept suggestions for what the object really is, e.g. a piece of folded cloth.

> 'What kind of cloth?'
> 'Where might you see something like this?'
> *In a window . . . on a table . . . in a Harry Potter film.*

Then ask questions such as,

> 'What does this remind you of?'
> 'What does this look like?'

S2

p. 101

Try to encourage the children to make creative links between the shape in front of them and their imagination, bearing in mind children's experience of a slice of cake, piece of pizza, slice of melon, wedge of cheese, rocket cone, flag, pickaxe, witches' hat, . . . You can ask for suggestions from anyone or go round the circle looking at each child in turn. They can of course 'pass'. Keep the cloth carefully folded and hold it up so children see it from various angles. Change the orientation, turn it clockwise, then anticlockwise. Is it a windsock or nose-cone? Rotate through 90 degrees; is it a witches' hat or ice cream cone? Notice how orientation matters.

Children may only be familiar with images of a triangle or a square sitting on their bases. In textbooks and workbooks this is predominantly what children are offered. What happens when this object is shown resting on its point in an obviously unstable or metastable state? Is there a base now?

Touch is important to many children. If possible, use something like an old velvet or velour curtain. Anything that looks good, does not crease and could pass for a magician's cape!

STEPPING AROUND A FOLDED CIRCULAR CLOTH

For some children it is now no longer a triangle or square: typically the square will be called a diamond. You can lay the shape down on the floor and walk around it. Then, facing the children, hold up and rotate the shape, with your tummy as the centre, in the vertical plane. These are not identical experiences.

So now we have engaged with the representation of the shape in front of us. We have made our own mental links and heard the ideas of others, many of which we can readily accept. The unusual ones might help us see the shape in a different and novel way. Do not discount 'weird' replies, but do probe if you wish. Draw the children's attention to the differing views by reminding them of what different individuals have said. Collect some responses if you wish. At a later stage they could use wipe boards to draw what they imagine.

Put the folded cloth on the floor. (The colour needs to show up clearly against the colour of the floor.) Count the number of sides, running your index finger along the edge/side. For the sector with a small part of the circumference visible make a short wobbly sound, make a long monotonous sound for the straight sides.

Oooooooooooooooooo o o n e, Ttttttttttttttttttttt t t w o, THRE E E E.

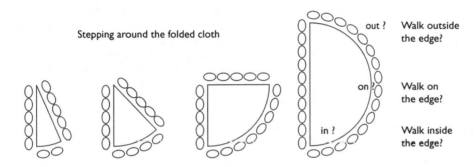

Stepping around the folded cloth

out ? Walk outside the edge?

on ? Walk on the edge?

in ? Walk inside the edge?

Ask if anyone can explain the significance of the noises? Long sound for a long side, short sound for a short side. Monotonous sound for a straight side, Wobbly sound for a curved side. Two long sides and one shorter curved side. What can they say about the two straight sides (equal radii)?

'Are there three sides?'
'If so, then is this a triangle?'

Measure length with 'fairy steps' with no space between heel and toe, or a shoe or some other object you might wish to use as an arbitrary unit. Tabulate or record if you wish. Ask a child to record or walk the steps for you. You model this first.

'When I unfold the cloth by one fold how many sides will there be?'
'How long will they be?'
'Can you predict the sounds I'll make?'

Then unfold the cloth slowly.

'Were you right?'

Repeat the perimeter measurement using the same units as before.

FOLDING AND UNFOLDING CLOTHS

Let children make the sounds as well. Count the number of thicknesses of cloth at the circumference. Notice that the two straight sides stay the same and the curved side doubles in length. If the cloth is thin enough you might be able to fold it into sixteenths. Eighths will have eight thicknesses; quarters will have four.

At some point the number of sides will go from 3 to 2! 'Have we lost a side?' Can they point out that 2 radii have become 1 diameter? Use the NNS *Mathematical Vocabulary Book* (1998) to check language.

Hold up this semicircular shape, rotate it in different ways and ask for imaginative suggestions of what it reminds them of.

The last unfolding will return the cloth to its full circular shape, now with only one side and a curved one at that! Again we can ask: 'What does this look like and what does it remind you of?'

Children really need to hold and fold the cloth themselves if this work is to be well consolidated. It could happen now, or on another occasion, but the kinaesthetic experience needs to be available to the children.

Some children may say that all sides must be straight and that a circle does not have a side. Interestingly, to draw a circle in LOGO one approach is to draw a 360-sided figure which looks very like a circle:

```
To circle
Repeat 360 [FD 10 RT 1]
End
```

• If you use material such as cotton or linen, the creases leave lines which show the six equilateral triangles.
• If you are keen, and so inclined, you could iron the cloth to emphasise the folds.
• Children enjoy playing with the cloths, recreating the activities and using them for other games, so they will need to be washed and ironed periodically.

At the end, ask them what they liked best and what they remember.

• What next?
• What could we do?

Fold up the cloth again to put it away.

Review the main points you want to get across as you conclude the activity. It could be fractions, or the relationship between radius and circumference. What about lines of symmetry (infinite)? You can easily get an estimate for 'pi' by comparing the distance around the circle (circumference) with the distance across it (diameter). π (pi) $= C/D$.

Fairy steps will give you a value near to 3. Stepping in, on or around the edge will change this value. Why?

What about other cloths? Squares, rectangles and hexagons are all interesting to use. It is well worth collecting some from a car boot sale and then carefully preparing them. They can be left out for the children to use by themselves. Consider getting hold of a large thin circular cloth to use for parachute games. Fold a hexagon in half into a trapezium, then fold up one corner to make a rhombus, fold over the other corner into an equilateral triangle and last, if you can, try folding this into a right angled triangle. Most adults, never mind children, find the unfolding process hard to predict and express surprise at each stage.

Extension activities could include discussing lines of symmetry, fractions and the number of layers of cloth and using table-top versions.

SQUARES AND RECTANGLES

Starting with a square piece of cloth is simplest and may give you and the children more confidence. With a single fold the square can be transformed into a rectangle or a triangle. A simple rectangular cloth such as an old curtain, sheet or quilt cover can be folded and unfolded in order to explore changes in size and shape. We can also reveal other properties of shape relating to perimeter, area and symmetry.

Starting with the rectangular cloth, fold in half 4 or 5 times and begin work on the concepts of area and perimeter by stepping round the folded rectangle using 'fairy steps' or a shoe or any other measuring device. Get a child or adult helper to record the results for each unfolding of the cloth.

> Ooooooooooooooone
> Tttttwo
> Thhhhhhhhhhhhree
> Fooooour

Notice two longer sounds (long sides) and two shorter sounds (short sides) in the form long, short, long, short, or a, b, a, b. This can give rise to children eventually articulating a formula for the perimeter of a rectangle as $2(a + b)$. Write down what the children say or even better get them to write it down for all to see.

A

p. 148

> It's two lots of long and short.
> You go along then across twice.

Notate and record depending on the age, interest and responses of the children.

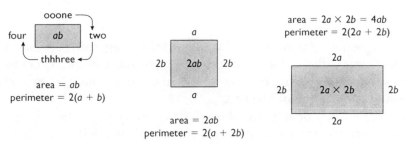

area = ab
perimeter = $2(a + b)$

area = $2ab$
perimeter = $2(a + 2b)$

area = $2a \times 2b = 4ab$
perimeter = $2(2a + 2b)$

Exploring the perimeter of an unfolding cloth

How can you measure or estimate the area? If we think of area as 'covering' a surface, we can get children or adults to stand on the cloth. First, ask them to estimate how many people can stand on the folded-up cloth. One useful rule is that your feet must be on the cloth and no part of your body can touch the carpet/floor. Count them on to the cloth and count them off, tapping their shoulder as you count. This will make things easier if there are more children involved.

Use a cloth large enough for the whole class to stand on when fully unfolded – a good group-bonding opportunity.

Questions to ask with the cloth folded:

- 'How many will fit on when we unfold the cloth by one fold?'
- 'What will the shape be?'
- 'Can you say what the lengths of the four sides will be?'
- 'What will the perimeter be?'
- 'What changes and what stays the same?'
- 'How many thicknesses of cloth are there now?'
- 'How many will fit on now?'

EXPLORING PERIMETER

Interestingly, you cannot keep doubling the people as their shoes will fit but their hips, bottoms and torsos will not. You can avoid the risk of 'people chaos' by putting only their shoes down. You might prefer to design a cloth that, when folded 4 or 5 times, can be covered with a sheet of A4 paper or card. Then children can easily see the doubling of the area each time the cloth is unfolded. Another alternative is to use square beer mats to cover the cloth and their sides to measure the perimeter.

Finally, there is the problem of selecting measuring devices. You can use huge tarpaulins with children lying down on them to estimate how much space would be needed to accommodate the whole class when camping. *Ah yes, but what happens when someone in the centre wants to get up in the middle of the night?*

Any of these activities can be transferred to the table top by using thin cloth or paper. Here is a table for the unfolding of a rectangular cloth (ratio 2:1) folded in half five times.

Folds	Length	Width	Perimeter	Area	Perimeter if $a = 2$ and $b = 1$	Area if $a = 2$ and $b = 1$
5	a	b	$2(a + b)$	ab	6	2
4	a	$2b$	$2(a + 2b)$	$2ab$	8	4
3	$2a$	$2b$	$2(2a + 2b)$	$4ab$	12	8
2	$2a$	$4b$	$2(2a + 4b)$	$8ab$	16	16
1	$4a$	$4b$	$2(4a + 4b)$	$16ab$	24	32
0	$4a$	$8b$	$2(4a + 8b)$	$32ab$	32	64

N9

p. 50

Other suggestions for materials include windsurfing sails, as they may have coloured and clear sections. Parachutes have a great track record as cloths to use in circle games, but they need much more space than can be found in most classrooms, so use them outside – or book the hall.

You can try out any or all of the above with ordinary paper, tissue paper, a hand-kerchief, or a thin silky scarf as a desktop activity while you follow the directions. Toy cars, Play People, plastic animals or Multilink Cubes might work as space fillers. Using pieces of paper and toys is useful to help you to plan and think about the activity but is not as much fun as the real thing. However, by all means consolidate and extend the children's knowledge and understanding with a desktop activity: remember children can also take folded paper home to show what they can do. The children will get great benefits from the scale of the big cloths, drawing their fingers along the edges of the folded cloth, stepping around the cloth and making up sounds to differentiate between sides.

> For a LOGO activity, the turning of the external angle at each corner needs careful work – and a desire to become a Dalek!
>
> Get children to estimate the angle and have a computer, turtle or Roamer to try out their ideas. The robots come to grief over the folded cloths so use large sheets of paper, masking tape or chalk.

WALKING OUT IN LOGO

Use playground chalk on tarmac, or masking tape on carpets or wooden floors, to make a shape, for example a triangle, square, rectangle, pentagon or hexagon. The child or adult can then walk around the shape following the straight sections of tape (sides), working out when to turn and by how much at each corner.

The teacher can play the role of a Dalek (Dr Who's sci-fi robotic adversary, that talks with a funny voice and either goes forwards or backwards in straight lines or stops and turns).

- Extend your right hand and point directly in front, while using the left hand to hold your nose.
- Make a continuous whine or sound when travelling in a straight line (along a side).
- Then stop at each corner and turn the appropriate amount (angle) until you are facing down the next section emitting a 'nick, nick, nick' noise to represent the turn.
- Notice the significance of distinguishing between moving forward a distance and then turning through an angle.
- Also notice when you try this that you are turning through the external angle.
- Remember that linking auditory response to mathematical ideas and visual activity supports those children with an auditory learning preference.

N9

p. 53

LOGO can provide us with exciting problems to solve in 1D, 2D, or even 3D. You can start by encouraging children to produce patterns using the REPEAT command. Children quickly feel in control and can achieve novel (for them) results with little effort. Trying to understand why the pattern has developed in this particular way is more problematic, but worth pursuing.

Most children can learn to define their own commands for simple shapes and save these in their own computer file for re-use. This building up of ideas is central to LOGO work. With TRIANGLE, SQUARE, PENTAGON and HEXAGON, worthwhile patterns and scenes can be built up especially if the shapes can be resized and even transformed. This is particularly easy with some versions of LOGO.

There is a danger of thinking that mathematics should be taught formally, with an emphasis on instruction, where reading is a major part of the learning activity. However, Edward de Bono began challenging formal views of learning and teaching over thirty years ago and his work has been taken up by many current writers. See, for example, Claxton (2002). Formal traditional schooling closes rather than opens children's minds: 'Mind like parachute: works only when open.'

Children need to learn how to use variables in their procedures to generate the sizes they want. The three different-sized chairs, beds and bowls in 'Goldilocks and the Three Bears' is a popular project. Some other projects could include:

- Brick wall (rectangle, brick, row of bricks/course and wall).
- Houses scaled up and down.
- Leaves and trees (holly is more interesting than might appear at first and nearly always has to be walked out).
- Generalising polygons and going on to stars, steps and stairs.
- Spirolaterals, growth patterns and work on fractal geometry.
- With multiple turtles and dynamic control further excitement beckons.

S4 **Unusual and unfamiliar**

UNUSUAL ACTIVITIES

Surprises

Starting with something unusual, including surprises and traps, is powerful because the more stimulated or interested we are, the more likely it is that an event will persist in our memory. At night, we recycle the events of the day. Some thoughts 'stay with us'. Sometimes we wake up with the solution to a problem. Often, the thoughts that sleep has brought surface into consciousness ready for use as we start the day. Teachers who are creative and innovative in other curriculum areas need to find ways to transfer their creativity to maths. We need to transfer our successful and exciting teaching styles into our maths teaching.

We all like pleasant surprises. Although schools need routines, these can become too predictable and boring. One way to engage the attention of a class is to surprise the children at the start of the session. You could try:

N2

p. 8

- a bit of mathematical magic;
- pretending to be a famous mathematician (dress up as Ahmes if you are brave enough);
- cycling into the classroom (using the bike for work on gears, ratios, etc.);
- using a puppet to explain a new idea or introduce a new game; or

N6

p. 38

- teach without speaking, a technique that can lead to using 'Silent Way' or mime.

You could count and perhaps speak in a different language. The patterns and structure emerge. Beat out a rhythm or pattern which the children copy: 'Name that riff', then analyse it. Make up a rap, song or poem to help learn some facts.

It is better if your opening gambit has some relevance to the work to be done. Do something surprising once a term; it should enhance your reputation, you might even enjoy the risk and try it more often! Try a double act with another teacher.

A set of what?

Reveal objects one at a time from a box, bag, stocking, cloth or old suitcase. Passing the objects round can work as a circle activity. What do they have in common? Why these objects? Are they a set? You can try:

- a set of socks of very different sizes, lengths, colours, materials and designs;
- a set of flutes, recorders and whistles of different designs, pitches, lengths and materials (plastic, metal, wood);
- a set of usual and unusual fruit;
- a set of triangles or quadrilaterals made from Meccano, Geostrips, plastic or cardboard.

This can result in work at many different levels such as, for example: simple sorting; matching; ordering and comparing; work on logic and sets; using Venn and Carroll diagrams to classify materials; generating a binary key or tree diagram; making a concept map to clarify understanding of the properties of the set of objects.

For example, a collection of strange dried fruit, pineapple, pine cone, sunflower head, flowers, plants and leaves, could be used for work on Fibonacci series. See www.mcs.surrey.ac.uk.

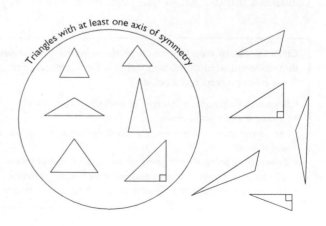

Triangles with at least one axis of symmetry

What's in the bag?

Feel inside the bag, comment and pass on; use as a circle time activity. Try 2D and 3D shapes from a set of 3D shapes or everyday objects or shapes made from Polydron. Wrap the object up like a present and pass round the parcel. Put light or heavy objects inside, for example, cat bells, sand, gravel, lentils, nuts, bolts, cotton wool, pot-pourri, essential oils, garden flowers and herbs (guess the smell). (I have used a French Smell Lotto available from some perfume factories in France.) Ask for children's comments, suggestions or questions.

Questions

Starting with questions is a natural starting point, but ask one pupil to write down, clearly and in order, all the questions asked about an object as it is passed around. You might use post-it notes, wipe boards or an interactive whiteboard. Give no answers, just collect questions. Then discuss how the class might find the answers. Where could they look? Whom could they ask? What observations, measurements, investigations, might they be able to conduct? Starting from their questions about an object or set you have collected gives you some control of direction and content but demands their interest.

Unusual objects

Unusual and interesting objects can stimulate discussion and a lot of work. For example:

B

p. 161

- a 6 m python skin and a windsurfing sail will produce questions relating to measurement;
- old letters, photos and documents could give raw information for a family adventure/detective game;
- newspapers, books and magazines, both old and new, have inspired data handling and work on the media;
- fossils, old coins, Russian dolls, sea urchins, starfish, old family photos, dodecahedrons, crystals.

Projects and topics

Projects and topics will get off to a more exciting start if they begin with an unusual activity or object. Explore the local area of your new school at the weekend. Ask the children to bring in fascinating objects or to search the Internet as part of their homework. Perhaps introduce a new face to the classroom. Visitors can come to talk about life, work or interests, or you can make a visit to a local park, shop or factory. Memorable examples include:

- an architect parent working on cantilever bridge design, explaining forces, tension and compression with carefully made models to a fascinated Years 5/6 class;
- conducting a local tree survey for the District Council, measuring, recording and mapping trees, which generated really useful data;
- making a representation of 1 000 000 using 1 mm square graph paper strips 1 cm wide round and round the classroom;
- children in a special school designing a maths trail for other local children and adults to use;

Working with large numbers

A biscuit wrapper claiming more than 3 000 000 sold each week, generated questions such as:

- How many lorryloads would that be?
- What would be the weight of 3 000 000 Tunnocks?
- How much would they cost?
- If everyone in class ate one a day how long would they last?
- If everyone in ___ village ate one a day how long would they last?

- How many seconds have you lived?
- How much does the school weigh?
- If we all held hands could we form a circle around the outside of the school?

- children classifying, drawing, researching and, with the school cook, making recipes using fruits and vegetables used by the Aztecs as part of a project on the Aztecs;
- working on a 'value for money' shopping basket with a local supermarket manager, comparing brand and size costs per 100 g (cola drinks cost more than diesel; medium-sized tins of beans are sometimes cheaper per 100g than a large tin).

Maths trails

Maths trails and the local environment are excellent for planning mathematical visits. Go to the local shops, look for the local park and interesting buildings and don't forget to look at the potential offered by the school grounds. One primary school in the centre of Plymouth has developed a marvellous range of areas over a period of more than ten years. These include a butterfly garden (symmetry), herb garden, different brick, stone and paving patterns (tessellation), small tree collection (Fibonacci), fossil and rock trail (time line), mini beast area (real data), recycling area, and board games from around the world (evaluated and selected by the children then professionally made to playground scale). These facilities can be used in and out of lesson time. In such an environment, maths trails are easy for teachers and children to design.

Bag of bits

N6

p. 38

A bag of bits is an interesting starting point. Ask every member of the class to bring in a carrier bag with 5 or 6 items, more if they wish. The items should be of interest to the owner and stimulate the senses in some way. If you don't think they can or will do this then provide your own bags; but this is not as personal.

Start a bag of bits where the children provide most of the resources and the teacher is not the limiting factor. This is a good way to start work on sets and Venn, Carroll and tree diagrams. Real objects from the real world versus 'psychologically clean' objects made for schools. An interesting variety is likely to appear when different people bring very different things: they cannot avoid bringing something of themselves. This works with people of all ages.

Unusual sets

Unusual and interesting sets can be planned with the five senses in mind. The set should stimulate a wide range of children: include bells, rattles, squeakers, rough, smooth, shiny, heavy, light, a range of scents and different smells.

- Have you used a wide range of objects? Enough things? Things that do not belong and are clearly not members of the set. Include traps or unknown objects that do not fit the classification.
- Have any of your things got properties or qualities that relate to shape and space, numbers, measuring, problem-solving or data handling?

Traps

Teachers can set the occasional 'trap' for children to fall into. They can play 'devil's advocate', and deliberately confuse and challenge children to confirm and deepen their understanding.

- Make a 'spoof' announcement: 'PE will be at 22.30 this Sunday.' What's wrong?
- Run a program that randomly produces wrong answers: $2 \times 3 = 7$. Help!
- Use 'Broken LOGO', where RT 90 results in RT 85 or 95 and FD 100 results in FD (90 + random 20).
  - What is happening here?
  - Is the computer broken?
  - It was okay yesterday.
- Use plastic shapes, such as Dienes Logic Blocks, as 'alien' money. Act normally.
- Use software to present numbers from another number system or base (binary or hex).

Organise groups of 4 to 6 children around a table, each with their own set of 5 or 6 things (giving 20 to 36 in total). Cover the table with a large sheet of plain paper.

- Pick an object. Pass it round. Say something about it.
- Hide an object. One person has it and knows what it is. The rest ask questions about it.
- You, or a child, think of one of the objects in the set on the table. They whisper what it is to a friend who says nothing. The rest have to guess which one you or the child is thinking about using less than 20 questions. Yes/no answers only.
- One of the group can sort out the objects by some secret property that matters to them. The rest must try to guess the reasoning behind the way the objects have been sorted. What have the objects in each set got in common?
- Use a feely bag, box or container to hide objects in so they can be felt but not seen. Hide one unseen, unknown object. One child can guess what it is by feeling, talking about what they feel. Others can ask questions and also guess what the object is.
- Try this with more than one object at once.
- Find, make or buy 3D puzzles to put together or take apart.

BREAK STATES: BRAIN GYM AND OTHER RHYTHMIC PATTERNS

Break states

Break states are just that. A way of breaking the current state to change activity, release tension, revitalise, relax, start or effect a smooth transition or ending. Some teachers use a whistle, piano chords, march, play Simon Says, get children to mimic the teacher's gestures, play Chinese whispers or sing instructions to their class and the children sing back.

Brain Gym

Brain Gym aims to connect the left and right sides of your brain. This should help improve motor co-ordination. The activities can be used to manage transitions, sustain motivation, boost interest and energy levels. They are quick and effective ways to change the physical and mental state of your class at the start, during or at the end of a session. Use, modify, develop, collect, share and enjoy.

'Double Doodle'

'Double Doodle' uses cheap paper and pens (or large wax crayons or coloured chalk).

- Draw large shapes first clockwise and then anticlockwise, then change hands and begin again.
- Try using both hands together.
- Try to produce the mirror image.

It is useful to work on balancing clockwise and anticlockwise movements. Many children really find it very helpful in developing first their gross motor control and then their fine motor control, which improves control over pencils, crayons, scissors and handwriting.

Look out for those children who initially can only go one way *either* clockwise *or* anticlockwise. It is possibly related to handedness.

> **Ways of giving instructions**
>
> - Tell them. (*Instruction*)
> - Show them. (*Demonstration or modelling the activity*)
> - They tell or show one another.
> - Provide a tape recording of the instructions.
> - Use a card with words, prompts, colours, pictures, some of the objects stuck on.
> - Offer paper, labels, string and pens to support making Venn, Carroll and tree diagrams.

Sky-writing uses 'Double Doodle' techniques in the air.

- It is cheaper, faster and you can assess the whole class very quickly.
- Try letter formation, spelling words, numbers, formulae, shapes, in fact anything.
- Say the letter, word or idea as you move your hands.
- Try going larger and then smaller, slower then faster.
- Try using both hands to create mirror images or to produce the same pattern with both index fingers tracing out characters in the same direction.

'Deux Mains et Deux Pieds'

'Deux Mains et Deux Pieds' uses hands and/or feet, clapping, stamping, patting the table or lap, finger clicking, vocal sounds or whatever to produce a rhythmic pattern that pupils can repeat. It can be done with the children sitting at the desks, or standing behind their chairs.

- Imagine you are Freddy Mercury at Wembley. 'We will, we will rock you.'
- Very complex rhythms can be built up and sustained just using hands and feet.
- Start by walking on the spot. Count 1, 2, 3 and 4.
- When this is secure, try it softer, louder, slower, faster.
- Try emphasising one beat (1st), or two beats (1st and 3rd).
- Clap hands on 1 and 3. Then on 2 and 4.
- Try just 1 or 4 or 1 and 4.
- Stamp or clap just to the emphasised beat; hear the rest.
- Ask the music teacher, go to Samba School, collect rhythms. 'Life is rhythm, man.'

O5

p. 80

'Alphabet Edit'

'Alphabet Edit' uses the alphabet, or any series of numbers, letters, words or symbols that you want to learn, written on an OHT, a sheet of paper or on the board.

Under each letter, word or symbol put:

    L   put up your left hand
    R   put up your right hand
    B   put up both hands

This is much harder than it looks, but strangely restful and invigorating.

Say the letter, number, word or symbol as you do the movement. Start slowly then speed up as you get better. Try number sequences such as 'times' tables, squares or prime numbers.

A	B	C	D	E	F	G	H	I	J	K	L	M	N	O	P	Q	R	S	T	U	V	W	X	Y	Z
L	L	R	L	R	B	R	L	B	B	L	L	R	L	R	B	R	L	B	L	R	R	R	L	B	L

3	6	9	12	15	18	21	24	27	30	33	36	39	42	45	48	51	54	57	60
L	L	R	L	R	B	R	L	B	B	L	L	R	L	R	B	R	L	B	L

Adapted from activities from Dennison and Dennison (1986), Smith (1998), ATM (1987) and Liebling (1999)

TEAM BUILDING AND PERSONAL DEVELOPMENT ACTIVITIES

- Mime passing a precious, rare, delicate or dangerous object while sitting in a circle.
- Mime passing an object to the next person (you could use a crumpled piece of paper, cloth or sponge or nothing).
- The group has to guess what object is being passed on. For example, a precious jewel, dying bird, beautiful rose, jelly, beetle, snake, small furry creature, hand grenade, sharp knife, dirty nappy, full glass of wine, hot cup of tea.

Mime

Mime action, expression and gesture while sitting in a circle. Perform an action, for example, brushing your teeth, combing your hair, blowing your nose, sneezing. The next person repeats the action, then adds their own.

You or the next person or anyone in the group can say what they think the action is or they can stay silent and try to work it out. The next person repeats the previous actions and then adds their own. As a variation, try 'My granny went to market and she bought . . .' which is a good memory game.

Help one another. Try to encourage good performances of the mimes and increasingly subtle use of gesture, facial expression or action: for example, cleaning a window using precise movements in one plane with a pretend scraper and clearly defined glass surface while looking carefully to avoid any drips or smears.

'It's a Tick, It's a Tock'

'It's a Tick, It's a Tock' is a game where a phrase is heard and passed on. It needs a group to be sitting in a circle.

- Begin demonstrating the game with a warm-up, by turning to the person on your left and saying: 'It's a tick.'
- That person asks you, 'It's a what?'
- You repeat 'It's a tick.'
- That person then repeats this to the person on their left. They say: 'It's a tick.'
- The person on their left asks them: 'It's a what?'
- They repeat: 'It's a tick.'
- Convinced, this third person turns to the person on *their* left and repeats the whole process, gradually passing the short question-and-answer game around the circle.
- It will come back to you when the person on your right finally says to you: 'It's a tick.' You ask: 'It's a what?' They repeat: 'It's a tick.'

You can stop here and introduce the second part of the game. This time turn to the person on your *right* and say: 'It's a tock.' They demand: 'It's a what?' You repeat: 'It's a tock.' And so on as before, but going anticlockwise this time. The full game begins when you start the *Tick* going clockwise and the *Tock* going anticlockwise. At some place in the circle the two patterns cross, causing confusion and fun. You can change any of the rules. Do it with different things and actions.

Puppets

Make use of socks with elastic bands, buttons, beads, etc. to make hand puppets.

- The use of puppets is an excellent way to increase confidence, to encourage use of voice, to express feelings and to learn to act for both children and teachers.
- While writing on the blackboard, have a glove puppet on your non-writing hand. It can look over your shoulder at the class.
- The children can confide in the puppet and respond to questions put by you in the puppet's voice.
- Children can learn to read and tell stories using puppets and make up their own scripts and scenarios for role-play.
- Make your own collection of puppets.

Activities that connect both sides of the brain include:

- Describing (left) a picture or diagram (right).
- Visualising (right) a written description (left).
- Converting text or data (left) into a picture, graph or diagram (right).
- Algebra and logic or proof (left) into graphics or geometry (right).

M1 Measures and measurement

USING EXOTIC FRUIT

Some extra thought needs to go into planning lessons on measures and measurement. One challenge, for example, is ensuring that children have the technical skills such as being able to read weighing scales or angle measures sufficiently well to complete the activities we plan for them. Practical mathematics lessons pose the same challenges as practical science lessons. As with science, the majority of children really enjoy practical lessons about measures and measurement, but the technical skills and the mathematical ideas need to complement each other.

In the early stages of teaching, it pays to play with unfamiliar equipment yourself as part of your lesson preparation. If you think about what you want the children to do, set yourself the same demands and ask yourself the same questions. This will let you identify more clearly the potential challenges that your lesson creates. Some types of equipment do not always perform as you would expect: some so-called weighing balances will do everything *except* balance two objects that weigh the same amount!

c

p. 170

One book that tries to match children's developmental stages against mathematical concepts is Deboys and Pitt (1988). It is best not to assume that your lessons will ensure *all* the children go through *all* these supposed stages in a controlled manner. There is a lot of evidence to suggest that children learn in unpredictable ways, even when we are very prescriptive about our lesson content. The information in Deboys and Pitt can be used to remind us that in activities such as weighing, for example, there are easier and harder concepts and skills for children to learn. We need to be sensitive to conceptual and skills development, rather than stick rigidly to a list, and ensure that in our lessons we ask children to work from simpler to more sophisticated concepts. It is unreasonable to expect a child to try to read a scale to the nearest 100 g when they still find it difficult to work out the value of an unnumbered graduation. Considering halves and quarters of an object, for example an orange, is very different from considering half a kilogram (500 g, 0.5 kg, 1/2 kg, 50% of a kilo, 500/1000 g).

A collection of exotic fruit will provide the focus for a week's work covering: observational drawing and mixed media in art lessons; measures work and money in mathematics; countries of origin and transportation in geography; seasons, germination, dispersal and growth in science; the establishment of orangeries and heated greenhouses in eighteenth- and nineteenth-century British country houses in history (possibly a local National Trust visit); healthy eating and personal food preferences in the PSHME (personal, social, health and moral education) curriculum; and describing shape, colour, smell, texture and taste in English.

It is useful to buy a couple of examples of each fruit: mangoes, passion fruit, melons, etc. They can be put on display for two or three days beside a selection of drawing paper of different colours and textures and a range of colouring media.

MEASURES

Use a question board for children to write questions about the fruit on card or post-its that can be answered later. Children can think about paper texture and media before being allowed to use any. Although relatively expensive, oil pastels are ideal for smudging, blending and mixing to match the colouration of the fruit.

Children can make a colour palette, choosing a single colour and producing some subtly different shades. Use a card rectangle with a rectangular hole in it as a viewfinder to help children look closely at one part of a piece of fruit and work on the pattern and colours rather than try to draw the whole fruit. On another occasion, cutting one piece of each fruit to expose the inside allows for a new round of observation and colour mixing, this time looking at the inner structure, seeds, etc.

Another strategy is to sketch the fruit quickly, take a bite and sketch again, repeating this process until only the core is left. This series of sketches tells the story of the fruit being eaten.

For mathematics there are several choices including: number and graph work involving cost; taste preferences involving data collection; or direct comparison of fruit by weighing.

- How many might fit in a box?
- What is the circumference of each piece of fruit?
- Then find the average: display each measurement using an appropriate length piece of string or tape. This method will give a good sense of the mean, mode and median values.
- A study of cost could be combined with a visit to a local greengrocer or supermarket to learn about supply, countries of origin, transportation, storage conditions, shelf-life and so on.
- Fair trade issues and profit margins can come to the fore if you compare prices paid to growers and others at each stage. You might need to get this data from an independent source such as the Office of Fair Trading or the Consumers' Association (you can use the Internet for this).
- Take a close look at what information supermarket till receipts provide. Compare different supermarkets.

Use costs per item for younger children or the cost per 100 g or per kilo for older children. Children or teacher can select two very different fruit, which would need to be weighed with accurate scales. Calculating the cost per kilo of a papaya at 320 g and a honeydew melon at 1.41 kg would present a difficult challenge for most children. You might consider preparing for this sort of calculation, and others that will be needed, during a two-week period leading up to the time when you buy the fruit. A simple bar chart could show the cost on the vertical axis of several named fruit arranged horizontally across the chart. Calculations showing the price per kilo could start with a table of results. This could lead to a bar chart with the cost per kilo shown vertically and the fruit arranged from least to most expensive horizontally.

For younger children, likes, dislikes and taste preferences are a good place to start. In mixed ethnic groups you could have some children who are very familiar with a particular food while others in the same group have never tasted it.

WORKING WITH FRUIT

Select three or four different fruit for each small group of children. Try very small pieces of fruit using cocktail sticks or wooden forks to pick up the samples. You will need to teach hygiene and preparation methods, and also do a risk assessment regarding sharp knives, food allergies, etc. A parent who works as a local chef or green-grocer could be a help. They might be able to demonstrate the food preparation for you or have some recipes to share. Children can sample the prepared fruit and talk about their preferences.

If you want to link this with English work, get the children to use language of comparison with sentence prompts on paper or on a flip chart. Have some paper slips ready with a selection of useful nouns and adjectives for children to use when describing the taste, smell, texture of their fruit – but be prepared for very sticky fingers, so don't use best writing books yet.

It is also useful to have some articles by food writers available for children to read at some point. Don't forget to include children's and teenage television programme websites, paper-based magazines and e-zines. English extension work could include comparison of the genre for 'foodies' with other types of writing.

Fruit	Honeydew melon	Medjool dates	Pineapple	Papaya	Pomegranate	Mango
Origin	Spain	US	Costa Rica	Brazil	India	Puerto Rico
Weight	1.41 kg	180 g for 10 fruit	1.02 kg	320 g	75 g	480 g
Price £ p	1.49	1.99	1.49	1.09	0.59	0.99
Price £/kg	1.06					2.06

Examples of supermarket fruit, prices and countries of origin

- To calculate the price of the honeydew melon in £ per kg divide the price paid (in £, £1.49) by the weight (in kg, 1.41 kg).

- For the mango the price is 99p and the weight is 480 g.
    - divide 99/480 to get the answer in pence/gram;
    - multiply by 1000 to get the price in pence per kg; and
    - divide by 100 to change the pence into £.

For younger children in Years 3 and 4, just use different types of fruit juice. Include cordials that have to be diluted. One school in Bristol grows a variety of food with the help of the local Allotment Association and the teachers make elderflower cordial in the summer with the children.

ESTIMATION

Maths activities can focus on volume, capacity and ratio. The week before you plan to carry out the practical work, buy different-sized cartons and also buy from different shops. Compare volumes and product details on the packaging. Compare quantities and prices. Labels offer a plethora of information. During each lesson introduction tackle one estimation problem for five minutes then move on to your main work for that week. Put the cartons on display with some notes about the discussion. Ideas will build up during the week and the children will be fully prepared for the following week's work.

Start the preparation by introducing two products from two different shops. Discussion can focus on comparison of prices using two separate one litre packets of orange juice, but at different prices. On another day focus on blackcurrant cordial and the instructions for dilution. Provide some of the information, for example a two litre bottle of Ribena claims to provide 66 servings and the product before dilution contains 22% juice.

- Which juice do the children actually like?
- What dilution do they prefer?

Offer straws for tasting.

- What is a serving?
- Can the children estimate how much concentrate to put into a standard school beaker?
- How many litres is equivalent to 66 servings?
- What proportion is concentrate, what proportion is water?

Another lesson introduction could include a discussion about personal taste preferences and how to plan a group activity. You and the children could design a paper chart that will help them record their taste preferences in small groups, starting the following week. If they were blindfolded could they taste the difference between different drinks? How could their accuracy be recorded? It's easy to let activities become too difficult for the children, and much harder to keep a clear focus on an enjoyable activity that helps improve just one or two skills at a time.

Children need plenty of practical experiences of measuring but this experience is not easily integrated into knowledge, understanding and skills. Children need to be taught estimation strategies for indirect measurement and they need plenty of practice of estimating and approximating in situations where direct measuring is inappropriate or impossible. They also need to be able to use measuring instruments effectively in those situations where direct measurement is useful. Adults often use strategies for estimation based on mental images – i.e. if we have a lot of experience of swimming 25 metres we can 'imagine' the distance when asked to estimate how far it is across a field.

To help children measure effectively

- estimation needs to be incorporated into every attempt to measure;
- the activity should have a purpose to which the child is committed;
- a variety of non-standard units need to be used for measuring;
- build up experience of using a unit that is smaller than the object to be measured before posing the problem of what to do when the unit is larger than the object to be measured;
- the use of non-standard units needs to be continued alongside standard measures, and should not be seen as a *precursor* to the use of standard units;
- help children to create mental images of familiar standard and non-standard units;
- techniques for using measuring devices need to be taught and practised frequently;
- accuracy will only be forthcoming when the children are committed to the task.

VISUALISING AND ESTIMATING

In many of the situations where we need to measure, we cannot use any instruments or measuring devices. When driving cars or walking through busy shopping areas pushing a shopping trolley we have to make judgements as we go:

- Is there sufficient distance between me and those around me to avoid collision and leave us all feeling comfortable?
- Is there a suitable gap in the traffic to allow me to continue at this speed?
- Is there sufficient space to allow safe manoeuvring and parking?
- When buying food (e.g. at a delicatessen counter), we do sometimes ask for so many grams or ounces of a particular food, but we are just as likely to point and estimate what will be enough for our purposes.
- When preparing food with familiar routines and recipes, we are more likely to estimate than to measure quantities in grams or ounces (a handful of raisins is about one ounce, a cup of uncooked rice is enough for two people, . . .). On special occasions, of course, with expensive foods or unusually large numbers of guests, we may prefer to measure carefully.

People can be good at certain types of estimation and poor at others. Many people are best at length estimation, with measures such as area, volume, capacity, weight, time, density and speed posing major problems of accuracy. The accuracy of estimates of objects depends on, among other things, the arrangement and nature of the objects being considered. Accuracy will also often vary with changes in the situation or context. Strategies used in familiar estimation tasks often go unnoticed and so unfamiliar tasks may pose a problem simply because we lack a known strategy.

The strategies for estimating the length of a piece of cotton for sewing on a button, or mending a tear, for example, are different from those for estimating the distance between two buildings across open fields.

And some estimating needs to be done without the objects in view. For example, agreeing to give someone a lift home from work may take you out of your way and it may be necessary to estimate how much extra distance or time will be added to the journey, to be on time.

Many estimates have to be based on *remembering, imagining, inferring* or *simplifying* in some way. People usually have several strategies for estimating and can call up different strategies for different situations.

Estimating a distance that can be seen (look out of the window – how far is it to the large building over there?) may prompt someone who spends a lot of time on a running track to estimate the distance in terms of visualising a 100 m track. For another person who is a regular swimmer, the estimate may be in terms of a number of swimming pool lengths. The nervous energy involved in preparing for a 25 m swimming race plays a part in strengthening the image of the distance and may make it easier for a person to visualise the image in other situations.

Because we continue to use non-standard measures as adults, we need to give children practice in this alongside teaching them to estimate using standard units such as kilos, metres and centimetres.

STRATEGIES FOR ESTIMATING

For the reasons given above, the enthusiasm and emotional commitment of children to a measuring task often influences their capacity to recall and relive previously relevant experiences that can be brought to the task. Think about situations where you have to estimate. What strategies do you naturally call on for estimating a measurement? Do they depend on whether you can: *touch, see, can't touch, can't see*?

When working with children to develop their understanding of measurement, in particular length, the solid world of 3D objects can be used as a starting point, rather than the flat 2D world. Teachers, parents and children can look at and talk about everyday objects such as buildings, trains, boats, planes, containers, cupboards, shelves, food and clothes. These objects can be represented by making models of them out of material such as Lego, Multilink, Plasticine, paper, cloth and toys.

During this activity, adults and children will use words associated with describing size. For example:

- they might describe a building as – a tall tower block, a narrow supermarket, a long row of houses, a short row of shops;
- they might talk about a narrow boat, or a boat too wide to fit in between the lock gates;
- roads can be wide, or straight and narrow or long and winding;
- we need to pass *through or over* some objects such as bridges, gates and doors;
- kittens and puppies have whiskers to let them know if they will fit through the gap.

Children need to have experience of objects or models of them and hear and use appropriate language (Dickson *et al.*, 1992). They may use words such as big, little, large and small, and this imprecise language can be refined steadily by encouraging the use of more precise words such as tall, short, wide, narrow, broad and long. These words are always subjective, and compare the object with some other (not necessarily defined) object or norm. For example, peas might be small, little, 'petit pois', sweet and tender, normal or big, large marrow fat peas, starchy, soaked dried peas, or mushy peas. How do the words describing sizes used here compare with the same words used of a dog, lorry, tree, flower, shoe or house? How small might be a little pea, little flower, little wing, little shoe, little dog, little tree, little lorry or little house on the prairie? All refer to subjective, relative smallness.

> Think about the different strategies you use for estimating:
> - length, distance, physical objects where length is the most important dimension
> - volume and capacity
> - area
> - weight
> - time
> - money
> - numbers of objects.

- Make a 'tocker' using the lid of a jar with a piece of Blutack inside the rim. Estimate how long it will tock (rock backwards and forwards). Try it out. How good was your estimate?
- Draw a shape on squared paper. Now draw it again, with every line twice as long as before. What happens to the area? What happens to the perimeter?
- Look out of the window. Choose three objects: something close; something far away and reachable by walking; something in between and reachable by walking. Estimate your distance from each chosen object. Estimate their heights or distance from the ground. How do you estimate in each case? How do your methods of estimating change for different situations? What are your friend's estimates?
- A beetle is planning a new garden design. The beetle needs a fence to keep out the hedgehogs. Use squared paper to help the beetle work out the least amount of fence it will need to enclose a garden of 9 square units. What about a more adventurous garden design of 16 square units . . . a really adventurous design of 20?
- Make a pop-up birthday card for your best friend. How will you make sure the pop-up is the right size for a picture and/or message?
- Make a container that is a tenth of your volume.

GIANTS AND TINY PEOPLE

Comparison of objects is often cited as a natural first stage of children's interest in size (Williams and Shuard, 1996). Sometimes the description becomes a specific word or definition such as long boat, narrow boat, tall ships, high-rise flats, jumbo jet, Big Mac, long-sleeved pullover, short skirt, wide-brimmed hat, shorts, long trousers, briefs, long johns, deep blue sea or deep pan pizza.

Using the idea of people much larger than we are and people who are much smaller than us, as well as normal human scale (for example, as portrayed in *Gulliver's Travels*), allows us to think about the appropriateness of everyday ordinary household objects as seen from three different perspectives.

The teacher can leave giant footprints around the classroom, on the ceiling or put a series of tiny handprints on a window (the enlarge/reduce facility on the photocopier can be helpful for this). Use a clip from a video, read an episode of *The Borrowers* or an excerpt from a story such as *The BFG*, *Mrs Pepperpot* or *Thumbelina* to get started.

C

p. 174

- Stretch a long string horizontally across the classroom to represent a size line, perhaps dealing with capacity to start with.
- At one end, display small objects with sizes in the order of millimetres, millilitres or grams and talk about how tiny people would use these objects.
- Put human-scale objects in the middle and objects for giants at the other end with litres, metres and kilograms.
- How many litres of water would a giant need to drink each day?
- You could take objects out of a big suitcase, sack or box, talk about them and put them in a suitable place on the size line.
- Are they big or little?
- Who might use them? And for what?
- A clear plastic cup becomes a shower cubicle or an eyebath.
- A woven basket, which is small from our point of view, becomes a bed for a tiny person or a thimble for a giant thumb.
- A box of eggs is probably not enough for a giant's breakfast, but one egg might feed a family of tiny people.

Length
- Draw round your hand and cut the shape out. Measure your hand in cubes, matches, orange rods, pennies.
- Would you rather: have your height in pennies or your reach (from fingertip to fingertip) in 5p pieces placed edge-to-edge?

Area
- How many 1p coins does it take to cover a piece of A4 paper?
- What about 2p coins?
- How many teddy bear counters can fit on a paper cut-out of your hand? Your friend's hand?

Volume
- Use up to 20 Multilink Cubes to make an animal. Now build your animal twice as big.
- How many cubes did you need the second time?
- Make some solid cube shapes using Multilink. How many cubes did you need for each solid cube?

Capacity
- Estimate how many cups of beans are needed to fill a large jug?
- Find 5 containers and put them in order in terms of how much they can hold. Now fill them and see if you were right.

Weight
- Find 10 things that weigh less than a block of wood.
- Find 5 things that together weigh the same as 20 Multilink Cubes.

Time
- How long does it take you to count a hundred pennies?
- How many hops can you do in one minute?

Making miniature gardens, making a map of an adventure island, designing a space station or making a design of their ideal bedroom in a box fascinates many children. It appears that they enjoy the challenge within a finite small space that is under their control. I remember asking the children to collect small objects to fill a matchbox. They were amazed at the diversity of objects and the variation in the total number of objects that some had managed to cram into their boxes. This was a great vehicle for counting, graphing and discussing the results. You will, however, have to prepare a risk assessment first.

You might start with a story to set the context. 'What questions would you ask someone who was 4 inches to 7 inches high? What is that in cm?'

Try 'hot seating' where one child offers to role-play the tiny person while the class ask him/her questions.

Ask the children to make a list of household objects and their possible uses by a tiny person. Their resources might be a box of bits such as:

> key, button, yoghurt pot, bead, pin, paper clip, treasury tag, elastic band, aluminium foil, tea bag, string, cotton, safety pin, piece of chewing gum or Blutack, toothpick, match, cocktail stick, straw, plastic bag, cotton reel, nail, screw.

Consider both the structure and the function of each object.

- Now reconsider, imagining yourself to be the tiny person. What function would the object now have?
- How could the objects be used or linked together to solve the problems a tiny person might encounter? Suggest other everyday objects to add to the list.
- Design and make a prototype of one item of furniture, play equipment or clothing for a tiny person.
- What would be the advantages and disadvantages of being a tiny person? Write a list based on a PMI assessment (plus, minus and interesting).

Mass
- What would be too heavy for a tiny person to lift?
- What would a giant consider to be heavy and use for weight training?
- How might a tiny person or a giant use a 6 inch nail?

Length and distance
- A piece of thick string in our imagination could be used as a heavy-duty washing line or a piece of dental floss.
- What would be considered a long way?
- A journey originally meant how far you could go in one 'jour' or day.
- How far would that be for a giant or tiny person?

Area
- How would tiny people or giants use a human-scale bed sheet, carpet tile, hat?
- Could the children make dolls' clothes and giants' gloves?

Time
- Would time be different?

- How long would it take to get from one place to another?
- What of gestation period, life expectancy, heart and breathing rates?
- Do small animals live as long as large ones?

Capacity
- A wine bottle (75 ml) could be one mouthful or enough for a big party.
- How much would a giant or a tiny person need to drink to feel full?
- What would their daily water requirements be for washing, cooking and drinking?

Volume
- What would be the volume of the giant or tiny person?
- Volume is how much room an object takes up in space or how much water it displaces. What sort of containers might do for a bath?
- How much water would they hold, with and without the person in?

M Measures

FIXED AREA AND FIXED PERIMETER PROBLEMS

'24 Paving Tiles'

This is a problem of fixed area. If you prefer, try using 24 Multilink Tiles or square tiles. Arrange the 24 tiles in various rectangles. Can you work out the perimeter of each rectangle? Make a table of these results. Use paper with small squares on to sketch out your ideas. As an alternative, arrange 24 eggs into a rectangle in a large egg box. How many ways are there? A simpler version uses 4 half-dozen egg boxes. How many different ways can you arrange them?

> What shapes can you make with an area of 24 paving tiles when each tile has an area of 1 sq cm?
>
> What rectangular patios or paths for a garden can you make with 24 square paving tiles?

2 different patios with 24 tiles

12

2 | area = 2 × 12 = 24 units^2 | 2

12

Perimeter = 2 (2 + 12) = 28 units

6

4 | area = 4 × 6 = 24 units^2 | 4

6

Perimeter = 2 (4 + 6) = 20 un

O2

p. 65

C

pp. 172–176

'24 Sheep Hurdles'

This is a fixed perimeter problem.

*   You can use toothpicks or lollipop sticks to model fences or hurdles.
*   You could work from outside in, with a 24-link measuring chain.
*   What shapes are best, why, for whom?
*   How many sheep are you planning to farm, 10, 30 or 100 sheep?
*   With a fixed perimeter of 24, what shapes are possible?
*   Is a square better than a rectangle?
*   What of a hexagon, octagon or circle?
*   Will the area stay the same?
*   Does fixed perimeter also mean fixed area?
*   How much do any of you know about moorland sheep farming?

> You are a sheep farmer trying to look after your sheep. You are concerned for their health, safety, feeding, breeding and lambing. As a moorland sheep farmer you have 24 wattle hurdles (2 m × 2 m) to build enclosures. What useful shapes can you make on open moorland to look after the sheep?

It is useful to have an envelope of clues and cues that can be collected by children who feel unable to start, or who get stuck. Clues could be given to all groups or revealed one at a time as needed. Groups could use tokens to buy clues if they decide they really need help. The following suggestions are designed to encourage discussion.

*   Do not bother to record anything but talk, listen and show others your ideas in your group.
*   When you are satisfied with your solutions, you can write them up, record and display them.
*   The minimum response is to be one word on a piece of paper or one picture or drawing.

Be prepared to share knowledge and discuss the rest of the context.

*   Make up your own story as a shepherd and then justify your actions.

Be prepared to challenge and be challenged on your understanding of perimeter and area, especially, 'What is the largest area you can enclose with 24 hurdles?'

VOLUME AND CAPACITY PROBLEMS

Building with a fixed number of cubes

This is a fixed volume problem. One useful activity to demonstrate working with the language of length is to take a number of cubes, for example 12.

If you arrange as $1 \times 1 \times 12$ standing up as a tower block, this looks and feels very different from a low-rise building of, say, $12 \times 1 \times 1$.

The rule here is width $\times$ depth $\times$ height: $2 \times 2 \times 3$ is a three-storey tower block, but $3 \times 2 \times 2$ has only two storeys.

- Can you design a lighthouse, a cinema complex, a nursery school?
- Design something you would like to live in it.
- What might each of your buildings be useful for?
- What of $2 \times 1 \times 6$ and $6 \times 1 \times 2$?

> Build houses and dwellings with a fixed number of pieces, such as Click Cubes.
>
> If you select a number, for example 12, 16 or 24, then the factors will give you a clue as to what sizes of houses you could build.

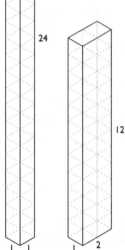
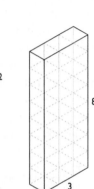
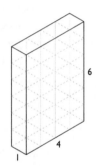
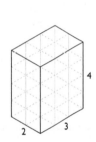
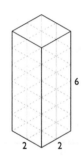

Cuboids with a fixed volume of 24 units³

'Maxbox' or 'Boxes without Topses'

What is the best box without a lid that the children can make from a sheet of paper or card? They should be systematic and cut four equal squares from each corner to fold up the sheet to make a box.

- What happens when they cut a 1×1 square out, 2×2, 3×3 and so on?
- Use paper with large 2 cm squares that will give a sheet of 10 by 14 units.
- They can use the Multilink Cubes to fit the squares so that they can calculate the volume.
- For older children centimetre squared paper and Centicubes will work.
- The children should tabulate and then graph their results.
- Work out the capacity of each box.
- How much material is used and wasted.
- Make a box to hold sweets, fudge, Turkish Delight or a present.

M2 Data handling and using the media

DATA HANDLING STARTING WITH THE MEDIA

There is plenty of information about BBC radio and television at www.theinternet forum.co.uk/bbc/. Some children will be viewing terrestrial and satellite programmes. Some will be watching and listening to non-English speaking channels such as Sunrise Radio (www.sunriseradio.com/).

A curious potted history of radio in the UK is available from the aptly titled site www.naffcaff.co.uk/anorak.html.

Sky has published the results of an extensive survey of Asian viewers and listeners, with details at www.skypressoffice.co.uk/. Information is also available on the government site for digital television at www.digital television.gov.uk/. Simple statistics about who watches which channel may uncover some interesting viewing trends that can be followed up by an exploration of favourite programmes. Websites such as www.upmystreet.com/ will provide a host of details to explore.

> In your local paper, where would you look to find out:
>
> • Which chemist is open late?
> • What's on at the local cinema?
> • Who won the local football competition?
> • When the swimming pool is open?
> • Who got married recently?
> • What other sort of information is available?

There are lots of local and regional papers available for analysis. Collect copies of a local or national paper. What different sections are there? How does the newspaper help you navigate the pages? How do the columns vary in widths, typefaces, font sizes? Where are the articles, the advertisements, the news in brief, home news, international news, television details, weather, and so on?

Information	Home news	International	Television	Advertisements	Weather
Pages of coverage					

C

p. 170

Invite an editor from the local paper to school to show the process of building a paper – maybe it could be based around a news story involving the children in your class. What questions are the children likely to ask? Will they know the language of newspapers? Can they talk about how the paper is laid out, font sizes and styles, ratio of pictures to text, main headings, a comparison between different daily papers? They will know more of this specialist language if they are involved in keeping the school website up to date or if the school has its own newspaper. It is not unusual for young children to be interested in the effect that news and newspapers have on people. One six-year-old girl recently asked: 'Why is the news about so many sad and bad things?' How would you answer her?

When is it better just to talk about the news? When is it better to classify and organise it? Children need to see that there is a purpose to collecting and organising information. The best way to do this is to use information that they care about and then show them that people find it hard to get a clear picture of what is going on unless we sort things into categories and do some counting.

> Where do you look for things which cost less than: £5, £10, £50?

Advertisements

Advertisements give useful opportunities for working with different sized numbers. Read a few advertisements with the children. What sort of things are on sale? How does a local newspaper or a free-ad paper work? How are the advertisements organised? How do you put an advertisement into the paper? How do you buy something? Is it wise to buy?

What type of things can be bought for less than £5? Try to classify the types of goods in each price bracket.

What are classified advertisements?

Is it easier to find what you want here? Is it worth buying second-hand goods? Why? Why not? Depending on what you want to do with the prices you could either look at why certain prices seem to be popular (£4.99, £9.99, £29.99) or you could remind the children about rounding prices up and down so that they can investigate prices rounded to the nearest pound. Car and house prices give sums of £100s, £1000s, £10 000s and £100 000s to work with.

Radio and television listings

Ratings give the number of viewers in millions to 2 decimal places (based on a sample survey). This affords some opportunities for work on millions in a meaningful way, but also necessitates the use of being able to convert 17.42 million into 17 420 000, and approximating with figures such as 7.98 million being nearly 8 000 000, short by only 20 000!

If you take the viewing figures for the top ten programmes for each of BBC1, BBC2, ITV, Channel 4 and Channel 5, how much work can be done? Can you find viewing figures for all the digital channels? Many children will be motivated to list their top ten programmes. They might enjoy trying to schedule a selection of programmes for, say, two hours from 16.00 to 18.00 on weekdays for one week.

> • What factors might affect television viewing figures?
> • Compare figures from different times of the year, e.g. summer and winter.
> • How have viewing figures changed over the last few years?
> • What factors affect viewing?
> • What is available now that wasn't available five years ago?
> • What are your predictions for the future?

Using television programmes

Start by making a video of some advertisements for children's toys. This is especially easy to do in the run-up to Christmas. Encourage the children to talk about what is being advertised and how it is being sold. What pressures are placed on children and parents to buy the 'in' toy? Are children aware of the concept of 'pester power'? Are these toys value for money? How much packaging is involved? Can the toys be found in local papers advertised for sale at knock-down prices in their original box afterwards as an unwanted present? Do the children have access to shopping channels? Which video clips could you use to improve children's powers of discrimination? Who pays for the advertisements? Are perfumes and aftershave good value for money? What do the advertisements promise?

> Imagine a new channel run by and for children:
>
> • What would you schedule?
> • How long would your favourite programmes be?
> • Would you permit advertising?
> • What would you transmit and for whom?
> • When would you transmit?
> • Who would you expect to be watching?
> • What do children want to watch?

Travel brochures

These are easily available and lots of travel companies are only too happy to get rid of multiple copies of last season's brochures. A class set can give lots of opportunities for planning holidays and the problem-solving tasks that this type of activity produces.

- Plan a weekend break.
- Plan a school trip with the children.
- What limit should be placed on funds?
- How far can a family travel on £200 per person?
- What kinds of holidays do the people in your class like?
- Who goes on holiday and who doesn't?
- Who likes to go to the beach, the theme park, the swimming pool?
- Where did the children go last year?
- What was the furthest distance travelled?
- How could you collect and organise the different types of information?
- Use a good Internet travel portal.

Information and communication technology

Using information and communication technology (ICT), review the usefulness and difficulties associated with using someone else's data compared with gathering your own. How easy is it to be overwhelmed by data? How do you decide what to do with the information when you have collected it? Get children to plan a data collection form before they collect and put their data into the computer. Trump cards and other packs provide good sources for data handling. Use hand-held data recorders to collect data about the weather, surroundings or the children themselves. Use Excel or any other spreadsheet program for collecting, handling, transforming and interrogating data.

Consider using a simple piece of software such as Sort Game or a binary key program where children can build up the information as they collect it and represent it in various meaningful ways.

Do computer games such as driving or flight simulators, or the whole of the SIM range involve information handling? Children can use web creation software to make their own multimedia presentations.

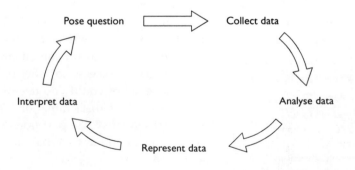

REDUCE, REUSE, RECYCLE

Can the current curriculum prepare our children to take an active role in preventing global warming, protecting the environment and learning to live more lightly? It is no good waiting for someone else to solve the world's problems for us. We need to start now by doing something *today*.

To quote Ghandi, there are enough resources on the planet for everyone's need but not for everyone's greed.

Think about how you can reduce, reuse or recycle paper, aluminium, steel, plastic, glass, water and electricity.

• Aluminium can be recycled *indefinitely*, with no loss in quality, making huge savings in energy use when compared to producing new aluminium. Of materials recycled today, aluminium is the most valuable.

Every day 40 million aluminium drinks cans end up in landfill sites. Find out the average weight of an aluminium drinks can. What might 40×365 million weigh? www.alupro.co.uk.

• *Save a tree* by recycling a one metre cube stack of paper. Less than half the paper in the UK is recycled and more than 5 million tonnes each year are dumped in landfill sites. How much paper does your class use in a week, in a year? How many newspapers do the families in your class buy every week? How many trees a year? Share or pass on comics, papers and magazines. Use both sides of the paper to write or draw on. www.eco-schools.org.uk.

• *Packed lunch anyone?* Home-made sandwiches in a box; crisps from a larger bag in a small container; a local apple or pear and a drink in your own bottle. Compare the cost and packaging with your normal packed lunch. You will be surprised at how much waste, and money, you can save in a week. Collect the packaging from your packed lunches for a week in a cardboard box. Try to use a smaller box each week. www.wastefreelunches.org.uk.

Buy local, think global and support your local economy. How far does your food travel? Who can produce a packed lunch where the ingredients have travelled the shortest total distance?

• *Carrier bag madness.* We use 8 billion plastic carrier bags every year. How many is that for each household? How many bags a week? Try reusable boxes or cloth bags instead of carrier bags. Try to buy loose goods such as vegetables and put them straight into a bag or basket. The Irish government put a tax on carrier bags and their use has been reduced by 95 per cent, resulting in less plastic litter in the streets as well. www.wwf-uk.org.uk.

• *Put a brick in it.* Putting a brick in your toilet cistern will reduce the water used when you flush it. Find the volume of a brick. Use the Internet to find out how many people live in the UK and how many homes there are? Estimate how many times the 'loo' is flushed in your house each week. By putting a plastic bottle filled with water in your toilet cistern and forgetting about it, you might save more than 2000 litres of water a year. www.globalactionplan.org.uk.

Even more significant is the combined use of water and electricity to heat water for showers and baths. Taking a shower instead of a bath could save 25 litres of hot water a day. How much is that a year?

Material adapted from Scott (2004).

M3 Statistics and probability

STATISTICS AND PROBABILITY

We use statistics in a number of situations:

- to organise data to reveal and extract information;
- to compare sets of data;
- to find trends in a data set;
- to predict what might happen in the future, using current information;
- to show changes over time;
- to persuade people and to argue about ideas;
- to 'collapse' data to make life easier, without losing the information that a large database contains (e.g. loyalty cards at large supermarkets to monitor what you buy and when you buy things).

> **What language is used for describing the probability of events?**
>
> - chance would be a fine thing
> - the luck of the draw
> - what are the odds of . . .
> - no chance
> - even Stevens
> - fifty-fifty
> - odds on
> - iffy
> - dead cert
> - a definite maybe
> - very likely! (which often means the exact opposite)
> - no way José (not so familiar now, but may appear from time to time on TV and elsewhere).

Statistics can help us simplify information so that we can have a better picture about what is going on in the world. Statistics can also be used to represent ideas in a particular way in order to convey values, attitudes and beliefs. Children need to see how information is used to present biased arguments.

At Key Stage 2 children are taught to process, represent and interpret data, as well as learning to solve problems involving data. They can interpret data in a range of different formats including tables, list and charts, which can be found in everyday settings in and out of school. They learn to construct and interpret frequency tables, including tables with grouped discrete data: for example, by finding the children with shoe sizes in the ranges 3–5, 6–8 or 9–11.

They have opportunities to collect a wide range of data from different sources including the Internet and from software packages. They learn to represent and interpret data by using graphs and diagrams. They use pictograms, bar charts and line graphs.

C

p. 170

They learn that mode is a measure of popularity (*à la mode*) and that range is a measure of spread of data and they can use these two ideas to discuss different data sets. They learn to tell the difference between discrete data such as shoe size and continuous data such as hair length in centimetres. They can draw conclusions from statistics and graphs and they can learn to recognise when information is being used to mislead.

They can discuss and explore ideas of certainty and they develop an understanding of probability through classroom situations. They learn to discuss events using a vocabulary that includes words and phrases such as:

- equally likely
- fair
- unfair
- certain
- unlikely.

REPRESENTING DATA

Children need to make plenty of use of physical objects such as stacking cubes to represent counts, before they move to direct recording using tables and charts on paper. They need to experience the full range of modes of representation:

- Tally marks can be used against a picture or a label (jam sandwich, packet of crisps) to show how many children like each type of food.
- Physical objects can be organised in some way (stacking cubes in a tower).
- Block graphs are used to display discrete data: to begin with, one block represents one item; later, one block can represent more than one item (but a key is needed).
- Pictographs are used to display discrete data with a symbol such as a car or a face (again a key is needed to show the 'value' of each symbol, e.g. a plate to represent every 10 people eating lunch, half a plate to represent 5).
- Bar charts are used to represent discrete data such as shoe size, but the length of the bar represents the number of items; a scale is useful to show the length of the bar; each bar must be kept separate (a single line could replace the bar).
- Pie charts represent data divided into different sectors. If software is used, then pie charts can be employed successfully with quite young children. The pencil-and-paper calculation is difficult for many children though: the task requires the ability to use a protractor, familiarity with fractions or percentages, knowledge of 360 (degrees) and the ability to calculate, for example, how many degrees are required to represent data such as the sixth of the class who like goldfish. The visual result is powerful and pie charts are useful for data comparison.
- Scatter graphs and line graphs require the use of axes and the ability to plan a scale that matches the paper. They demand the comparison of two data sets and the reading of both the horizontal and vertical axes at the same time. Children with dyslexia can find the mental processing involved too stressful and frustrating unless the activity is carefully managed.

The activity of producing graphical representations of data is only valuable if it is complemented by activities where children are faced with interpreting graphs from data which they both have and have not produced themselves.

The questioning process is a key activity too. At first, the teacher can pose questions and invite children to seek answers. Gradually though, at the upper end of Key Stage 2 the teacher can introduce data from various sources, for example newspapers, and ask children to develop their own questions. This then allows children to be much less vulnerable to misleading data and encourages them to form and test their own ideas.

It can be useful to think of teaching probability in three stages:

- as it arises naturally from non-mathematical experiences;
- by placing events on a probability line without the use of numbers;
- by comparing and calculating probabilities in relation to a probability line extending from 0 to 1.

EVERYDAY PREDICTION

A useful beginning for work on probability is to get children to collect phrases used at home and heard on the television and radio. This work could start, for example, with English work on superstitions in literature. Collecting data illustrates just how pervasive the language of chance is and the degree of concern we express about chance, luck and risk in our lives. The children can make a drawing to go with a favourite phrase they have discovered, for use as part of a simple probability display.

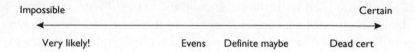

Impossible				Certain
Very likely!	Evens	Definite maybe		Dead cert

The collected phrases can be written in large letters on hinged card. Each group of children discusses their collection, chooses a single favourite and discusses where it should be put. One child brings it out and hangs it on a washing line stretched across the classroom. Class debate then follows about the group's decision. The children's attention can be drawn to the variability, inconsistency and richness of language to express human hopes and fears.

Red sky at night, shepherd's delight.
Red sky in the morning, shepherd's warning.

Mackerel sky, not twelve days dry.

Rain before seven, clear before eleven.

Morning sun in August never lasts the day.

Swallows flying low is a sign of rain.

When the wind blows east, the fish bite least.

Cut 'em in May, they'll grow in a day.
Cut 'em in June. It is too soon.
Cut 'em in July and they will die. [Thistles!]

If the ash is in leaf before the oak then we will get a thorough soak.
If the oak is in leaf before the ash, then we will only get a splash.

Mist on the moor, brings sun to the door.
Mist on the hill, brings water to the mill. [*Pre-industrial revolution*]

or

Mist in the valley, brings sun to the alley. [*Post eighteenth-century version?*]

How can we test this folklore? Are they right more often than not?
Do they only apply to one locality or country? How universal are they? Why?

> There are several areas of activity to promote in the Key Stage 2 classroom:
>
> - the language of chance;
> - looking at language and the way it conveys mood, feelings, and ideas ranging from impossible to certain;
> - using a probability scale with words;
> - developing a numerical scale from 0 to 1;
> - using both theoretical and empirical approaches to chance events to illustrate the difference between the two.

THEORETICAL AND EXPERIMENTAL PROBABILITY

Later, as work progresses, a standard scale can be added. The idea is to move from a casual to a more scientific prediction of events but not to completely disregard the casual everyday responses because they have strong cultural and literary roots which can be explored and exploited in English work. A problem emerges when trying to use the scale to predict the probability of future events, for example: 'I will have tea when I get home.' At the top end of Key Stage 2 the children can often enjoy exploring pessimistic viewpoints, and it becomes difficult to ascribe anything to do with people's behaviour that can be placed further along the line than 'likely', for example: 'Your mum might lose the front door key and you will have to get your tea at your friend's house.'

Many children enjoy exploring the idea that nothing is certain except death. This can lead to interesting cross curriculum issues – but hamper the mathematics!

In mathematics we need something more consistent than that offered by everyday language. The children can look at coins and drawing pins and other objects that can produce statistical results. A drawing pin will either land point up or point resting on the table surface – but are the two outcomes equally likely?

'Pass the Pigs'

'Pass the Pigs' is a useful game to explore probability. When thrown, each pig can land in 6 different positions, each with a different probability of occurring! The temperature, the surface onto which it is thrown, and the way it is thrown can all affect the outcome. Only experimental methods give any predictive power.

Coin tossing

Coin tossing is easier to predict as only two, equally likely, results are possible. More repetitions should mean greater convergence with theoretical predictions. We can deduce theoretical probabilities by reason and logic alone. When we start to toss coins, the empirical results may be very varied for a few tosses (e.g. 7 heads and 3 tails in 10 tosses). The children can then observe how the empirical results tend towards (a correct) theoretical prediction as the number of events increases.

It is important to explore children's views of the probability of the next event, so that you are aware of their thinking: many young children believe that adults are 'better' at throwing a six than they are. Drawing cards from a pack of playing cards gives the chance of a picture card, a heart, an ace, a black card, red card and so on. This works well for combining probabilities. For example:

> a heart: 13 in 52 or 1 in 4;
> an ace: 4 in 52 or 1 in 13;
> the ace of hearts: 1 in 4 $\times$ 1 in 13 = 1 in 52

or

> a red card: 26 in 52 = 1 in 2;
> a Queen 4 in 52 = 1 in 13;
> so a red Queen has a 1 in 26 chance of being drawn from a full pack.

What happens to the odds when we have tried but failed 10 times to draw the predicted card?

Two approaches are possible:

- Theoretically I can argue that a coin has two sides and that if I flip the coin, it will land on a flat surface to show either a head or a tail. So the theoretical answer is 1/2 for a head and 1/2 for a tail.
- I can do the same thing as an experiment and record the results. In 10 flips I may get 7 heads and 3 tails, giving 7/10 and 3/10, so the experimental result may not fit the theoretical one. Maybe I just need to flip the coin a few more times?

PROBABILITY WITH TWO DICE AND PREDICTION

Throwing two dice gives opportunity to both gather data and consider the theoretical possible outcomes. Drawing a probability tree makes this easier. The throws can be graphed in a number of different ways to show different aspects.

Two large dice, one blue, one red, both thrown together 36 times. What is the most likely total from adding the two dice scores? Least likely?

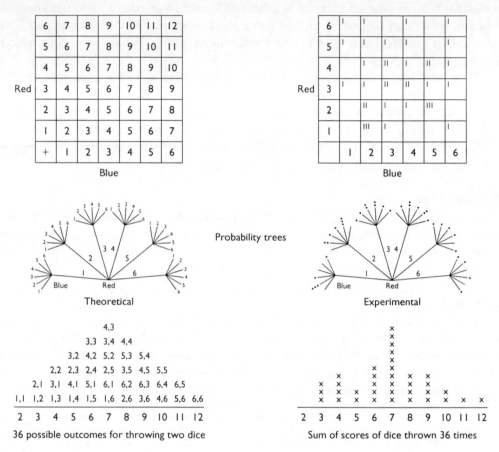

Probability trees

Theoretical   Experimental

36 possible outcomes for throwing two dice   Sum of scores of dice thrown 36 times

Theoretical and experimental results for two dice thrown 36 times

Probability is a way of expressing our responses to events in the world around us. In practical situations, planners need to know how many people are likely to use roads, buses, rail and air services. Building, contents, car, health and life insurance has to be based on risk assessment by collecting large amounts of data and spotting trends. Weather forecasters need to be able to make the best predictions possible about future weather patterns. Probability can make use of information that is derived from statistical sources. The language of probability is very familiar to children and is derived from social settings, for example, trying to win the lottery, a horse race, or from card or table-top games. They can learn to evaluate the manipulative power of probability.

In terms of development, teachers can explore children's:

• intuitions – what they say and think;
• experience and why they think certain things happen and others don't;
• responses to experiments that help them understand;
• understanding as it changes over time.

Part II

Developing interactive teaching strategies

In Part II we take a closer look at the knowledge and skills that teachers display when they work to maximise opportunities for interactive mathematics teaching. We look at the strategies that teachers use to maximise the effectiveness of classroom activities. We provide links between the mathematical activities in Part I and the more sophisticated teaching strategies discussed in Part II.

In the interactive classroom there is a strong focus on creating narratives with individual children and groups in order to strengthen links between children's mathematical activity and mathematical reasoning. Obviously, teachers' and children's questions play an important role in helping to develop narratives of mathematical thinking. Effective teachers encourage children to view the discussion of errors as a valuable opportunity for learning and they use sophisticated strategies to challenge the predominant view that the primary purpose of discussing errors is to emphasise personal failure.

In Part II we look at ways of responding to preferences in learning style. We look closely at the impact on learning when a variety of different resources is used to tackle a mathematical idea or activity. We argue that creating dissonance (by creating situations where things are not quite what they appear to be) is valuable in making children's thinking more robust and comprehensive.

We discuss the impact that assessment and classroom feedback have on motivation and learning outcomes. We emphasise the growing trend amongst teachers to provide *assessment for learning* wherever possible. We offer a framework for thinking about mathematical activities which we believe can enhance children's enthusiasm for mathematics. A useful strategy is to plan mathematical activities around three dimensions:

- fantasy and reality;
- inside and outside the classroom;
- rule focused and problem focused.

The best mathematics classrooms emphasise the 4Rs of learning, where classroom organisation and management encourage learners to be resourceful, resilient, reflective and robust (Claxton, 1999, 2002).

A MODEL FOR INTERACTIVE TEACHING AND LEARNING

In this section, successful mathematics teaching is presented in terms of a six-part model (shown in the following diagram), based on a variety of sources and ideas including discussions with Ruth Merttens (1996) in relation to the Hamilton Maths Project.

We can think of successful mathematics teaching and learning as made up of three main parts. Each part plays a role in all stages of the daily maths lesson (DML).

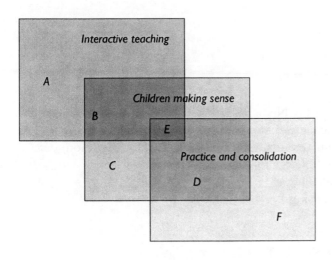

The areas A–F can be summarised as:

A What teachers need to know about interactive teaching to be effective.

B How teachers and children can interact to make sense of mathematical ideas and activities.

C How children can make sense of mathematical ideas through practical activities, independently where appropriate.

D How children can consolidate new ideas and build up resilience and resourcefulness through more independent working including homework.

E How teachers can intervene to review practice and consolidation activities and to monitor errors and misconceptions.

F How children can maintain fluency, application, speed and automaticity.

The three main parts of the model are:

- interactive teaching;
- children making sense;
- practice and consolidation.

We get a sense of the complexity of teaching and learning in classrooms when we look at their interrelationships.

- Sections B and C acknowledge the need for different levels of interaction with children if they are to develop as mathematicians.
- Section D suggests consolidating new ideas and developing personal qualities through more independent working.
- Sections E and F have been combined in the text. Section E acknowledges the need for high teacher–child interaction to review practice and consolidation, perhaps dealing with specific errors during feedback and assessment. Section F implies a more secure knowledge base, which nevertheless requires practice for fluency and automaticity – perhaps through quick-fire questions in a lesson introduction or some practice activity for homework.

In the following pages, we look at Sections A to F in a systematic way and, where appropriate, we include activities and suggestions about these different ways of working.

A What teachers need to know about interactive teaching

This section considers:

* the philosophy and structure of the NNS, the balance between a focus on numeracy and the need for a broad, balanced and relevant mathematics curriculum;
* how research has informed our understanding of mathematics education;
* how the choice of resources influences mathematical thinking;
* resources for counting and calculation;
* differentiating to maximise learning.

THE NNS: PHILOSOPHY AND STRUCTURE

The NNS was organised through the application of constructivist learning theories and Bruner's (1974) suggestion that the most effective curriculum is based on a spiral of experience, where constructs are repeatedly revisited and where the content is chosen to suit the increasing age, experience and interests of the learner. The intention is that the curriculum is always intellectually challenging and problematic, rather than simplified. Successive visits to the same mathematical idea are made distinctive through the teacher adjusting the pitch or level of difficulty so that each turn of the spiral allows the learner to rethink, consolidate and extend their mathematical understanding. The most useful NNS section to look at in terms of coverage and development is the one with the sheets laid out term by term. These sheets show a high level of repetition both within each term, so that key ideas are revisited before and after the half-term, and across the three terms in each year.

The assumption is that the pitch or level of difficulty will be adjusted by the class teacher at each visit, mainly as a result of feedback from assessment and review activities and partly in response to the required pace, which is driven by the government's targets for eleven-year-olds. Many key learning objectives relate to mental calculation *strategies*, which can be revisited frequently. Strategies, such as rounding numbers up and down, can be pitched to the nearest 10, 100 or 1000. Doubling of single-digit numbers can be followed by work on simple two-digit, three-digit and four-digit numbers such as 30, 40, 50, 100, 200, 300, 1000, 2000, 3000. This can be developed further by doubling of fractions and decimals. So revisiting a strategy is an opportunity to practise strategies in new and more demanding contexts.

Each half-term block contains the units of work and the locations of example activities to support the teaching. Apart from the Reception curriculum, the examples are presented as double-page spreads with three years at a glance. The example activities allow the teacher to tune in to the expected level of difficulty for each age group in relation to the levels of difficulty for preceding and succeeding years.

Although each lesson stands separately, very often groups of lessons are organised *as units* to allow for the introduction of several new ideas and the development of a variety of strategies. Some schools choose to have one day per week where the maths lesson follows a different format from the more structured NNS 'daily maths lesson'.

Progression and progress in the NNS

It can be helpful to keep these terms separate. Progression can be defined in terms of moving through the prescribed curriculum, whereas progress reminds us to focus on the development of individual children's understanding. Some mathematical strategies, such as using complements to ten to solve mental calculation problems or rounding up and down, are introduced at certain points in the NNS and will reappear in many different years of the programme. Progression can be thought of in terms of whole school decision-making about how to pitch the level of difficulty across the full age and ability range.

Obviously, if we take a constructivist view of learning then progression in the curriculum *must* influence children's progress powerfully. Children can progress only when the curriculum makes sense to them and that is determined by how the teacher plans each successive mathematical experience. Unless very explicit links are made by teachers, the majority of learners find it very difficult to manage the dual tasks of learning new content and strategies, and also using their learning in new situations. Generally, insufficient time is spent on helping learners make connections between different mathematical ideas and in showing them how to use mathematics to tackle problems in other curriculum areas.

The effective teacher chooses from a range of possible interactions with the children, such as questioning, explaining, describing and demonstrating. Opportunities should be created for children to make sense of the mathematics, and children therefore need to use the same skills as their teacher. Both teacher and children should describe, demonstrate, model, question and explain to others what they think and do. The theory of learning on which the philosophy of the NNS is based combines the personal construct theory of Piaget with the socially-focused and language-focused theories of Vygotsky. Piaget argues that people learn by engaging with the physical environment in such a way as to produce internalised constructs or concepts of their experience in the world. Piaget's is an interactive model where people acquire constructs and have to manage apparently conflicting perceptions of the world. For example an early concept that heavy objects sink and light objects float is challenged when a child discovers the reverse is also true, demanding a reconstruction that admits the new knowledge without rejecting the old.

Learning is consolidated when contradictory ideas are integrated into a new, more complex construct, which contains both the earlier construct and the apparent contradictions. In the previous floating and sinking example, in order to deal with the apparent contradictions we need to incorporate the idea that shape matters as well as weight, and introduce more elaborate ideas about whether or not an object can displace its own volume when placed in water.

A three-part philosophy for maths lessons:

* **Interactive teaching** through explaining, describing, demonstrating, modelling, questioning and telling.
* **Children making sense** through practical activity and discussion.
* **Practice and consolidation** through individual, group and whole class activity.

Merttens (1996)

Piaget never really addresses the influence of groups and language interaction on individual learners in ways that would be helpful to teachers. According to Vygotsky we make sense of experience through linguistically rich social engagements with other learners and teachers. The NNS builds on Piaget's constructivist theory by incorporating Vygotsky's work on the social aspects of learning and the central role of language as the structuring process of experience.

> Most of our encounters with the world are not direct encounters. Even our direct experiences, so called, are assigned for interpretation to ideas about cause and consequence, and the world that emerges for us is a conceptual world. When we are puzzled about what we encounter, we renegotiate its meaning in a manner that is concordant with what those around us believe.
>
> Bruner (1986: p. 122)

The need for a broad, balanced and relevant mathematics curriculum

The NNS was introduced for the express purpose of focusing on number and mental calculation in order to raise children's standards of mental and written computation. While its philosophy is workable and coherent, the NNS has led to an overemphasis on the formal practice of 'number' in many classrooms, despite the broad definition of numeracy contained in the NNS framework.

We argue here that the NNS philosophy and its model of interactive teaching and learning is a valuable basis for promoting the learning of mathematics, but the time is ripe for returning to a much broader and better-balanced mathematics curriculum. The emphasis of the NNS is on interactivity in the classroom, both in terms of engagement with practical resources and activities, and in terms of discourse. It is useful for all of us to monitor the strategies we use to support children's mathematical learning.

The checklist below offers a simple way of reflecting on some of the key strategies. We can tick the boxes in response to two questions:

- Which of these did I use today?
- Which of these did I help the children to use?

Additionally, a colleague can use a similar checklist during a lesson observation to record the best examples that you use.

	Model	Explain	Question	Discuss	Respond	Assess	Support	Manage
Intro								
Main								
Plenary								

Pre-school children are able to use and respond to a wide variety of images and symbols to represent their lived experience. In school, representing one's thinking through images and through pictorial and graphical representation is crucial but problematic. This has been explored, for example, by Marion Bird (1995), Martin Hughes (1984) and Carol Aubrey (1997). The NNS philosophy is to develop children's ideas by making discussion central to classroom activity.

Margaret Donaldson (1978) showed that the child's experience of the world of school can become discontinuous with the rest of the child's experience: school often fails to make sense. Where children are helped to make sense of the world of school, they can perform as well in school as they do in more familiar environments. Bruner extended Vygotsky's social constructivist model, which suggested that the social interaction of teacher and child allowed the teacher to predict appropriate experiences for furthering the child's understanding. Bruner (1974) developed this in terms of 'scaffolding'. Three crucial elements co-exist in this philosophy of learning.

1   The language function of the teacher–child–mathematics interaction is central to the learning process. Discussion is the key to learning and the child is a respected partner in discussion of mathematical ideas. In this philosophy the giving or transmitting of knowledge to learners is not the teacher's primary occupation. Teaching *how* to learn (mathematics) becomes the primary activity and language is the primary focus.

2   A highly interactive teacher–child relationship is required, with great importance given to the social aspects of the relationship. Vygotsky's views on language as a vehicle for the transmission of culture are taken very seriously. The culture of the mathematics classroom is seen as a crucial influence on the child's understanding and engagement with mathematical ideas.

3   Language, writing and numbers are human sign systems, which serve an interpersonal communication function and a cognitive constructivist representation function. Language is the vehicle through which the structuring of mathematical ideas takes place. Language supports and shapes the social and interpersonal relationships that make the learning of mathematics worthwhile and meaningful.

From this point of view, the learning of mathematics is seen more as the result of discourse, less as a body of knowledge to be transmitted to the learner: we have to learn the talk! Learning mathematics is regarded as a highly interactive, interpersonal process where the adult practitioner supports the child's entry into mathematics as a particular form of discourse, moving from mathematics as an activity that is embedded in social and practical situations in the early years, towards a more abstract, symbolic understanding of a self-contained system that will allow children to relate the particular examples of mathematics to more general and abstract mathematical rules.

USING RESEARCH TO PROMOTE LEARNING

In his book *Math for Humans* (1999), Mark Wahl explores the contribution that Gardner's (1999) 'Eight Intelligences' can make to mathematics teaching. Providing for a full range of learning styles is only possible over time and with careful planning, when we ask ourselves: 'In how many different ways could I get children to engage with this mathematics in the classroom?'

Used occasionally, as part of lesson preparation or review, this checklist can support the development of alternative approaches and ways of representing mathematical ideas and supporting thinking.

Children who are strongly:	Think	Love	Need
Linguistic	in words	reading, writing, telling stories, playing word games	books, tapes, writing tools, paper, diaries, discussion, debate, stories
Logical-mathematical	by reasoning	experimenting, questioning, calculating, puzzles, logic games	things to explore and puzzle over, science materials, museums
Spatial	in images and pictures	drawing, designing, making, visualising, doodling	art, moving images, illustrated books, Lego, construction materials, galleries
Bodily-kinaesthetic	through body sensations	dancing, running, jumping, climbing, building, touching, gesturing	movement, role play, drama, building materials, sports, physical games, tactile materials
Musical	via rhythms and melodies	singing, whistling, humming, tapping feet and hands, listening	sing-along time, records, tapes, concerts to play musical instruments
Interpersonal	by bouncing ideas off others	leading, organising, manipulating, mediating, partying	social gatherings, group games, clubs, friends, apprenticeship
Intrapersonal	deeply inside themselves	setting goals, meditating, dreaming, being quiet, planning	time alone, secret places, self-paced projects
Naturalist	about their environment	working in nature, exploring and learning about plants and animals, feeling a part of the world, being outdoors	to be in nature, opportunities to observe and identify flora and fauna, interdependence, life cycles and bio-rhythms

One way of reviewing our preferences and teaching styles is to take a familiar activity that we enjoy teaching and reinvent it by planning new activities that cover a wider range of intelligences. Think of an activity to write in the appropriate box(es) and about the materials and activities that you might use to teach this activity. Continue by inventing new activities for the empty boxes.

Intelligence	Teaching activities	Teaching materials	Instructions
Linguistic			Read about it, write about it, talk about it, listen to it.
Logical-mathematical			Quantify it, think critically about it, conceptualise it.
Spatial			See it, draw it, make it, visualist it, colour it, map it.
Bodily-kinaesthetic			Build it, act it out, touch it, dance it.
Musical			Sing it, play it, rap it, beat it out, listen to it.
Interpersonal			Collaborate on it, teach it, interact with it.
Intrapersonal			Connect it to your personal life, dream about it.
Naturalist			Classify it, observe it, link structure and function in living things, look for rhythm/cycles, describe the whole.

Tables based on Sylwester (1995)

Developing interactive teaching strategies

THE EFFECT OF RESOURCES ON THINKING

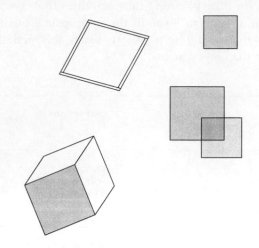

- A paper square shows squareness by virtue of its edges.
- Four equal length Geostrips have their squareness determined by the interior angle.
- Two pieces of gel can be used to illustrate squareness in their overlap.
- The faces of a cube have a squareness that can be imagined, even when the eye does not see a square.
- Combining resources is a powerful strategy, e.g. a number line with Cuisenaire Rods or Play People.

Resources emphasise different mathematical attributes

- When we look at a paper square, its squareness is strongly visible in the 'edge-ness' of the paper.
- When we use four equal-length Geostrips, hinged at the four corners, the square-ness appears as a special position obtained only when the internal angles are held carefully at 90 degrees.
- When we use two pieces of gel and form a square in the overlap, the squareness appears in the darker shade of the overlap.

Only by using different resources in a range of contexts do we realise that:

- Squares are solid – except when they are not.
- Squares are skeletal – except when they are solid.
- Squares are two dimensional even when they are the faces of a three-dimensional cube.
- Squares can be seen as a special case of a rhombus, and so on.

The ability to recognise squareness builds up in us, together with an awareness of the contradictions, until we gain a robust and persisting view of the generality of square-ness. In the physical world most views we get of the faces of a cube are not square – we abstract the squareness despite what our visual sense tells us we are seeing.

The conclusion to draw is that we should use a range of resources within lessons and teach children to move between them. We need to point out how each resource shapes our perceptions and our thinking, by allowing certain viewpoints while limiting others.

The tired discussion about whether to start teaching 2D or 3D to young children is irrelevant. Children need to be taught to 'see' the 2D in the 3D and vice versa: they need to print triangular patterns with the face of a tetrahedron dipped in paint, and to guess an object's shape from its shadow cast by an OHP.

N9

p. 50

S3

p. 111

Representing mathematics

Mathematics remains abstract even though objects such as a protractor are tangible. We come to realise that the resource is *not* the mathematics. The abstract nature of mathematical ideas demands that we need to shift the way we think about and use resources.

- We can measure our height with a tape measure but the tape measure does not become our height.
- We can represent the addition of two numbers using Multilink or Dienes Blocks, but the pieces of plastic and wood are not numbers.

What we do is represent numerical, algebraic and geometric relations through the use of pictures in our minds, lengths of wood, lumps of plastic and marks on paper.

The power and the challenge of mathematics lie partly in its abstractness and the fact that it can be generalised to many different situations.

- A number sentence such as $a + b = c$ is a general statement that can apply to many different types of number including:

  - integers
  - decimals
  - negative numbers and
  - vulgar fractions.

- An equation such as $y = mx + c$ represents *every* straight line that we can imagine or draw on a piece of paper or some other flat plane.

O2

pp. 58–65

Most young children and adults need to use a wide range of resources and work with lots of specific examples of a mathematical idea before they can use general mathematical statements with confidence and understanding.

To be successful learners of mathematics, we need sufficient particular examples of mathematical ideas, including real and apparently contradictory examples, before we come to know a general mathematical concept securely. We also need a mastery of language if we are to manipulate and shape our thinking in ways that allow us to use mathematics in social contexts, in the classroom and beyond.

The way we present mathematical ideas to children, which we convey through language, is a combination of our unique understanding of the mathematics and how this is represented by a resource. As teachers and learners, we connect everyday experiences and mental constructs through the structuring and organising facility of language: this allows us to abstract the mathematics as we work with a variety of resources.

When we develop our teaching skills we discover that some resources and equipment serve us better in the classroom than do others. During the early stages of teaching mathematics, it can be a relief to have some 'easy to use' resources, especially for those people who are reluctant teachers of the subject.

Later, when we have developed greater confidence, we can be more critical of all resources and be prepared to look more closely at the impact that resources have on different learners. Reluctantly perhaps, we may even accept that a favourite resource, which may speak to us very clearly, is not helpful to some learners. Teachers are challenged on a daily basis to adopt teaching styles that do not readily harmonise with their own preferred learning style. Teaching mathematics challenges us to provide access to mathematical ideas and strategies for learners whose learning style may not be our preferred style – and sometimes that means giving up favourite resources and using equipment that is not our preferred choice.

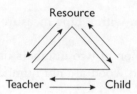

The triangle represents the complex interaction between a classroom resource, the teacher and the child. The effectiveness of a resource in supporting learning can be thought of as the extent to which it is an accurate representation of the teacher's and child's mental structures and ways of thinking about mathematics. A resource is useful when it:

- can accurately model the mathematics;
- connects with the teacher's thinking;
- supports the child's mental frameworks.

S2

p. 104

For example, teachers can observe play, identify a child's current preoccupation with schema and use this knowledge to promote language that supports the child's continued exploration and extension of the schema. Getting this intervention right is an extremely skilled professional activity. It follows then that there is no inherent mathematics within a resource. Leaving children to play with equipment is of little benefit unless the play is complemented by other ways of engaging. Equally, without opportunities for play, the usefulness of a resource to support thinking is seriously undermined. The benefits to learning that can be derived from play are limited by too much imposed structure and inappropriate adult questioning and intervention.

The benefits of using complementary resources

The exciting possibility opened up by a careful choice of different resources is that we create different experiences of essentially the same mathematical concept. For example, when introducing work with quadrilaterals, very different aspects of quadrilaterals can emerge when using different resources. Different resources allow different degrees of freedom and impose different restrictions. An investigation can start with questions such as: 'What happens when squares overlap?'. Restrictions force attention and can create changes in our awareness. For example, some children will only look on a pinboard for squares that are aligned with the horizontal and vertical arrangements of pins.

By specifically requiring children to create a square that is not aligned in this way their attention is forced on to new ways of thinking about the board and also about what counts as a square. With a pinboard, the elastic bands form the sides while the pins form the vertices in a rigid lattice arrangement. The contrast with long loops of elastic is dramatic, because we ask children to hold the elastic loops and use their fingers to create the vertices, which are free to move in space. The sides are created dynamically by pulling the elastic into tension under the control of our movements and squareness is achieved only by careful positioning of the fingers.

With the 'overlapping squares' problem, we could give each group a different resource to work with. We need to select resources based on a choice of which particular aspects of squareness the resource reveals.

- What does each resource add?
- How does it restrict us?

Using contrasting resources in the same lesson is a fairly new development for many teachers in Britain, where the assumption has often been made that using a range of resources leads to confusion. However, using a variety of resources and approaches within a single lesson allows children and teacher to focus on similarities and differences between resources and their distinctive contribution to a concept such as 'squareness'. A more robust and well-rounded conceptual understanding can be established if the differences are explored actively as part of the lesson.

Resource	Vertices (corners)	Angles	Sides (edges)	Whole shape (face)
Long elastics	The bit you hold	Variable	Variable (elastic limit)	Variable, does not have to be plane
Geostrips	Paperclips hold pieces together	Angle can be varied to change shape	Fixed by length of strip and where it is clipped	Varies when shape is moved
Overlapping gels	Fixed/variable	Fixed/variable	Fixed/variable	Fixed/variable
Template	Fixed	Fixed	Fixed	Fixed
Pin-board and elastic bands	Determined by position of pins	Finite	Defined by elastic band	Finite
LOGO	Variable	Need to know angles to define shape	Variable	Variable

Which resources:

- result in a permanent record?
- produce only transient results?
- feel dynamic and support a kinaesthetic knowing?
- seem static and rigid, offering visual knowing?
- are elegant and beautiful and produce aesthetic results?
- make you laugh and feel happy?
- can make you feel calm, excited, involved, detached, lost inside the activity?

Long elastics, pinboards with coloured elastic bands, coloured gels with an OHP, graphic/geometry and LOGO software, tissue paper squares, gummed paper squares, square template to draw around or in, square foam pad with one colour of ink, garden wire with soapy water, Geostrips, plastic Meccano.

N1

p. 2

RESOURCES FOR COUNTING AND CALCULATION

Moving from counting to calculation

Many children use stairs as a resource to explore counting and for many people, a particular flight of stairs holds strong memories of childhood counting activities. Children quickly discover that all objects can be counted and that pebbles, stones and fingers can all be used to represent and organise counts. Children learn how to let numerals stand for objects in different ways. In cardinal counting, one physical object represents and is represented by a 'thought object' – a single countable entity held in mind. A string of such thought objects becomes represented by the ordered string of number names: one, two, three, four, ...

We quickly learn that it is possible to count objects such as cups and saucers which are physically present as well as to count people who will visit for a cup of tea, but who are as yet only present in our mind's eye. Later we learn to use the Arabic numerals 1, 2, 3, 4, ... to record counts in numerical form. In the classroom, we often use sets as part of cardinal counting. We can group a set of objects together and attach a numeral as a tag. The last number counted can also be used to represent the number in the group. Most young children are psychologically able to grasp the concept of cardinal counting by the age of three or four. By age five, many children can carry out accurate counts of small sets of objects and record the result symbolically in idiosyncratic ways (Hughes, 1984).

N1

p. 5

Children need to be able to recite the number names in order and know that the count needs to begin with one. They need to make a one-to-one correspondence between the number words (one, two, three, ...) and the objects to be counted. Most young children need to touch the objects in order to count accurately. For young children, the word can become mentally associated with that object. George, aged three, could easily count three cushions. However, when asked to bring two cushions, he would fetch the second to be counted, rather than two. Children eventually learn that objects can be counted in any order. I worked with David, aged five, who could count when I counted with him but refused to begin on his own. I asked what the problem was. He said he could count pretty well, but he never knew *which* object to start with, unless I or some other adult began the count for him. His counting was temporarily hindered because of his misconception that order matters in this form of count. Finally, we need to learn that the count has to stop when we have counted every object once and once only. The last number in the count is also the number given to the total.

Young children quickly learn to count in a wide range of different contexts. They also learn that there are very many different ways of representing a count.

Five little speckled frogs, sat on a speckled log

One, two, three, four, five, once I caught a fish alive, ...

The accurate counting of sets of objects is an important skill but it is an inefficient route into calculation. We need to ensure that children also develop ordinal counting strategies, since these are a better route to the skills of calculation. The ordinal counting process starts with memorising the unique set of counting names, from zero or one through to ten and beyond. Children develop ordinal counting skills, for example, through nursery rhymes and songs, where the counting words are learned in order but are not applied to objects in a set.

Many adults spontaneously count when they play with babies, counting fingers and toes, buttons on coats and steps when negotiating stairs. Most five-year-olds are able to replicate counts with considerable accuracy if they have had opportunities to practise, although many children and adults find that counting backwards remains a more difficult process than counting forwards. For example, 'Five little ducks went swimming one day . . .'.

It is crucial for children to calculate, rather than count, to solve number problems. Ordinal counting is the route to calculation. It is developed in school through number lines and later with the 0–99 or 1–100 hundred square. We introduce counting from numbers other than one, counting down from 5 or 10 to 1 and then introduce different counting patterns, perhaps beginning with counting in twos, tens and fives, followed by more difficult counts based on steps of 3 and 6, 4 and 8, 7 and 9.

Where cardinal counting and sets are useful for representing quantity, the number line is much more effective for representing calculation. Number lines also provide a better representation of what adults do when they calculate. The NNS (1999) booklets on mental and written calculations are a good source of information, as is Thompson's (1997) writing on early number acquisition.

Cuisenaire Rods are a powerful resource for exploring number and calculation. They were brought to Britain in the 1950s by Caleb Gattegno, who, in 1953, met the Belgian teacher George Cuisenaire who had devised them. The rods are coloured pieces of wood or plastic, of one centimetre square cross-section. The numbers are represented by colour. One is represented by white, two by red, three by light green, four by pink, etc. Rods can be used to represent addition and difference and subtraction. They are also useful for representing multiplication as repeated addition and equivalent fractions. By renaming the white one centimetre rod as 0.1, the red as 0.2, and so on up to 1.0, the rods can be used to carry out decimal calculations.

Resources, activities and explanations are all provisional. That is, they might work for a particular teacher, group of children and context but they might not: 'The teacher and the taught together create the teaching.' The teacher has to take responsibility for directing the teaching, for shaping the physical and linguistic context in which the teaching and learning takes place and, through the choices of resource and language that the teacher makes, for the effect these decisions have on children's understanding and motivation. Teachers need to be open to choosing new approaches, different resources and different ways of framing the mathematical discourse.

> Cuisenaire took us to a table in one corner of the room where pupils were standing in front of a pile of coloured sticks and doing sums which seemed to me to be unusually hard for children of that age. At this sight . . . I knew at once that here was one of those events whose significance is measured by a complete change in one's life.
>
> Gattegno (1963)

When laid end to end, the rods represent addition and subtraction:

━━ ━ ━━

- pink plus red together are the same length as dark green 4 + 2 = 6.

When arranged as rectangles the rods can represent multiplication and division:

  Get this many (5) pink rods and make a rectangle

- five pink rods can make a 4 by 5 rectangle, which is equivalent to 20.

One advantage is that the rods emphasise inverse operations. Addition and subtraction are shown as 'undoing' each other, as are multiplication and division. Multiplication is shown as repeated addition.

Developing interactive teaching strategies

New resources and new articulations offer the chance of a fresh thinking frame and can help build resilience in learners by challenging dependence on preferred ways of thinking and working. It is like giving children a new pair of spectacles to wear: new glasses shift the perspective by changing the visual field and the focus.

Dienes Blocks are useful for showing addition and difference. Extra care needs to be taken when using them for subtraction.

Find the difference between 234 and 122.

The more resources we can use effectively and the more varied representations we draw upon, the more choice we have in our teaching styles.

Educators made a huge mistake in the 1970s and 1980s. Teachers were encouraged to leave children to play with Cuisenaire Rods, Dienes Blocks and other equipment, instead of directly demonstrating their use. We thought, at that time, that instructing children about learning their tables would be unproductive. Instead, we thought that the maths would somehow rub off through indiscriminate activity with equipment. Having spoken recently to Kay, a newly qualified teacher, it is clear how frustrating it is for recently trained teachers not to be able to bring basic mathematical knowledge immediately to mind. Lack of fluency undermines Kay's confidence as a teacher of mathematics and is an unnecessary burden to carry into a new career.

When we set out to create a new thinking frame involving new resources and discourses, we need to bear in mind:

- the questioning techniques and the discursive language we use;
- how well we engage with the children mentally and emotionally;
- what the children already know;
- how well we reinforce connections between relevant secure knowledge and the new ideas we are introducing;
- the opportunities the children have for describing and reporting their experience back to us to keep us in touch with their learning and the relevance of our teaching;
- how well the resources model the mathematics;
- how the mathematical activity connects with the children's lived experience inside and beyond the classroom;
- opportunities for practice and consolidation in different contexts;
- how open we are to modifying the learning frame to suit children's learning styles.

Dienes Blocks are useful when working with index notation. A 1000 block when viewed from a distance looks like a single cube. If the large block is worth 1 then what are the flat, the long and the single worth?

0.1	0.01	0.001
0.1^{-1}	0.1^{-2}	0.1^{-3}

Of course, we have our own frames for thinking about our teaching, based on our own attitudes, beliefs and levels of confidence. When our own thinking frames are limited, as they are when our confidence is low, when we cannot admit to being wrong, when we expect the children to make do with second-rate teaching, then our thinking frames limit children's opportunities for learning.

The idea that we need to select from a range of resources and a range of discursive styles to suit our teaching style leads on to a consideration of children's learning styles and to differentiating between different children and their learning styles. Does my teaching allow children to be different and respond in different ways or do I demand a standard set of responses and behaviours?

A single cube viewed from a few centimetres appears huge, like a 1000 block. If the single is worth 1000 then what are the long, flat, and the block worth?

10^4	10^5	10^6

Planning how to differentiate between different learners requires an intuitive feel for how children learn best and what interests and motivates them. This intuitive awareness is supported and guided by factual information about what they already know. Intuitive awareness develops through regular observation and conversation between teacher and learner concerning the learner's interests, needs and progress. 'Differentiation is a planned process of intervention in the classroom to maximise potential based on individual needs' (Dickinson and Wright, 1993). Intervention, like mediation, which is itself an intervention, should be 'as little as possible but as much as necessary . . . and can be by *task, resource, support, response, outcome* or even *role*' (Liebling, 1999).

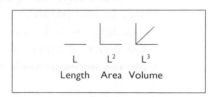

L $\quad$ L² $\quad$ L³
Length $\quad$ Area $\quad$ Volume

DIFFERENTIATING TO MAXIMISE LEARNING

Selecting activities to maximise learning is a planning and teaching process that allows children to be different and supports their excursions into new areas and ways of working, ensuring the teacher has the maximum impact on learning.

Differentiation by task
Children benefit from being told, at the start of a lesson, what they are meant to achieve and what is expected of them, what constitutes a good outcome and how much time they have for the task. Give them the 'big picture'. Many teachers now display and discuss specific lesson objectives with the children at the start of a lesson and set different tasks for each group. Some teachers match the task to children's ability. Others match tasks to learning preferences (e.g. VAK).

For example, using differentiation by VAK, we might plan an activity with triangles as follows:

S3

p. 108

O2

p. 64

- **A visual task** – sorting a box of paper/card triangles; or children making their own triangles from Geostrips.
- **An auditory task** – two children sit back-to-back; one tries to make the triangle described by their partner.
- **A kinaesthetic task** – arrange a collection of triangular shapes on the carpet, one child draws a triangle on their partner's back with a finger. Can their partner find the same triangle from the collection on the floor? Alternatively, walk around a large triangle marked out on the floor or playground with chalk or masking tape and then draw the same triangle on paper or make one with a pinboard and elastic bands.

> Rods support kinaesthetic and visual activities. Use rods to solve this number sentence:
>
> $$\square \, \bigcirc \, \square \, \bigcirc \, \square = 24$$
>
> Can you find three rods that *add* to 24? If all rods must be different, does that change the problem?
> Can you find a small, a medium and a large rod to make *a hop, a step and a jump* to 24?
> Now try to find three rods that can be *multiplied* to make 24. You could start by making different cuboids that use the equivalent of 24 white cubes.

Developing interactive teaching strategies

Differentiation by resource

You might like to give instructions for a task, but offer very different resources to complete the task. This can result in very different outcomes because resources emphasise different aspects of mathematics, which can then be discussed and the nature of the resource explored.

'What happens when squares overlap?'

N2

p. 8

Children could select or be given one of the following resources: pinboard with coloured elastic bands, pegboard with coloured pegs, templates, squares of coloured plastic gel and an OHP, gummed paper squares, squares of tissue paper, or foam squares and ink or paint pads. They explore the problem using their own resource and prepare a contribution for the plenary when we compare results and the strengths and limitations of each resource.

Plasticine, clay and Blutack can be used to quickly shape a 3D object. A knife can be used to slice through the object in different ways to explore symmetry. This can be extended by drawing or painting cut-up fruit or vegetables, such as a tomato, broccoli, star fruit or red cabbage. Use charcoal, pencil, crayon, watercolour or oil pastel on a variety of papers, or chalk on black paper.

Numbers can be represented very differently using different resources. Target boards, number lines and hundred squares, and 'Silent Way' activities offer different routes into the same basic concepts such as complements of 10 or 100, multiples of 5, doubling and halving.

N4

p. 24

Differentiation by support

N5

p. 32

This can be from peers, support assistants and parent helpers. One way to ensure regular and reliable support is to pair children as maths partners. Give partners a specified helping activity for a few minutes in every lesson for half a term, so that the helping ethos gets properly established.

Arrange for a group or a pair to report back in a plenary about their findings, sharing ideas and supporting one another. This allows different group members to play different roles. Co-operative or team teaching with another adult and small-group tutoring can also enhance support. Everyone wants to work alone at some point and a few children prefer to work alone most of the time. The DML assumes that a teacher often identifies a target group to support during lessons. Many untrained adults who work in classrooms see their role as simplifying tasks for children rather than supporting children as they work on difficult tasks. This approach tends to reduce the level of challenge and take away from children the opportunities for thinking. Training is needed so that helpers are made aware that their job is to create physical and mental space for children to think.

Some teachers use tape cassettes with pre-recorded instructions and ready-made OHTs as support. Good software offers powerful support, especially so-called ITS (Intelligent Tutoring Systems; www.rm.co.uk).

Differentiation by outcome

Give the same problem to a group of children and, if they each work on it individually, you will end up with different strategies employed, different solutions and different ways of reporting their findings. This is differentiation by outcome and it offers opportunities for children to demonstrate diversity of thinking and strategy. Practical tasks that will provide diversity you can explore with the group are, for example:

- Tell the story of 24.
- What lies between 0 and 1 on the number line?
- 'All the 4s' and other investigations.

O2

p. 58

You can encourage differentiation by outcome by discussing preferred ways of responding. You can then ask for different forms of response, such as spoken (with or without notes), an OHT, written, dramatised, a poster, graphical, mimed, sung to music, etc. In this way you are encouraging a creative, risk-taking culture in your classroom to complement the more restrained responses that are needed on other occasions.

Differentiation by response

We can think about a child's response to the task: how the child begins to tackle the task or what the child produces as an end result. It is particularly interesting to observe how the child engages or fails to engage with the task. The latter is an important response to the task and can provide a lot of feedback for diagnostic use.

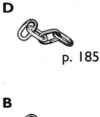

D

p. 185

We can also think about the teacher's response to the child and what the child produces. This can include oral and written feedback during the task, celebrating the child's achievement publicly, suggesting the next step, or providing guidance about the next step or the next task.

B

p. 165

As a result of both types of response, the child could:

C

p. 175

- Write in a learning log or booklet, which can be sent home for parents to comment on as well as the teacher.
- Produce an action plan negotiated with or without the teacher, which contains targets to be achieved.
- Arrange one-to-one conferences between peers (response partners) or with an adult.

I used to arrange twenty-minute consultations with every member of my class about six weeks into the year. We protected the time and they valued the opportunity for a prolonged dialogue. The other children had to learn to work quietly without my help during these sessions, which could also be linked to assessment and review lessons and target setting.

Differentiation by role

You might prefer children to lead with their strengths, as this can help to build their confidence so they are more prepared to work in another area where they are less confident. Children can be offered different roles within a group trying to solve a problem, working on an investigation or reporting to the class about their work. The different roles provide opportunities for individuals to contribute to the group and prove their worth. Offering children a specific role within the group is a powerful tool for both you and them. Make up roles and titles such as recorder, tabulator, secretary, note-taker, statistician, calculator, decision-maker, treasurer, banker, information-gatherer, resource-manager, artist, spokesperson.

The briefing might go like this:

> I'd like this group to report back to the whole class during the plenary today.
>
> You can have up to 5 minutes for the presentation.
>
> One person or maybe two could do the talking (presenters).
>
> One or two people can prepare the poster or OHT (note-taker, secretary, artist).
>
> One person (strategist) might think about what strategies you used to work on the task or complete it in time and prepare the presentation.
>
> You may want to show how these strategies might be useful elsewhere (bridging).
>
> Someone else needs to manage and organise the whole group and remind people who is to do what.

O3

p. 75

The teacher can give children their roles, or put the roles on cards with an explanation and let individuals select or draw the cards at random.

With a group investigation for the whole class, you can appoint a 'spy' whose role is to notice what the other groups are up to and report back to their group, keeping them informed of what resources and approaches others might be using. Spies may be allowed to move around or may have to stay with their own group. Sometimes a spy is also a trader who trades information with another group in exchange for resources or useful information. This approach works well with simulations and role-play games where groups are in competition, but can be used equally well when other groups are engaged in a similar activity.

S2

p. 105

Obviously children can take different roles from session to session or week to week. It may take a few sessions to get into a new role and appreciate its value.

Children need to find out what they are good at. They need also to try other things, which they may not be so good at, and grow in confidence. Through different roles within a team, children become aware of the power of a team approach, mirroring the real world. They can learn to appreciate the strengths of others and create opportunities to use everyone's talents.

B Teachers and children interacting to sustain learning

This section covers:

- encouraging children to discuss mathematical ideas;
- the role of questions and questioning;
- using questions to promote discussion;
- using assessment, feedback and marking to promote learning.

Interactive teaching demands restraint on the teacher's part to balance observing, listening and informally assessing on the one hand with the roles of telling, explaining, demonstrating and modelling on the other. Because children need to learn the language of mathematics and become fluent in mathematical discourse, it is useful for teachers to adopt a strategy whereby 'the one who knows the most does the most listening, while the one who knows the least does the most talking'. This notion, which might seem odd at first, helps the teacher to provide space for children to practise sharing ideas and giving mathematical explanations, which initially will be incomplete and untidy. This approach provides an ideal context for teachers to monitor and assess children's thinking.

Dialogue helps us to express our thoughts and leads to new ideas, and of course dialogue is interactive. Memory is a weak faculty. It is not a good idea to try to learn mathematics by memorisation alone. Interactive dialogue helps children to *restructure* the mathematics we teach them by strengthening connections between VAK learning processes, thereby minimising dependence on memory.

Suppose we try to create discussion that is intentionally one-sided, with the teacher being pedagogically strong but mathematically self-effacing – meaning that the teacher's role is to lead the discussion very firmly in an intended direction, but that the intention is to speak hardly at all and certainly not to provide explanations and answers to mathematical questions. The intention behind employing this strategy is that, in discussion with an individual child, a small group or the whole class, the teacher speaks briefly to help sustain the exploration. When the children speak, the teacher's attention is in listening rather than intervening. It is the children who carry on the mathematical discussion as much as they can.

This strategy is only possible if teachers strictly limit their own role to sustaining the social process and modelling how to support discussion through active listening. The children learn to take risks in their thinking without fear of being told they are wrong. They engage in extended discussion and learn to contribute more fully to the ideas that are being worked on.

DISCUSSING MATHEMATICAL IDEAS

The teacher can initiate the activity by selecting some mathematical ideas that the children have already explored and which need to be consolidated. For part of the lesson, the teacher encourages this extended critical thinking and discussion of mathematical ideas. It is not about ensuring that children can recall facts. Rather it is about encouraging children to explore mathematical ideas, even if that means tentatively discussing half-baked thinking.

An interesting starting point is to try the following approach, used successfully by one American teacher. He placed a chair at the front of the class to create a 'master class' scenario. The chair was occupied voluntarily by a child who had a problem with some maths. They posed their problem and the class discussed possible strategies in a lively debate. This idea of hot seating can be developed into role-play.

There are some cultural issues that might make this more challenging in a British context. In Britain, for decades if not centuries, difficulty in maths has been used to indicate stupidity. In many British classrooms children who have difficulty with mathematics tend to see themselves as useless. This cultural response destroys confidence and resilience, but is not the norm in some other European cultures where being stuck can become a useful focus for discussion without the risk of a personal sense of failure.

When children's ideas and difficulties are the focus of public discussion, we need to remember that we have to balance the role of instructor with that of listener, so that children get an opportunity to rehearse ideas publicly without experiencing personal criticism. If the main role of the teacher remains the instructor who corrects errors, then many learners don't learn to correct their own ideas and many will not risk speaking and thinking out loud. The teacher can often deal with errors and misconceptions obliquely, by pointing out inconsistencies and by inviting children to question each other's ideas.

If the teacher maintains the role of speaker, then inevitably the main role for children is a listening one. If, however, the teacher enters a mainly silent but positive facilitating role, children will soon learn to adopt a speaking role. By taking on the role of active listener the teacher works to help children describe and discuss the mathematics. The mathematics can be treated as if it were an externalised object rather than an example of children's personal worth. Geometry can be a good place to start this type of activity since discussion of geometry often requires visualising, and visualising invites plenty of explanation.

In the early stages, teachers need to place less emphasis on children being able to *explain* their knowledge and ideas and, instead, allow children to demonstrate and show what they know in lots of diverse ways. Teachers need to be challenging however, and children also need to be strongly encouraged to articulate their knowledge – but from a secure experiential base where other ways of knowing have been used extensively.

QUESTIONS AND QUESTIONING

- What is gained and what is lost by asking children questions?
- What are the purposes we have in mind?
- Do we hope that children will learn to ask good questions by copying our good questions?
- Can you think of a time recently when you were asked a question that was helpful, or perhaps intrusive and unhelpful?
- What did you notice about the question/er?

When we consider questions, there seem to be two types of professional challenge for the teacher: one is about technical skill as a questioner, but the other is more fundamental. Our questions are shaped by our assumptions of what children are like as thinkers and what rights they have to think their own thoughts. Do we believe in the integrity of children's thinking? Do we believe that children are inadequate thinkers whose thinking is inevitably flawed? Or do we believe they do not have the right to think independently from us? Our questions will inevitably reflect our viewpoint. If, instead, we suppose that children's emotional and intellectual processes work pretty much like those of adults, then we can use reflection on our adult experience of being **S4** questioned as a starting point for our research into the best ways to pose questions to children.

p. 115

Questioning and questions are at the heart of classroom power and responsibility. What do I expect a child to do in response to my questions? This depends of course on more than just the questions. Can children choose to say, 'I don't know' without being embarrassed or knowing that I won't be annoyed? Can they get up and write on the flip chart without asking permission? Can they pose me a question before they answer mine? Can they suggest that another child answers instead of them? How do I feel about my authority as a teacher if children take control of the questioning process in these ways? What choices do they actually have in my classroom?

Open and closed questions

One distinction that teachers are encouraged to make is a technical one between 'closed' and 'open' questions, where 'closed' is usually taken to mean that only one answer is possible. 'Open' is used to imply many answers are possible. As a teacher, it can sometimes be difficult to work out whether a particular question is open or closed, partly because we may be thinking about how to acknowledge children's freedom to work in the classroom in ways that are useful to them, as well as thinking how to stimulate mathematical learning by posing problematic questions.

For example, after several lessons on quadrilaterals, I would hope that I am asking a closed question when I ask 'Is a triangle a quadrilateral?', but it may not be received as a closed question by some children. I may think I am asking an open question if I ask for the names of some quadrilaterals, but this might not feel open to some.

Teaching older children to write down questions that spring to mind can help them to concentrate on *what is being said* rather than spending their energy holding on to their question and holding up their hand. Stop for one minute to give everyone the chance to ask questions for you to write down and respond to later. Alternatively, ask a learning support assistant to collect questions quietly as you work with the class. Giving children a specific time to write down questions can help capture good questions for exploration later. Collecting questions can become a 'break state', creating a shift in attention. After some complicated work, ask for questions on post-it notes and get the children to put them on a flip chart where they can be left for a couple of days. Children will volunteer answers unexpectedly in later lessons.

Questions	Open	Closed
Whole class		
Small group		
Individual		

Where do you tend to direct your questions? As a self-check, use a table like the one above. Record your preference for closed or open questions, and your tendency to ask questions in certain situations. Talk to a colleague about how to get the ticks more evenly distributed. It is really useful to be able to move at will backwards and forwards between posing a question that tends to demand a single answer and a similar question that invites a wider range of responses. The NNS *Mathematical Vocabulary Book* (1998) contains some useful examples of open and closed questions.

S3

p. 108

Closed	**Open**
What is the difference between 6 and 4?	Give me two numbers with a difference of 2.
What are four threes?	Tell me two numbers whose product is 12.
What is an equilateral triangle?	Draw some different sorts of triangles and then talk to me about them.
How many centimetres in a metre?	Give me two lengths that make up a metre.

I remember David Fielker giving a demonstration lesson on triangles with a group of Year 3 children from Fowey primary school.

Showing a large cardboard triangle to the group, he asked, 'Is this a triangle?' *Yes.* 'How many sides has it got?' *Two.* – A pretty much unanimous answer from the group, which created a frisson of puzzlement in the observing teachers. How was David going to handle such an odd response?

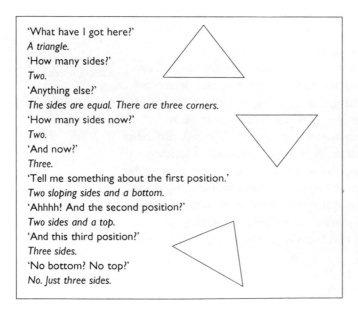

'What have I got here?'
A triangle.
'How many sides?'
Two.
'Anything else?'
The sides are equal. There are three corners.
'How many sides now?'
Two.
'And now?'
Three.
'Tell me something about the first position.'
Two sloping sides and a bottom.
'Ahhhh! And the second position?'
Two sides and a top.
'And this third position?'
Three sides.
'No bottom? No top?'
No. Just three sides.

What excited me in David's discussion with the children, which went on for fifteen minutes or so, was that David was entirely neutral to the answers he received. He was simply curious, and used each child's answer skilfully in deciding what to do next. He didn't use the children's answers to drive them towards a conclusion or way of thinking that he had previously determined. He did pose them increasingly challenging questions. The result was a strengthening of their mathematical thinking rather than consolidation of some factual information.

Valerie Walkerdine's research, which she discussed in *The Mastery of Reason* (1998), demonstrated the social power of the mathematics classroom. Walkerdine showed that children pay particular attention to the words and actions of the teacher, even to the extent of giving mathematical answers that they know are wrong, in order to follow social rules and give teachers what they think is being asked for.

It is very natural for children to treat teachers' questions as signals about what is socially appropriate. Even when I am sure that we are all focusing on the mathematics, it is easy for me and the class to get into a game of *guess what the teacher wants you to say* – a sort of linguistic 'Hangman' game, where my questioning makes it seem as though I am chasing one specific answer. They struggle to give the socially 'right' answer even when it does not make mathematical sense. Once I get the 'right' answer from them, I can be deluded into believing that they were thinking entirely mathematically. Perhaps mathematical 'Charades' would be more fun and more successful?

Part of the technical skill of the teacher is to focus the learners' attention, but:

- Where does my attention go once I have asked my question?
- Do I become preoccupied with thinking about the next question?
- Am I missing the meaning behind the children's answers?
- Do I give children time to answer or am I impatient for a response?
- Do I follow up answers to encourage and extend thinking?
- Do I encourage children to do some of their thinking out loud, by using phrases such as:
  - 'Think to me.'
  - 'Draw your idea.'
  - 'Tell me more.'
  - 'Can anyone say that differently?'
  - 'Does anyone else agree?'

The increased use of individual wipe boards and number cards by children provides them with more time to frame responses and offer up their suggestions together at the teacher's signal, 'Show me'.

The contexts in which teachers pose questions can provide different opportunities for both teachers and children. We can set questions that ask for quick recall. We can pose questions for children to research at home. Questions can be oral, written or visual. A spatial puzzle and learning the 3 times table feel like very different home activities. In lessons, oral and written questions pose different listening and reading demands. Quick-fire questions in a lesson are experienced very differently from a work-sheet that can be tackled over a few lunchtimes and put into a collection box when finished.

Quick-fire questions and careful exploration of a single question offer very different opportunities for learning. If a single question is followed by a discussion about what the question means, then we are unlikely to arrive at an answer for a long time, but children get the opportunity to discuss at length what the question actually means to them. Extending the range of questions and questioning benefits teachers too because they come to realise how differently children can experience this process.

Teachers use mathematically focused questions to:

- control children's behaviour;
- ensure attention;
- check that something has been remembered;
- check that something has been learnt;
- check that something has been understood.

Do these questions feel different? Could they prompt children into different ways of responding?

- How many different sorts of triangle can you draw?
- What is three more than minus twelve?
- What units do we use to measure temperature?
- Is 49 in the 7 times table?

- Most of us feel more confident and enthusiastic about what we are trying to learn when we are asked questions that we have a good chance of answering correctly.
- Most of us like questions that challenge and puzzle us.
- If we don't know the answer, then being laughed at or moaned at is the biggest turn-off.
- We like being given the opportunity to answer, even when we need more time to think than others do.
- Most children understand that teachers need to check whether the children have remembered what has been taught.
- Most children learn better if the teacher helps them to make mental connections between a question they are stuck on and some useful things they have already learnt.

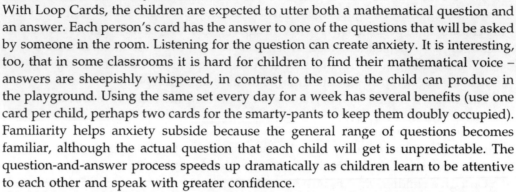

O5
p. 83

A powerful shift of energy occurs when teachers combine questions and questioning with wipe boards, Number Fans and Loop Cards. (Also see Follow Me cards at www.standards.dfes.gov.uk/numeracy/publications/ where there are card designs for line symmetry, missing numbers, etc.)

Number Fans and Loop Cards

With Loop Cards, the children are expected to utter both a mathematical question and an answer. Each person's card has the answer to one of the questions that will be asked by someone in the room. Listening for the question can create anxiety. It is interesting, too, that in some classrooms it is hard for children to find their mathematical voice – answers are sheepishly whispered, in contrast to the noise the child can produce in the playground. Using the same set every day for a week has several benefits (use one card per child, perhaps two cards for the smarty-pants to keep them doubly occupied). Familiarity helps anxiety subside because the general range of questions becomes familiar, although the actual question that each child will get is unpredictable. The question-and-answer process speeds up dramatically as children learn to be attentive to each other and speak with greater confidence.

The power of the teacher's question is changed dramatically when every child has an individual Number Fan or a wipe board and pen. Without these personal items, children can hide or get lost (depending on your point of view) in the classroom horde. In the conventional question-and-answer routine, the teacher can only manage to hear a few answers before feeling the pressure to move on and maintain the pace of the lesson.

In contrast, when everyone has a wipe board and pen, *everyone* can produce an answer to each question. It is interesting that the slate, a symbolic piece of Victorian classroom drill equipment, has provided opportunities for rich and varied mathematical exploration.

With the wipe board and the Number Fan, everyone has the opportunity to respond to a question and all responses can be seen. Every child can feel involved (or feel that there is nowhere to hide) and the teacher has options about where to put the confident, quick children (at the back) so that the less confident and less accurate ones cannot see that some children have been flourishing a correct answer for several seconds before they get their act together.

Teachers get immediate feedback on errors and misconceptions and can allow children to self-correct. In response to a few children flourishing 14 when the rest are showing 49, the teacher can provide an oblique prompt, 'I said seven *times* seven'.

In contrast to quick-fire questions and answers, you could write three carefully chosen questions on the flip chart at the beginning of a lesson and invite children to give you an answer at the end.

Establishing rapport

Direct questions to individual children and always use their name:

'Januk, please, three more than minus four?'

'Cerys, what's the first prime after 95?'

'Destiny, can you tell me, please, what's one *more* than a quarter of twenty-four?'

USING QUESTIONS TO PROMOTE DISCUSSION

Responding to children's statements

I don't know what to do; Can you show me how to start?

- What do you know?
- What could you do?
- Have you seen a problem anything like this before?
- Can you try something?
- Can you make the problem easier by changing something?
- Could you write something down, use a number line, calculator . . .?
- What equipment or apparatus might help you?
- What questions could you ask?
- What might your answer look like?
- Give me a guess.
- How will you record your response?

I'm stuck. I can't do any more.

- Can you describe the problem in your own words?
- Talk me through what you have done so far.
- What do you already know that might help?
- Could you try simpler numbers or different numbers?
- Do you think there are any more answers/ solutions?
- Could using a number line or grid help you?
- What happens if you put things in order?
- Can you see any patterns?
- Would drawing a picture, table, diagram or graph help?
- What have other people done?
- Compare your ideas with someone else.

Is this okay? Have I done enough?

- Show me or explain to me what you have done so far.
- Can you find a pattern or a rule?
- Is there a quicker, more efficient way of doing this?
- What is there left to do?

What am I supposed to learn from this? What is the point?

- How did you get your answer?
- Can you describe your method/pattern/rule to us all?
- Can you explain why it works?
- What could you try next?
- Would it work with other numbers/ shapes?
- What strategies did you use?
- Could you use them elsewhere in mathematics? [In other curriculum areas, at home, in your hobbies, sports or interests?]
- What have you learned or found out today?
- What was the most interesting thing you learned today?

    Adapted from NNS *Vocabulary Book* (1998)

Using questions is especially useful for establishing yourself in a new class, where you might need the children to make and wear name labels for a week or so. This strategy demands simple questions with quick answers. Even so, children can lose interest while waiting for another individual to respond. Also this strategy can encourage competition and noise with some children loudly 'whispering' the answer while others wave their arms frantically, causing disruption and putting pressure on the slow or thoughtful child who is expected to answer.

It is possible to turn questions into discussion and invite replies from anyone who wants to speak.

> 'Hannah, what's seven sevens?'
> *Fourteen?*
> 'Seven *lots* of seven is what I asked! Alice, can you explain what seven lots of seven means? Louis, can you help out here?'
> *Seven times table?*
> 'Yes, go on!'
> *Umm, seven lots of seven means what is the seventh number in the seven times table.*
> 'Brilliant! What's the answer, Louis?'
> *Don't know!*
> 'Anyone got a way of finding out? Clare, do you want to say something?'
> *Seven, fourteen, twenty-one, twenty-eight, thirty-um, um.*
> 'Thirty-five. Go on!'
> *Thirty-five, forty-two, forty-nine. It's forty-nine!*
> 'What is?'
> *What you asked us. What seven sevens make! The answer's forty-nine!*

We need sufficient confidence to let the discussion wander and enough skill to prevent it drifting too far from the original question. We could follow up with: 'If fourteen is the answer, what is the question?'

You can avoid closure by not signalling whether answers are correct or not. Initially children will push you hard to give them confirmation and will not like the lack of closure.

> 'Simone, if you spend eighty-four pence, what change should you get from five pounds?'
> *Four pounds sixteen?*
> 'Merryn, is that right?'
> 'Alex, do you agree?'
> 'Can someone say how they do it mentally?'
> 'Seema, what's your answer?'
> 'Shall we ask Simone to explain how she did it?'
> 'Destiny, can you say how you would work it out?'
> 'Can you show us on the number line?'
> 'Would anyone like to ask Simone a question about how she checks to see if she's right?'

If the class is used to a single mode of working, *you ask – they answer*, then you might get some grumbling the first few times you remain non-committal, refusing to say whether answers are right or wrong. When you consider how much more work the children have to do while listening to each other, checking each other's answers, being ready with an opinion, providing their own answer and perhaps justifying how they arrived at

> Collect children's questions throughout the lesson, by writing them on a flip chart, or encouraging children to write them down on cards or post-it notes. This shows that their questions are taken seriously and allows time for reflection. You won't know the answers to all their questions, but you will have a record and you or they can respond later.

it and explaining why they think a certain answer is correct or not, then it is worth continuing to avoid closure and involving more children in the exploration of a single question and the initial response.

Lack of closure keeps the topic open and running. It allows thoughtful, perhaps slower, children to join the conversation part way through because sustained commentary on a single question allows more thinking time and provides alternative ways of working out the answer. It invites children's commentary and requires child-to-child listening. It encourages children to commit to decision-making, rather than relying on the teacher to verify answers. It signals that different approaches are all right and that we can tackle calculations idiosyncratically.

So the rhythmic change of pace during this part of a lesson could be:

- rapid question and answer for two minutes, noting who does not get involved;
- slow exploration of a single question, encouraging responses from more children;
- Loop Cards for ten minutes (careful listening for your turn);
- wipe boards for five minutes (everyone involved at every stage);
- a slow discussion based on an error or misconception that emerged during one of the earlier parts of the lesson;
- a quick-fire quiz for two minutes using key strategies;
- finish with an exploration of some questions posed by children, collected during the lesson on a flip chart or wipe boards.

ASSESSMENT FOR LEARNING

Assessment and feedback

Giving verbal feedback to children during lessons has a profound effect on their future performance. As teachers we find it relatively easy to give feedback to children on how well they have responded to our teaching and the classroom activities we provide. We find it much more difficult to give feedback that is focused on their learning. In order to focus the feedback on learning we have to listen carefully to the children's contributions to discussions. Feedback that focuses on learning requires a discourse that children and teacher can both use.

Teacher and child need to have a common language for discussing the child's thinking, decision-making, strategies, errors and misconceptions. The teacher needs to focus on the child's thinking, listen to what the child reports, give feedback on the effectiveness of the child's thinking, and comment on the child's decision-making and on the way the child's thinking has impacted on the mathematical activities that the child has tackled. All this might take place in a 20-second exchange. The feedback is effective when it helps children to be reflective about the quality of their thinking and their actions. Effective feedback allows children to act immediately to improve the quality of their thinking and their work.

When giving verbal feedback there are both surface issues and deep issues to be dealt with. Surface issues relate to the children's immediate responses and behaviours within a lesson. These surface issues are often behavioural and may include the sorts of behaviour that are strikingly obvious to visitors who drop in to observe us in our classroom. They include general levels of noise, mobility around the room, and children's awareness and responsiveness to us and each other as well as to our questions and instructions. It is easy for surface issues to become the only ones on which we give feedback. In the early stages of teaching, many teachers find it useful to deal with surface issues publicly in the classroom. Later on, very public discussion of surface issues tends to become counter-productive, distracting children from deeper issues related to knowledge and understanding, and getting in the way of deeper learning.

So how we respond to and manage surface issues is tricky for teachers to get right. New teachers who are especially concerned to establish their classroom routines have to be sensitive about when to move on to different methods of classroom control. Reducing the amount of public discussion of surface issues between teacher and children must not lead to sloppy classroom practice, or ignoring inappropriate behaviour, so we are not advocating giving up on these issues. It is rather that feedback needs to engage children in the deeper issues of learning and understanding. This can happen more effectively when surface issues of classroom management and individual children's behaviour are kept to the level of private and discreet communication between teacher and individual child.

The surface issues that we need to emphasise when we are new to a class and new to teaching include:

- the layout of any work done on paper;
- what Helen Williams in her writing refers to as 'welly-boot questions', such as 'Where do I find a protractor?' and 'Who is in charge of the pencil sharpener?';
- when it is all right to talk and when to keep quiet;
- issues of written presentation, style and neatness;
- features of written work: how calculations are set out and performed;
- the quantity of work produced;
- when it is acceptable to copy and when not;
- effort and behaviour.

Experienced teachers working with a new class use brief opportunities in lesson introductions to remind children of the rules for the particular lesson. Inexperienced teachers may well find it beneficial to do the same. General rules can be on display in the classroom for reference, but specific rules for the lesson also need to be made clear and followed by both the teacher and the children.

Close observation of the techniques used by experienced teachers is particularly helpful in developing strategies for focusing feedback on deep learning. Experienced teachers often deal with the surface issues listed above quite privately with individual children or a small group, particularly when they need to be critical of a child's activity. They whisper their feedback about surface issues, often as they move around the room when children are engaged with individual, paired or small group work. Having already clarified classroom rules at the outset, they are less inclined to make a public example of individual children in order to maintain their classroom routines. What they say audibly in public in the classroom generally relates to thinking, learning and effective working strategies. The teacher clearly articulates how a particular decision or action by the child has led directly to successful learning. This means that the general 'teacher-noise' that children hear is mainly about learning, knowledge and understanding. In contrast, where children mainly hear pronouncements about neatness and the quantity of work required, they assume that these issues are the most important ones to focus on.

The key assessment features that promote learning were identified in a research study by Paul Black and Dylan Wiliam (2002). Their research found that effective teachers promote children's learning through written feedback and assessment. Effective teachers:

- provide effective feedback focused on learning, both when giving oral feedback and when writing comments on children's work;
- create opportunities for children to become actively involved in their own learning;
- adjust their own teaching to take account of the results of assessment;
- recognise the profound influence that assessment has on children's motivation and self-esteem, both of which have crucial effects on learning;
- create opportunities for children to assess themselves;
- ensure that children understand very clearly how they can improve on current performance.

Numerical marking or grading of children's work tends to reduce motivation and self-esteem. Where the teacher provides a mark or grade and an additional comment, the comment is generally ignored, however constructive it is.

The mark or grade carries the greatest impact, not the comment. Where teachers provide only a comment, this has an impact on learning, particularly where it is:

- constructive;
- relates to the learning intention;
- explains clearly what action the child can take to improve.

Children are often demotivated when assessment focuses on quantity and presentation rather than quality of learning. The effect of a continued and heavy emphasis on grading tends to encourage children to compare themselves with others and lowers individual children's self-esteem, demoralising less successful children. Marking that serves mainly managerial and social purposes is not very productive and does little to help children to understand how successful they have been in terms of learning.

To shift the focus from surface to deep learning, teachers are encouraged to:

- organise their classroom to make learning intentions clearly visible;
- work strategically to include opportunities for children to suggest success criteria for learning as part of the lesson introduction, the main activity and the plenary;
- publicise one or two success criteria during the lesson, making them clearly visible on a whiteboard and returning to them later to monitor success;
- question children in ways that encourage them to assess their own achievement in relation to learning, not just in relation to completing the current task;
- give oral feedback that focuses on learning rather than classroom activities, emphasising where children are being successful;
- give written feedback that consists of constructive statements about how the learning objective has been met and what the child can do to improve.

C Children making sense of mathematics

What we offer here are some planning ideas and activities that teachers can use to help support children as they make sense of mathematics and, where appropriate, work more independently. The section includes:

- real world-focused and classroom-focused activities;
- rule-focused and problem-focused activities, including ideas for using personal measurement to explore ratio;
- ideas for using fact and fantasy as starting points for mathematical activity;
- strategies for supporting practical activities, problems and investigations.

The DML requires teachers to create opportunities for children to work on tasks individually and in small groups with a minimum of teacher intervention, often after an initial period where the teacher has introduced an idea or demonstrated a particular way of working. Children benefit from less directly supervised activities because they need opportunities to develop their own thinking, to practise using resources, to rehearse skills and strategies, and to work independently.

THREE SETS OF AXES FOR THINKING ABOUT PRACTICAL TASKS

It is not easy to ensure richness and diversity of mathematical tasks over time. We have developed a model that employs three axes, or dimensions, which together act as a simple checking device when planning or reviewing the breadth of opportunity and experience that children are offered.

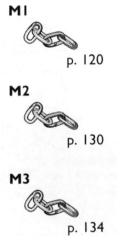

M1 p. 120

M2 p. 130

M3 p. 134

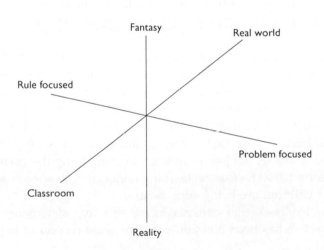

Fantasy
Real world
Rule focused
Problem focused
Classroom
Reality

Mathematics can be used

- as a tool to support work in subjects such as geography, science and PE;
- as a source of ideas for activities begun in English, history, art or music;
- as a focus for studying pattern, logic, reasoning, proof.

REAL WORLD-FOCUSED AND CLASSROOM-FOCUSED ACTIVITIES

Thinking about the real world–classroom dimension allows us to think about 'out-there' and 'in-here' activities. We can think of taking children out of school to supermarkets, rivers and beaches, or just into the playground. We can think of how to modify tasks for homework and class work. Many of us feel more confident starting with classroom-friendly 'in-here' activities because they are easier to manage.

The reality–fantasy dimension may be less obvious at first, but there is a strong fantasy interest running through childhood and into adulthood, as the continuing interest in traditional fairy stories demonstrates. The successes of the Harry Potter books and *The Lord of the Rings* are examples of our continued enthusiasm for fantasy and mystery. Devising activities based on giants, dragons, elves, fairies and fictional characters from story books is not only interesting to many children, but it also allows us to link mathematics creatively with English work, including the use of stories from a range of cultures and religious beliefs.

The rule-focused, problem-focused dimension is helpful because it reminds us that some rule-focused activities can be highly specific, table-top activities that require little in the way of resources or time. We might work with the whole class on making simple patterns using Click Cubes.

> Red, red, yellow, blue, white, red, red yellow, blue, white, red . . .
> 'I wonder how we could work out the colour of the 19th, 20th, 105th, 999th cube?'

Often the teacher needs to demonstrate how to enter an activity, perhaps by showing how it can be organised into a series of manageable steps. Then individual children and small groups can work with sticks of cubes, with the original task modified for different levels of ability. A task involving just three cubes and an answer grid provided by the teacher for recording results is a lot simpler than one using a strip of seven cubes and a challenge to find the colour of the 999th cube.

Children need to learn to use *known facts* to derive *new facts* that may not be immediately accessible to them. Few children will know their 15 times table but they can practise calculations such as 7×15 by using their knowledge of the 5 and the 10 times tables and by using strategies such as doubling and halving. Practical tasks involving a search for patterns and the practice of

---

When we look at ways of combining numbers we discover that:

$$5 = 3 + 2$$
$$6 = 3 + 2 + 1$$
$$7 = 4 + 3$$

How many other numbers can you write as consecutive numbers?

Think of a number

- If it is odd multiply by three and add 1.
- If it is even – halve it.

What strings of numbers can you make when following these rules?

Find the pattern here

I × I	=	I
II × II	=	121
III × III	=	____
IIII × IIII	=	____

Try other pairs, such as II × III.

- I'm thinking of two numbers.
- When I add them I get the answer 9.
- When I multiply them, I get the answer 20.
- Can you find my numbers?

When using calculators with a class, include simple warm-up activities to get started. Tell the children that you are checking to see if they can key in numbers accurately.

- Please follow the instructions carefully.
- Key in any three-digit number and then key it in again to make a six-digit number. For example, if you chose 341 then your calculator should now read 341 341.
- Now key in the following.
- Divide by 11, divide by 13, divide by 7. Now press equals. Are your fingers working properly?
- The reply from the majority is usually: *Yes. But!* . . . *How does it work?*
- Move on to another activity to leave them puzzled, but of course you can return to it later or leave it for homework.

O6

p. 90

rules will provide a good source of independent and small group activity. After whole class work on divisibility rules, children might explore divisibility by 9 individually and write brief statements of their findings.

> *I think 4671 is divisible by 9 because I tried adding up the digits and they make 18, and 1 plus 8 equals 9. I know that if the digits add to 9 then the number is a multiple of 9.*

RULE-FOCUSED AND PROBLEM-FOCUSED ACTIVITIES

In contrast to rule-focused activities, such as looking at digit sums in the 9 times table, many problem-focused activities do not specify the resources or the approach to use, and may take several lessons to complete. Instead of searching for a unique answer or the application of a rule, some practical activities invite a divergent range of solutions and methods to solve problems. In contrast, a problem such as planning an end-of-year class party will involve lots of choices about what to do and could take several lessons, during which children can collect data on food preferences and calculate the amount of food and drink needed.

In an imaginary farm children might work with plastic fences and farmyard animals, exploring ways in which they can keep the animals together or certain animals separate from the rest:

- What size of field or enclosure might each group of animals need?
- Does it matter which animals we put near the pond?
- Does it matter what time of year it is?
- Which seasons might prove problematic?

Teachers' questions can open up or close down the activity:

- What happens if the amount of fencing is limited?

Older children might be challenged by a fixed perimeter problem that asks what is a good arrangement of 24 two-metre long sheep hurdles on the edge of a moor. What questions might children ask to clarify the problem?

Problem-solving work usually leads to a range of possible solutions. Older children can solve problems such as how to raise money for charity by planning a school activity day for parents, or planning a holiday for a set amount of money for their family, ensuring that they cater for everyone's interests as far as possible. The teacher can also set some specific requirements: the planned holiday must include the use of timetables for a rail or air journey.

M1

p. 128

Open questions can exploit real-life contexts:

- How far can you travel for £20?
- How should we arrange the tables in the hall for the autumn fair?
- How should we spend the £850 raised by the School Friends Association?
- Where and how could we store lunch boxes?
- How could we mark the sports field or playground for Sports Day?

- How could we best organise, label and store classroom games and resources?
- How could we organise and carry out a local tree survey?
- What's the best way to organise a spring fair?
- How could we produce a large map of the school and grounds?
- Let's plan a day out or an adventure week.
- How could we organise a maths week or a maths trail?

Children can plan a beach party or rock pool study on a tidal beach that is only accessible at certain times, or use the Internet to research the air–sea rescue services, learning to read maps and calculate bearings to co-ordinate an imagined rescue at sea, and deciding which service (Lifeboat, RAF helicopter) is best positioned to help a stricken yacht or oil tanker (RNLI, 2004).

Addition and multiplication grids, with some numbers missing or obscured by ink blots and clouds, draw the child's attention to the rules of the grid and the number system. Addition and multiplication written algorithms provide opportunities for learning and applying very precise computational rules. You can give children examples of sums that you have done for 'homework', making, for example, a consistent error with about 25 per cent of the calculations. The children will enjoy marking your work and writing a comment underneath about how you can improve. Of course, in order to do this, they have to spot the error and explain it. You can give the children practice in spotting the very same errors that they tend to make.

> I have some
> 2p, 5p and 10p
> stamps. My
> parcel will cost
> 21p to send.
> What stamps
> should I use?

There are many examples of problems involving stamps and parcels that can be linked to the present-giving festivals celebrated throughout the year.

Personal measurement

Personal measurement can form the basis for a lot of work where children apply skills and knowledge of measures and measurement. The only cautionary note is that the majority of children at the top end of the primary school are conscious of their physique and research suggests that the majority of girls aged ten have thought about dieting for one reason or another. We can create some interesting problems by choosing the right questions, with the necessary sensitivity to individual children.

In the first century BC, the Greek writer Vitruvius provided architects and builders with guidelines about designs for monuments and statues. He brought together a lot of information about the human form in terms of ratio. For example:

> A third part of the height of the face is from the bottom of the chin to the bottom of the nostrils.

> The foot is a sixth of the height of the body.

Some of these ratios are easy to explore in the classroom by turning the data into a question that prompts an activity. Presenting the activity as a set of 'Is it true . . . ?' cards poses a research problem for children. The cards invite experimentation, careful measurement, calculation and a decision based on the evidence obtained.

Children have to do something with the information they collect rather than just practise measuring. They have to check the veracity of the claim and come to a conclusion. Do they think it is enough just to check one or two people or is it necessary to measure a range of people? There is a great variation in children's growth and development by Years 5 and 6 and teachers need to manage this activity with sensitivity. They may begin to think about children's and adults' bodies, suggesting that some of the ratios are true for certain age groups but not for others. You may want to see if they have a feel for statistical evidence.

> Is it true that:
>
> - You are as tall as 9 of your hands (from fingertip to wrist)?
> - The distance around your neck is twice the distance around your wrist?
> - The distance around your waist is twice the distance around your neck?
> - You are as tall as your reach (reach = both arms stretched out horizontally to the sides)?
> - Your foot is as long as your ulna (elbow to wrist)?
>
> In preparation for this work, we might need to revise the use of tape measures and the conversion and recording of centimetres and metres. It might be necessary to show some children how to collect and display data from a group of people.

FANTASY-FOCUSED AND REALITY-FOCUSED ACTIVITIES

We can assume children have an awareness of variation and deviation about a mean value if they use an argument along the lines that they need to measure a few people because there are some tall people and some small people in the class. Children may suggest that the statement might be true for some and not for others. There are opportunities to introduce some statistical language and ideas at this point, such as range, mode, median and mean.

There are further possibilities. Use the evidence that the children have produced to set the task of making clothes for a giant, from chicken wire, newsprint, paper and paint. (Roald Dahl's *The BFG* (*Big, Friendly Giant*) is a suitable giant because there is a story to be read as well, although Goliath is a useful alternative and offers a very different genre.)

Suppose the children have carried out the first activity and come to a conclusion about which ratios they think are true for humans. There is an interesting discussion to be had in an English lesson about whether the data could be applied to a giant. (Are giants human? Do giants have similar body proportions to humans?) The story of Goliath gives a height measure. From this it would be possible to compute hand and foot sizes, etc. based on what we know about body ratios and the studies of Vitruvius.

M1

p. 126

The creative and enjoyable stage for the teacher is to observe children's current interests. Think broadly and openly about interest in Harry Potter or the Hobbit, the latest collecting craze, a character from a new film or book that children identify with. Think about the action that is portrayed and turn the action into a challenge or problem that is manageable in the classroom within the constraints of 'literacy hour' and the 'daily maths lesson', with an outcome that involves the use and development of some mathematical knowledge or skill. Teachers can capitalise on children's strong connections with fantasy and what Jung calls archetypes (and which other writers variously interpret as archetypal stages of human development, such as: innocent, orphan, traveller, warrior, martyr, sage, wizard). There is no doubt that these are deep themes represented in many traditional stories, such as *Peter Pan* and Homer's *Odyssey*. The trick is to find a mathematical connection and exploit it. A good source of story books for mathematics is the *Maths from Stories* booklist at www.standards.dfes.gov.uk/numeracy/publications/.

Factual themes also work well. At least 70 per cent of Britain's imports arrive by sea and strong links can be made between mathematics and geography or history, for example, the Second World War and the blockade of Britain. Most children in Key Stage 2 are very concerned about a range of environmental issues, so factual information about depleted fishing stocks or oil tankers spilling their cargoes will strike a strong chord, as well as having a clear connection with the science of flotation and the invention of safety features such as the Plimsoll line.

STRATEGIES FOR PROBLEM-SOLVING

Many of the strategies that we want children to use in the classroom for tackling practical activities, problem-solving and investigations are easily recognisable from the strategies we use in our own lives. The following box lists several of the key strategies that make us effective problem-solvers.

How do I find out what I already know?	• Brainstorm and jot down ideas. • Work alone, in pairs or small groups. • Pool knowledge and experience rather than keep it to yourself. • Collaborate rather than compete. • Display ideas on posters. • Accept jottings and draft notes – no need to polish and refine. • Use lists, pictures, drawings, concept maps. • Have I seen something similar before? • Gather, refine and select. • Organise information to make it accessible.
How can I check that the problem really is what I think it is?	• Read through the problem. • Deconstruct the words. • Check the meanings of words. • Have mathematical dictionaries easily available. • Which words are important/unimportant? • Is all the information useful? • Take time to imagine and visualise. • Play around with images, be prepared for blind alleys. • Be flexible and prepared to give up a particular route. • Say what you are thinking. • Ask questions. • Imagine yourself inside the problem as a person or an object.
What do I prefer as a learner? To have the 'big picture' before I start or to avoid overload by doing a little bit at a time?	• Some people cannot start until they have heard the whole story. • Others just want to nibble away at small bits without getting overloaded with detail. • If you have the tendency to work in only one way, it is useful to develop your skills using the other approach. • It is also good to team up with people who think and work differently. • Break the problem up into mind-sized pieces. • Are there stages to this problem and its solution? • Put the pieces back together at the end of the activity and check you have really solved the problem.

N8 pp. 48–49

O3 p. 74

S2 pp. 104–107

MI p. 128

The above box is meant as a memory jogger: 'Oh yes, I'd forgotten I use that method.' The challenge for the teacher is to recognise the need to build children's skills and abilities steadily throughout a whole year. This can be done by using the three dimensions of reality versus fantasy, real world versus classroom, and convergent versus divergent, to ensure a rich diversity of activity types. In the same way, a balance is needed between number, algebra, shape, space, measure, data handling and statistics. When you have this part of your preparation comfortably under control, then you can use the box above to monitor the strategies you teach and the ones that children tend to adopt.

> • Keep one part fixed while you change the rest.
> • Don't try to change too much at once.
> • What if not?
> • Suppose the rules are reversed?
> • Then what happens?
> • If I don't like the way the problem is presented can I change it?
>   – A lot?
>   – A little?

What can I alter that leaves the problem unchanged?

Mental calculation methods demand a freedom of approach to calculation. Efficient mental calculation is only achieved when we are free to change the numbers involved in calculations to suit our own preferred methods. Fractions can be changed to decimals and percentages, pencil-and-paper calculations can become jottings on a number line. Numbers can be rounded up and down to something more manageable. Change the numbers, the routines, the shapes, the order of doing things. Learn to recognise whether you have changed the mathematics or just the approach. Subtraction and counting back is hard, so use counting forwards and finding the difference.

What remains constant and what is variable?

Can I extend what I know by making new maths from old or by playing with the ideas? Can I change the way I see the problem by trying to visualise it differently, by walking round the problem or looking for a diagram or picture by moving things around until I find something familiar? Try using extremely small or large numbers such as 0.1 or 0.0001 or 1000, or 1 000 000 to see what happens at the extremities. Can I see trends or patterns?

Trial and improvement

Try using the numerals 1, 2, 3, 4, 5 in a three-digit by two-digit multiplication. Which arrangement of digits produces the largest answer? Use number cards and physically move them around. Find approximations mentally then check with a calculator. Try anything you fancy and see what happens. Compare results for different combinations of numbers and try to improve on your previous answers.

One train leaves every hour on the hour from town A and another leaves from town B. The towns are connected by a twin-track railway. The journey from one station to the other takes four-and-a-half hours. If you catch a train in town A, how many trains travelling in the opposite direction will pass you during your journey?

Gaining access to problems

Some problems are hard to enter. A useful strategy is to make a representation. For example, in this train problem, it might be difficult at first to think about how to organise the count, unless a way can be found of modelling what actually happens. It will probably be useful to draw some pictures, get some toy trains and dolls to represent people, or pretend you *are* the train or the train driver and imagine the journey.

We choose particular problems because:

- we want to strengthen links with other curriculum subjects;
- they provide opportunities for consolidation and practice of recently acquired knowledge and skills;
- we want to strengthen particular strategies and ways of working.

The lesson introduction and plenary can be used to introduce and review specific strategies. Some teachers like to include brief investigative activities lasting a few minutes in most lessons. Others like to provide a lesson at the end of a unit where children can work on practical tasks and problems. Ruth Merttens' *Simmering* booklets (part of the Ginn Abacus scheme) provide a useful source of activities from Reception age onwards, which allow strategies to be kept 'simmering' in children's minds over several days.

D Consolidating new ideas and developing personal qualities

In this section we discuss:

- developing general and specific strategies with children;
- ways of strengthening mathematical strategies;
- problems with word problems;
- developing personal qualities that support learning including emotional intelligence;
- the need to provide bridging and avoid pillar learning.

DEVELOPING GENERAL AND SPECIFIC STRATEGIES WITH CHILDREN

Children need to be taught a range of strategies and to be provided with opportunities for the consolidation and practice of new knowledge and skills. We need to look at ways of increasing children's independence as mathematical thinkers. The more independent children become, the more time teachers can find to work with small target groups and support individual children who need guidance. Greater independence from the teacher is also essential if children are to develop both efficient personal approaches to calculation and also greater resilience and robustness as learners.

People often use the words 'skill' and 'strategy' interchangeably. In this book, we use *skill* for activities such as drawing a straight line with a ruler and pencil. A *strategy* is a decision-making process that usually requires a bundle of skills to support its execution. Deciding *where* to draw a straight line to show the bisector of an angle is a strategy in our terminology.

Strategies can be general, such as planning and looking for patterns, or they can be specific to mathematics, such as converting fractions to percentages to make a calculation easier, doubling and halving, or using mathematical knowledge of odds and evens to see if an answer is sensible.

O3

p. 66

Specific mathematical strategies that children need to develop include:

- knowing odds, evens, count on, count back, tens complements;
- starting with the largest number, knowing how to double, halve, near double;
- being able to use nines complements, approximate, round up, round down, estimate;
- finding the nearest ten or hundred, using divisibility rules;
- knowing that the order of operations matters for subtraction and division (2 minus 3 is not the same as 3 minus 2, 12 divided by 4 is different from 4 divided by 12);
- knowing that when more than one operation is used there is a priority of the operations (brackets, powers, of, division, multiplication, addition, subtraction).

General strategies to teach children include:

- checking the facts and questioning the rules before you start;
- planning to complete the task in time, being systematic, using trial and improvement;
- sharing the workload among the group, taking on different roles to solve a problem;
- looking for your own mistakes and explaining them to others;
- looking for patterns, making rules, putting things in order, ranking or comparing;
- checking that answers are sensible, comparing a range of responses;
- setting your own targets.

General strategies are best taught by example, with the teacher introducing them and modelling appropriate behaviour, then following up with activities where children have opportunities to practise the strategy in a range of decision-making situations.

THE NEED FOR A RANGE OF STRATEGIES

One way to ensure children develop strategies is to be explicit about the strategies we use when we tackle mathematical and other problems. Children are more likely to adopt general strategies if we communicate how we structure our own thinking. One example is the strategy of moving to and fro between considering 'the big picture' and considering things broken down into small(er) pieces.

Strategies can be exemplified with different resources. We can use the children themselves, counters, toy animals such as Compare Bears, squared paper, number lines and grids, complementary numbers using fingers and so on. By using these ourselves within lessons we model behaviour that children can adopt; and with continued teaching and practice we show how to use a range of strategies in different contexts. Collections of competencies that belong together in a bundle are called 'schema'. Schema can refer to habits and desires such as arranging food on a plate in a circular, spiral or layered pattern, or preferring to have custard beside rather than on top of a slice of pie in a bowl. We can observe children's active schema during play. Children's schema often reveal strong mathematical themes such as linearity, circularity and closure. Pre-school children often become involved in repetitive play for periods of time, taking every opportunity to tie up furniture with string, or use adhesive tape to connect every object in a room, or to organise toys in a very precise way. The schema can be seen in a dominant play theme often for several days or weeks at a time before its importance fades. Linda Pound (1999) provides plenty of examples of schema in her book *Supporting Mathematical Development*.

It is important to have a range of strategies at our disposal. No matter what age we are or what activity we are involved in, if we have no strategies at all then success could simply be a random event and hard to learn from. We might, if we are very confident, just try anything and see what happens, and this 'playfulness' in the face of new challenges remains important throughout our lives. It is part of legitimate peripheral incidental learning, which frequently occurs in the home.

Young children are skilled learners in informal family settings where they are peripheral to an activity. Having observed dressing and undressing in all sorts of situations, both directly and as a peripheral learner, a toddler confronted by new clothes will try to put them on, even if they are not child's clothing. A visitor in a foreign country unable to speak the language will try signs, sounds, gestures or pointing to get what they want. An inexperienced teacher may want to teach some lessons based on how they were taught.

We need strategies if we are to carry through what we want to do. Sometimes we have no available strategies to help us. This can happen when we panic or when we feel lazy. We may use the single strategy of getting someone else to do things for us: 'learned helplessness'. Guy Claxton reminds us that, as teachers, we need to recognise how easy it is to create learned helplessness in the classroom. One strategy may serve us well for a while, but should the strategy fail we are at a loss again. So, although starting with one strategy is fine, over-reliance on one strategy leaves us vulnerable and without a choice when we most need to be empowered.

Consider subtraction as an example. When vertical written 'sums' formed a large part of children's classroom work, teachers tended to emphasise subtraction strategies. Consequently children found mental calculation difficult since reliance on subtraction strategies alone is not enough for establishing good mental calculation methods. Children need to know more strategies than taking away and counting back to have good mental calculation abilities. These could include, for example, finding the difference by counting on. When children understand how to use empty number lines, they also have a tool to model this enhanced range of strategies. They come to recognise that they can choose the strategy that they think will work best in a particular situation.

We also need to model some problems for them so they can see that we use the same strategies as them. For example, if my brother is 70 and is 12 years older than I am, then how old am I? This is a difference problem and the difference has remained the same during our lives. However, the easiest way is to count back from 70, take away 10 gives 60, take away another 2 gives 58. Similarly £7000 − £6998 is a take away problem, but counting back might be harder for some than counting on from 6998 to 7000.

The challenge is to ensure that children are given opportunities to use practical examples of difference, such as:

- heights of children in the class;
- comparing the weight of two bags of apples;
- costs of groceries;
- different costs of toys.

Children should also use the number line as a potential modelling device to understand the links between:

- difference;
- counting on;
- constant difference.

Children then need to exercise choice over the strategies they use. If the problem looks hard, then try a well-worn and safe strategy. If we recognise the problem then we know what to do and it is not then a problem unless we hit a snag. The most interesting problems require a range of different strategies in a particular order. This is true of making a cup of tea, rewiring a plug, getting dressed or undressed, assembling flat-packed kitchen units, servicing a car, delivering a baby, or painting a watercolour landscape picture. A series of strategies is needed, often in a particular order and with a special trick, knack, 'le truc', such as wetting the paper, warming the pot, or adding one drop of paint at a time on the mixing palette. Children will only learn this flexible approach by being able to try, make mistakes, and try again – an error and improvement approach.

The DML, with its whole class introduction and plenary, allows the teacher to put ideas out in the open. This helps to increase meta-knowledge: we get to know what we know and how it is that we know it. Children need to be made explicitly aware of the strategies they are using because this makes the strategies more easily available. It is like spending time in technology lessons looking at the tools available on a toolboard: we can see what is available for use. Children can then be encouraged to use an increasing range of strategies and be rewarded for experimenting, taking risks, being creative and playful with them.

User of strategies, not victim of information

Reuven Feuerstein (1983) has worked for over half a century in diagnosing the learning needs of children – particularly those with learning difficulties. He looks at the strategies that children can use in terms of *modalities* (for example, checking facts, comparing ideas, orientation in space). Where these modalities are underdeveloped, he has created highly specific Instrumental Enrichment activities. These Mediated Learning Experiences are for the mediator (teacher) to use, develop and link with the learner. See also Sharron (1994) and Ben-Hur (1994). Feuerstein describes some children as having poor *spatial intelligence,* which relates initially to knowing where one is in three-dimensional space relative to other people and objects. Not only can this result in clumsy movements but in mathematics it poses problems when children are faced with diagrams showing relative positions and being asked to work out what is on someone's left or right, or what is in front or behind them.

People who have an undeveloped spatial intelligence can benefit from the use of toys, dolls and teddy bears to create views that could only be seen by another person or toy and that need to be interpreted. Programmable toys such as Bigtrak, Roamer and floor turtles also help to improve spatial awareness because, in order to control these robotic devices, it is necessary to imagine yourself spatially functioning and seeing the world from the robot's location. The child's decision-making processes are revealed when they have control of these toys. Their ability to spatially predict and understand changes in the toy's world-view can then be strengthened. The child becomes increasingly responsive to errors and usually shows little anxiety or embarrassment about making corrections.

Feuerstein's view is that many specific learning difficulties can be overcome by improving weak or faulty links between modalities that may be rarely or inappropriately activated (preventing successful interaction with the physical environment and other people). Some forms of dyslexia, for example, may result from poor synchronisation between the part of the brain that deals with reading a word and the part that makes meaning from it (Carter, 1998). Using the relatively simple VAK model, together with what has recently been learned from neuroscience, we have a model for teaching children to respond to mathematical ideas and activities by stimulating all the senses and trying to fire up as many different processing areas of the brain as possible (Smith, 1998; Smith *et al.*, 2003).

PROBLEMS WITH WORD PROBLEMS

Word problems continue to present teachers with difficulties in the classroom. Recent evidence reported in the review of the first few years of the NNS suggests that teachers in Britain are continuing to find it very difficult to help children develop the necessary strategies to successfully tackle word problems.

One solution to teaching word problems has been around for many years but has not been widely appreciated or publicised. As long ago as the 1970s, a Russian psychologist, Krutetski, published *The Psychological Capabilities of School Children.* He reported meeting a female teacher in Moscow whose children, on transfer to secondary school, scored more highly on word problems than any other children in that Moscow district. When he investigated, Krutetski found that she taught mathematical word problems as language lessons. Weeks passed before she focused the children's attention on the mathematics. In the initial weeks, the interest in maths was peripheral, dealing with terminology, special vocabulary, the mathematical effect of introducing the word *not* into a word problem sentence. The teacher took her time over a detailed analysis of the *language* of mathematical word problems.

Initially, each ten-year-old in her class was expected to explain what the words and sentences meant to them. Because the words meant different things to different children there was a need to spend time on the children's different interpretations. Next the teacher and children played with words and sentences, altering them and exploring the new meanings that the changes created. They played with word order and the effect on meaning was discussed. Negations were added and removed, synonyms and antonyms substituted. For weeks, individual children tackled only a little of the mathematics and rarely had to wade through an entire word problem to produce a mathematical solution, though the class would tackle a whole problem together, in order to practise the relevant strategies. Today, in Britain, this work benefits from the availability of individual wipe boards, coloured marker pens, and the teaching of text analysis in English lessons based on the Literacy Strategy.

In this Moscow classroom, work on mathematical solutions only began in earnest when the children were able to create, read and alter a range of word problems and had developed a good understanding of the associated language. By the end of the year, they out-performed all other eleven-year-olds in their school district in this area of mathematics.

Word problems pose particular difficulties for several reasons:

- They provide mathematical information in a very stylised way.
- Word problems often demand high-level general reading skills.
- They are a specialised form of communication in which words such as face, table, figure, may have both a general and a mathematical meaning within the same text.
- The mathematical ideas can be built up around contexts which are entirely beyond the child's everyday experience (I remember helping a nine-year-old in a Truro school who was struggling with a word problem about barges carrying coal along a canal).
- Negations and exceptions can play a powerful determining role in how to tackle a problem. (There are 250 children in a school and 70% bring a packed lunch. How many children do not eat a packed lunch?)

EIGHT QUALITIES OF SUCCESSFUL LEARNERS

Personal qualities needed for successful learning of mathematics

This discussion draws on several sources including the writing and ideas in Guy Claxton's *Wise Up* (1999). Claxton discusses the personal qualities of successful learners. The challenge for teachers is to ensure that classrooms are organised to make learning the easy option. It is not enough to assume that successful learning will emerge by chance from such complex settings and interactions.

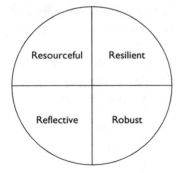

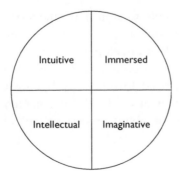

The new science of learning tells us that everyone has the capacity to become a better learner, and that there are conditions under which learning power develops . . . the new science of the learning mind has taught us the eight qualities that can make learning the easy option.
(Claxton, 1999: p. 332)

Resilient

Babies watch their mother's or carer's face carefully. They quickly learn the adult's facial expressions and emotions. Initially, adults synchronise their responses to fit in between the baby's utterances, creating the basis for the earliest form of communication. Baby and carer quickly manage to 'read' their dyadic situation. The process of becoming resilient depends on a dynamic balance between what we desire and what is available. The baby who grows into a resilient learner has learnt to do the best with what a good-enough carer makes available.

Problems can arise with an over-anxious or inconsistent carer who is insufficiently available or over-controlling (this could stem from lack of confidence, anxiety, depression, alcohol or drugs). When babies develop sufficient emotional resilience, they become willing to tolerate the feelings that go with learning. They gain the ability to cope with the excitement and frustration that can accompany strangeness. This development of resilience in the face of uncertainty or difficulty means that they are prepared to try, and to keep on trying. Most importantly, resilience helps to develop a belief in self. Being resilient suggests development of a mature resting place, a place that can be returned to, and a flexibility that can tolerate the anxiety experienced when reaching out into the unknown. In the best classrooms, the earlier resilience of the baby is transformed in older children into an ability to experiment with new ideas and challenges.

Robust

Alongside resilience, the learner also develops robustness, an ability to tolerate lack of success and feelings of frustration. Robust learners experience excitement at the opportunity of challenge. Robustness is characterised by phrases such as 'when the going gets tough, the tough get going'. A robust learner can handle disappointment or not knowing the answer. This does not imply that there is no emotional engagement, but that there is openness to the risk of disappointment based on the knowledge that learning can come from errors as well as from being correct. In the mathematics classroom, the robust learner expects *not* to know everything and overcomes lack of success by looking for the learning that is gained from setbacks.

For the teacher there is no need to assume that learners are weak and frail, to pretend that learning is easy or to make tasks simple. The teacher's most important work is to nurture the learner's robustness by ensuring that mathematical errors are not associated with low personal worth. Unfortunately, in the majority of schools, children learn that academic achievement is used for personal approval and that academic failure is used to devalue people. Many teenagers have a much poorer view of themselves as learners than four-year-olds entering formal school. Teachers must do more to nurture robustness.

Reflective

Successful learners are able to stop and take stock of the situation, to ruminate and be prepared to change their minds. They are able to select or suspend appropriate strategies and they work at developing meta-knowledge.

In the mathematics classroom they need some opportunities to think without being interrupted. They also need to reflect by having their thinking challenged in lively discussion. In the context of the DML, the plenary in particular provides opportunities to reflect and to think about process as well as product.

Resourceful

Resourceful learners develop a good range and variety of learning and problem-solving strategies. They are prepared to try out a strategy and change to another if the first does not work. Resourcefulness, resilience and robustness feed one another in a powerful learning loop. Lateral thinking (de Bono, 1974) is a valuable strategy that helps encourage resourcefulness. Lateral thinking in mathematics classrooms is nurtured through improvisation, experimentation, risk-taking, playfulness and exploring mistakes. Resourcefulness is supported by explicitly taught strategies and by providing children with the freedom to use risk-taking approaches to mental challenges and physical resources.

Immersed

Children need direct immersion in experience and the practical tools of exploration, investigation and experimentation that go with it. Children learn by doing and need to be encouraged to find their own tasks, to engage with the task, to get lost in the activity.

Immersion is often concerned with the physical world, but it also applies to social learning, involving imitation through interaction with others. Immersion promotes practical mastery of complex physical and social environments, through experimentation in the absence of conscious or reasoned understanding. Immersion is smarter than rational thought, especially when situations are complex, because unconscious natural learning is able to detect and deal with more complexity than conscious reasoning. In the mathematics classroom, teachers need to offer interesting, exciting, challenging, relevant and engaging activities. They also need to accept that children will want to change given tasks to suit their own interests. Role-play, parachute games, toys, puzzles, computer software and adventurous mathematical activities are powerful vehicles for becoming immersed.

S4

p. 114

Imaginative

The successful learner makes considerable use of fantasy and visualisation. Storytelling will enable children to create and explore hypothetical worlds. Young children often play intricate games, use role-play, invent fantastic situations and delight in imaginative play. Especially, but not exclusively, when children are young they need play and imagination as well as formal tutoring. In the mathematics classroom this translates into the use of visualisation activities, role-play, puzzles and games, computer adventure games such as Zoombinis and television programmes such as the *Number Crew*. The use of fantasy can be incorporated into mathematics and offers a useful contrast to logical and realistic approaches.

M1

p. 127

Intellectual

The successful learner is a powerful language learner, able to understand the subtlety of language, to apply reasoning and logic, to differentiate and segment experience in order to analyse and communicate ideas. An uncritical acceptance of Western society's lop-sided affair with clarity and articulation has resulted in the rejection and downplaying of intuition and fuzzy logic in favour of logical reasoning. Maintaining a balance between different ways of thinking is the key, together with the freedom to switch from one mode to another.

Intuitive

Intuition includes softer, more receptive types of thinking, where creative ideas are germinated and developed. Intuition is 'knowing', without conscious deliberation. There is a common fallacy that it is automatically better to move through successive developmental stages of thinking, with sophisticated logical reasoning seen as the most powerful form of thought, one which should replace previous stages and ways of knowing.

By contrast, the most successful learners tend to make use of different ways of knowing, with intuition remaining an essential thinking skill, particularly in complex mathematical problem-solving situations where it is important to stay with the 'big picture'.

DEVELOPING EMOTIONAL INTELLIGENCE

Gardner (1999), Goleman (1996) and those involved in the Highscope movement believe that children can and should be given more responsibility for their own learning, making their own decisions and solving their own problems than is possible within the highly prescriptive National Curriculum in the UK.

Long-term studies by the Highscope team in the US have clearly shown the long-term benefits to children who had the fortune to participate in the programme from an early age. Researchers compared the effects of permissive, traditional and Highscope early years education programmes. While the Highscope children did not make significant gains in comparison with traditional programmes for reading, writing and arithmetic, in the long term they did make better use of the opportunities society provided for them with gains which continued into adulthood. For the traditional group, good scores in the three Rs did not guarantee success in later life.

Academic prowess does not seem to be a good predictor of life success. Better predictors of a successful adult life include: learning to defer satisfaction; waiting for what we want; planning our own activities; deciding what we need to do a job; evaluating what we have done; and reviewing the whole process. These activities are key features of the 'Plan, Do, Review' model used by Highscope.

Aspects of emotional intelligence	Classroom strategy	Links to other sections
Accepting and controlling our emotions	Circle time, singing, dancing, painting, playing games	People maths, working with cloths N1 p. 2; S3 p. 108
Using meta-cognitive activities	Talking about and listening to people's feelings, asking why?	Discussion, modelling, sharing strategies B p. 160; D p. 177
Using activities that promote social interaction	Drama, role-play, games, discussions, field trips, co-operative learning	Unusual activities, children making sense through practical activities differentiation by role S4 p. 114; C p. 170; A p. 155
Using activities that provide emotional context	Simulations, role-play, drama co-operative projects	Giants and tiny people, unusual activities M1 p. 127; S4 p. 114
Avoiding emotional stress	Promoting self-esteem and control over own environment, making own rules, circle time	Verbal feedback, investigations, plenary, misconceptions B p. 167; S2 p. 100; E p. 189
Recognising the relationship between emotions and health	Ensuring that the classroom is a stimulating, emotionally positive, warm and safe place to be	

Developing emotional intelligence provides children and adults with a stronger glue that helps to make an integrated curriculum out of one composed of separate, logically defined disciplines. This is made possible within the mathematics classroom by teaching classroom strategies that develop emotional intelligence.

BUILDING BRIDGES FOR LEARNING

'Bridging' is an important strategy that teachers can both use themselves and teach to children (Ben-Hur, 1994: p. 19). Bridging is about forging connections between what Feuerstein (1983) calls modalities. It is a powerful strategy for making our personal knowledge more accessible to us. Frequently we fail to connect areas of learning. We tend to leave our knowledge and skills locked up in particular activities or areas of our life, leaving us able to find our way around a traditional library using a Dewey system but failing to recognise that the same knowledge could be useful when browsing the Internet.

Teachers can make bridges for children (for example in the lesson plenary) by making links from current work to other areas of the curriculum and to real-life situations. At the end of a lesson about pattern spotting, the teacher can help children to plan how to use the same skills for listening to a piece of music or to plan a movement sequence in PE. They can also suggest that children look at house numbers around their homes and think about how a postal worker might organise a bundle of letters so they can easily pop them into the right letter boxes as they walk along the street or through a tower block.

N7

p. 41

In arithmetic teaching we are getting better at bridging because the NNS curriculum focuses on repeatable strategies. So we are now more likely to see the need to bridge the boundaries of the number system: for example, to help children carry the same strategy over from earlier work with integers into later work with fractions, percentages and decimals. Learning to double 2 and 22 can be bridged and the knowledge gained can be used for doubling 200 002, 0.000 02, 1/2, 10^2, $2n$, $1/2n$ and so on.

Strategies can be extended or simplified across the primary age range, e.g. counting on in 1s, in 10s, millions, tenths, negative numbers, and so on. The same strategies work and keep working in many different contexts, but the bridging is seldom achieved without giving it attention and it needs to be explicitly taught within lessons where sufficient time is devoted to this strategy.

What is less obvious to children is the use of bridging across different areas of mathematics: from arithmetic to algebra, or from algebra to geometry, for example. Similarly, children need time to practise bridging across different curriculum areas, so that the knowledge gained in geography from 'using co-ordinates, angles and bearings to solve problems' can be used efficiently in mathematics; and 'looking for patterns' can be learned in music and bridged to dance, art and algebra. Bridging is not a trivial activity to be mentioned *en passant* in the closing moments of a lesson. But if you incorporate bridging into curriculum planning and use it frequently, the growth in children's understanding will be noticeable and other teachers will wonder why your children seem to know so much more than theirs do. Bridging widens the context within which a strategy might be chosen. Sound general strategies such as being systematic or planning become more efficient and effective in a widening range of situations.

When working across the different areas of mathematics, bridging helps reduce the number of separate facts to be learned, contributing to what Gattegno calls a science of education based on an economy of learning. The result of calculating 5×7 is the same as calculating 7×5. This small piece of information immediately halves the number of multiplication facts to be learned and children can be encouraged to look for other fundamental reversals that will make learning more economic. Reversibility is a fundamental feature of many mathematical processes and operations. Consider the relationships between the operations:

addition and subtraction	$3 + 2 = 5$	$5 - 2 = 3$	$5 - 3 = 2$
multiplication and division	$5 \times 2 = 10$	$10 \div 2 = 5$	$10 \div 5 = 2$
addition and multiplication	$2 + 2 + 2 + 2 + 2 = 10$	$5(2) = 10$	
subtraction and division	$10 - 2 - 2 - 2 - 2 - 2 = 0$	$10 \div 5 = 2$	

We can bridge reversibility from arithmetic to geometry. Which transformations have the power to undo each other? Well, translation, reflection and rotation are different ways of moving objects around.

Here is a picture of a mouse (0) reflected (1) and then reflected again (2). But we can send the mouse back home to (0) by another route. First we can rotate the image at (2) through 180°, which puts the mouse back on her feet again and facing the same way as in the original position. Next we can slide the mouse all the way back to the original position (0). So a vertical and a horizontal reflection are undone by a rotation through 180° and a translation (glide).

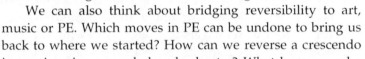
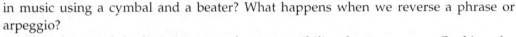

We can also think about bridging reversibility to art, music or PE. Which moves in PE can be undone to bring us back to where we started? How can we reverse a crescendo in music using a cymbal and a beater? What happens when we reverse a phrase or arpeggio?

It is also worth looking at areas where reversibility does not occur. Cooking, for example, is about creating chemical changes that are permanent.

Pillar learning

Pillar learning is the type of learning that takes place usually as a result of teaching where ideas are presented in simple form but left unlinked. Often this approach teaches through a series of advancing stages intended to produce mastery of skills and procedures in the hope that understanding of underlying structure, communality and links to other related areas will follow sometime later.

The teaching of fractions, decimals, percentages, ratios and probability are typical areas tackled in this way. The topics are often taught individually because it is assumed that they are difficult enough as separate topics, therefore together they must surely be too complex for the learner. They are often taught with few or no links, stories or bonds and with no connections made to origin, history, mathematical structure, application, common everyday uses, calculator functions or simple numerical equivalence. Such teaching can result in a few students being able to compute accurately but often this is true only for certain calculations learnt by heart. Most have difficulty converting between one form and another, such as 25% to 1/4 to 0.25 to 1:4.

Pillar learning appears efficient when tested by straightforward tests of recall of isolated skills, but when tested against application and understanding, a picture of confusion often emerges. To avoid pillar learning when teaching fractions, percentages and decimals for example, plan opportunities to make connections between them and look closely at the problems which surround conversion from one form to another.

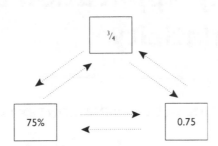

Can you perform all six conversions equally well? How do you perform them?

Number lines are particularly useful for showing these connections and avoiding pillar learning of number facts and skills. Number lines provide a strong visual image that can be used to bridge ideas.

25%	50%	75%	100%

We could begin by looking at a line extending from 0 to 100. In this case 25% is 25, 75% is 75 and so on, since percentage literally means 'of a hundred'. Later we could look at a line from 0 to 1. Some key points are likely to be known by heart (50% is a 1/2 and also 0.5) and they can be added to the line, with fractions written above and decimals below. If you know 10% you can deduce 20% and 5% through doubling and halving, so you can gradually add more information to the line and 15% can be found by adding 10% and 5%. Percentages, fractions and decimals can be linked through six different calculations. Known information (3/4, 0.75 and 75%) can be built up as trio facts. Previously unknown facts can be deduced through doubling and halving and other strategies. A look-up table presents the information in a different way.

N2

p. 14

Fraction	Decimal	Percentage
0	0.00	0%
$\frac{1}{4}$	0.25	25%
$\frac{1}{3}$	0.3̇3	33$\frac{1}{3}$%
$\frac{1}{2}$	0.5	50%
$\frac{2}{3}$	0.6̇6	66$\frac{2}{3}$%
$\frac{3}{4}$	0.75	75%
1	1.00	100%

E/F Consolidation and practice for accuracy, speed and fluency, application and automaticity

THE NEED FOR PRACTICE IN DIFFERENT CONTEXTS

In this section we discuss:

- the need for different contexts for consolidation and practice;
- developing fluency, speed and automaticity;
- children's errors and misconceptions.

Consolidation and practice form an important part of the model we introduced at the start of Part II. It is very difficult to get the right balance of activities, intervention, monitoring and feedback to ensure children can explore new ideas, practise skills and consolidate knowledge. In addition to creating opportunities for consolidation and practice, the teacher needs to monitor children's thinking and practical activity, paying particular regard to errors and misconceptions. The classroom culture may not always help in this regard. There is plenty of research evidence dating from before the introduction of the NNS that children were prepared to ignore right answers and disregard what they knew to be right, because they believed that mathematics is not supposed to make 'common sense'. As we discuss below, this adds an extra burden to teachers who are working to reduce children's errors and misconceptions in mathematics. We need to know more about how the culture of the classroom is currently shaping children's thinking.

Mathematical learning is particularly vulnerable to both under- and over-rehearsal. Too much teacher-directed practice is demotivating and can easily lead to an increase in errors; too little leaves the learner under-rehearsed with skills that are insufficiently embedded to be retained. Many mathematical ideas need 'simmering'. This is particularly true of calculation skills – short but frequent revisiting is necessary, not only because the procedures are complex and unused skills can become lost, but also because many need slight modification to fit different circumstances – such as working with decimals or money. The answer to a division such as $27 \div 5$ depends on the context – different contexts need different applications of the rules. It could be £5.40 each when £27 is shared equally between 5 people. The answer could be 6, if we are planning a car trip and the 27 people can fit 5 to a car. The answer is 5 if we cut string to make 5-metre lengths. The right balance of application and practice leads to fluency and automaticity – where the right skills are at each child's 'fingertips' and their minds are no longer burdened by *managing* the skill but are freed up to focus on the mathematical problems that have to be tackled. To develop children's fluency and automaticity, you can select from the activities in Part I. Try 'Silent Way' for oral/aural, target boards for computational, 'Story of 24' for representational and cloths for visual fluency.

O3

p. 66

N2, N5, O2, S3

pp. 8, 32, 58, 108

From Greek and Roman times there have been complaints of successive younger generations failing to learn mathematics properly. In England in Victorian times the newly formed Her Majesty's Inspectorate (HMI) found many examples of children failing to learn the arithmetic they were being taught. One inspector famously described elementary school mathematics as being 'beyond the capacity of the rural mind'. A modern, more sympathetic approach, which includes a social as well as a psychological perspective, recognises that, in addition to children's mathematical concepts developing, their mathematical concepts also undergo *changes*.

Nunes *et al.* (1993) writing about 'street mathematics' found that Brazilian street children worked for themselves and others as street traders, buying and selling fruit and other items to scrape a perilous living. Many of them displayed superb skills with money transactions, calculations, weighing, pricing, percentages and ratios, often much more advanced than the skills of children of the same age studying conventional classroom mathematics. Interestingly, the street children could not necessarily transfer their street-wise knowledge to solve classroom problems.

From a very different perspective, Martin Hughes (1984) confirmed the earlier work of his colleague, Margaret Donaldson (1978), that children as young as two and three years could often think and act mathematically, and yet could not always do 'school maths' when they began school a year or two later.

ERRORS AND MISCONCEPTIONS IN MATHEMATICS

So we need a social perspective to try to understand what is going on. Some mathematics, it appears, is difficult for children to learn *because* it is taught in school – not because it is mathematics, not because children are stupid, and not because mathematics is intractably hard. So as educators we have to ask ourselves what is it about formal schooling that makes hard work of learning mathematics? Why have we made it more difficult than it needs to be? Strange that learning some aspects of mathematics in school should be the difficult option rather than the easy one – especially when we think about how much money is spent on schools and training us as teachers. Nunes concludes that many of the mistakes that mathematically skilled street children made when subsequently taught school mathematics were 'due to the limiting effects of the classroom itself. These mistakes can no longer be attributed just to gaps and deficiencies in the children's mathematical reasoning' (Nunes and Bryant, 1996: p. 247). The classroom environment can push children into assuming that they must give up reasoning and common sense understanding and that the mathematics they use in classrooms does not need to make sense. Herbert Ginsburg, a Piagetian-influenced psychologist, undertook a thorough investigation of children's performance-related misconceptions in the 1970s (see Ginsburg, 1977). Although much of his work focused on formal written algorithms, many of his findings translate well to settings where mental calculation is emphasised.

> **Ginsburg's findings**
>
> - Children are generally trying to make sense of their world and apply what they know.
> - Errors result from applying strategies and rules rather than from carelessness.
> - The faulty rules underlying errors have sensible origins.
> - Sometimes rules become faulty when they are used in new and different situations.
> - Children try to apply addition rules to subtraction, multiplication rules to division and whole number rules to fractions in situations where the rules don't transfer.
> - Children don't expect school arithmetic to make sense, it is isolated from their ordinary interests and concerns.
> - Children demonstrate a gap between their informal and formal knowledge.
>
> Ginsburg (1977)

Misunderstandings, bugs, distractions

Ginsburg's work (1977) included hundreds of interviews with children working on mathematics calculation problems. Ginsburg focused mainly on written computation so his findings do not necessarily translate to the NNS with a 'daily maths lesson' focusing on mental calculation as a first resort. However, much of his work is still likely to be relevant to teachers who want to respond effectively to children's errors and misconceptions.

Evidence from interviews with the children and with their teachers showed that almost all children tried hard to get things right. Problems arose for various reasons. Children:

- tried to be systematic, but did not always understand the calculation algorithm and introduced bugs into their calculations, e.g. forgetting to add 'carry' digits in the succeeding column;
- mistook one type of calculation for another, e.g. they subtracted instead of adding;
- did not understand or use checking routines;
- did not believe that maths needed to make sense so were not surprised when answers did not fit with their common sense thinking.

Some errors can be the result of mind wandering, losing track of the process and original task, or not checking what has been done. To minimise these types of error the classroom needs to be a place where children know that checking their own work and each other's is a routine activity, not a special occasion. We can concentrate for only about twenty minutes at a time, so being able to stop your own work and spend a few minutes checking someone else's can be refreshing. The bonus is that we may spot an error in other work that we have not spotted in our own.

Encourage children to review their own work:

B

p. 165

Ask: 'Do you know where you have gone wrong?'
If the answer is *Yes*, then ask: 'Do you know what to do about it?'
If *Yes*, then suggest: 'Well, make your corrections then discuss with your maths partner so they can check your work with you.'

If the child has already talked to their maths partner then coming to you for help is probably a good idea.

'Which bit did you find hard?'
'Show me where you got stuck.'
'Explain your thinking up to where you got stuck?'
'What bits can you do?'

D

p. 177

Strategies imply decisions, choices and the chance to select an appropriate way of working or routine for a while until it either helps you solve the problem or you stop using it because it is not working for you. Strategies give children and adults the confidence to *control* information rather than *be controlled by* it, and to *use* information rather than *become a victim* of information. Strategies can offer the opportunity to create new knowledge and use trial and improvement to nudge our thinking forward.

Avoiding and remedying errors and misconceptions

Enabling the children to *explain* requires them to articulate their ideas, write them down, draw them, and show their current understanding and misunderstanding in some way. However, children should be allowed to 'pass' if explaining is proving too hard: leave the problem for another time. Our brains work on problems when we are away from them and even when we are asleep. It is a fallacy that learning mainly takes place in the classroom during lessons. Learning is more likely to occur if you resist telling a struggling child for the second or third time. Instead, ask *them to explain* where they are stuck, make a brief note in their book as a reminder of the discussion, then leave it for another day. It is not uncommon for adults and children to dream solutions to problems and to report a solution some time after the struggle to understand.

The teacher needs to encourage with *questions* such as: 'How did you get that? Can you show me another way? Did anyone else do it another way?'

As a teacher, you need to foster an atmosphere of *acceptance*. Children are allowed to make mistakes, it is all right and necessary to make mistakes and also okay to make them public and share them; others are likely to have made the same or similar mistakes. 'The man who never made a mistake never made owt' (Yorkshire saying).

Collect the children's responses and discuss them during the plenary. It is not essential to name the owner of the mistake, although it may be helpful if they can explain how they made the error. Often, the one who has shown their error or misconception is not alone in misunderstanding that particular bit of mathematics, so it can be more useful to focus on the mathematics and clear up the misconception in a whole class discussion.

At other times it is better to share ideas when trying to understand misconceptions. A useful strategy is to encourage the person who knows the most to say the least. The one who is in difficulty talks about their thinking and the teacher listens. Obviously this cannot happen if the culture of the classroom is all about getting things right first time. We can tell when this corrosive culture is in evidence because children who understand the maths act out the teacher's secret attitudes by laughing in public at those who make mistakes. If this behaviour happens in a classroom, it is because a teacher's attitudes are being acted out by the children.

Think about how you support children who are dealing with errors and misconceptions:

- Do you try to strengthen their independence by emphasising the importance of strategies?
- Do you involve them in explaining their thinking?
- Do you signal acceptance by telling them that interest in errors is what gets you out of bed in the morning – because errors are so interesting? But seriously, it should be okay for children to make errors in your classroom. Some children find it hard to separate comments about errors from criticism of themselves as a person, so it is important to make sure you give a clear message about where your criticism is directed.
- Do you use questioning that helps children explain, review, start again, take off on a new tack?

Developing interactive teaching strategies

Some common errors and misconceptions

- Counting on 3 from 7 and getting an answer of 9, is likely to be as a result of starting with and counting the 7. Teach counting on as jumps. How many jumps?

  'Start at 7 and jump on three more. Where do you land?'

  Count the spaces between the numbers, fingers or fence posts. When counting *on*, put your toes behind the line or finger on the start, zero or first number and then only count on when you move. Step and count . . . Stop when the count is achieved.

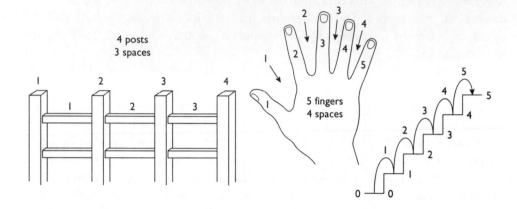

4 posts
3 spaces

5 fingers
4 spaces

N2

p. 8

- Some children may generate reading errors, for example by reading 206 or even 2006 as 26. This can result from misunderstanding the number system and place value.
- Some errors are produced in writing the numbers down, following the way they are said. For example: fourteen written as 41 or 410; one hundred and seven written as 1007. And some errors are caused by reading or writing down what is heard. Spend more time making and saying numbers.
- There can be confusion over what to do with fractions. When adding fractions, the child might try anything: for example: 3/4 + 5/2 = 86, or 14, or 59, or 8/6! Investigate how these answers have arisen.
- Children may misunderstand the order of a subtraction or division operation: for example, thinking that 3 − 7 = 4. We can combine numbers for addition or multiplication in *any* order, but for subtraction and division, the order does matter. Discuss and make clear which rules are the same and which are different for addition, multiplication, subtraction and division. Try out these rules for the four operations with simple numbers and also with very large and very small numbers.
- Children may assume that the outcome of division always gives a smaller value: that 4 ÷ 0.5 = 2. Or they may think that multiplication always makes things bigger, assuming that 4 × 0.5 = 20. These examples provide a good case for looking at limits and extremes.
- Children may line up numbers in columns from the left-hand margin ('We start writing on the left don't we?'). Or they may line up columns of numbers for operations against the right-hand margin, irrespective of the position of the decimal point. Emphasise how the place value system is rooted in the position of the decimal point although this is usually not written when working only with integers.

- Children may think that numbers are larger if there are more decimal digits: for example, 3.1694 is larger than 3.2. Or they may think that longer decimals have a smaller value, and thereby assume that 0.4 is greater than 0.610 23. Show that having more digits does not always mean more in terms of value. Work with exchange rates or food prices/100 g portion.

- Children may misread the scale on a ruler, starting at 1 (rather than 0) as a result of not understanding that the measure starts from 0. Use floor- or wall-size number tracks with zero as 'start', or always measure from the end of the ruler, using both dead-end and non-dead-end rulers. Is there any difference?

- When throwing dice, children may think that a 6 is harder to get than other numbers, not understanding the nature of equally likely and independent events. They need to understand that a lot of throws will be needed before we can be sure that the dice are not 'loaded'. Put a loaded dice in your box of dice to demonstrate. (Making weighted spinners is easier to do and see.)

- Children may assume that, because they have been taught to add a zero when multiplying by 10, they can use the same rule with decimals and numbers less than 1. For example, $2.3 \times 10 = 2.30$ and $2.3 \times 10 = 20.3$. Teach index notation as soon as possible. Encourage a 'feel' for numbers and teach what happens either side of the decimal point, making good use of links to the metric system.

- Children may assume that geometric shapes must always be positioned in a particular orientation. For example, they may think that a triangle with three equal sides and equal angles can only be labelled equilateral if it sits on a base line.

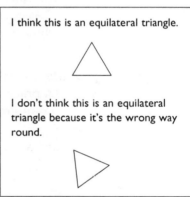

I think this is an equilateral triangle.

I don't think this is an equilateral triangle because it's the wrong way round.

Some further suggestions

- Make it clear that it is the *relative* position of the digits that is altered, and not the decimal point that moves, when multiplying and dividing by powers of 10. This is easy to show on some calculators, but is harder on paper. Try removing the decimal point from the multiplier or divisor and then repositioning it at the end of the calculation.

- Recognise the need to use precise mathematical vocabulary or notation. For example, avoid the use of 'take away' as the general word for subtraction, so that difference and counting on really are options too.

- Try making and using a maths dictionary (but don't be too pedantic).

- Discuss words that appear confusing: for example, 'difference', 'product' and 'half'.

- Explain Latin and Greek mathematical words, especially prefixes and suffixes.

- Teach the prefixes:
  - milli-, centi-, deci-, deka-, hecto-, kilo- for the metric system;
  - uni-, mono-, di-, bi-, tri-, tetra-, quad-, poly-;
  and suffixes such as:
  - -agon and -hedron.

Recommended sources

Askew, M. (1995) *Number at Key Stage 1*. [Another for KS2.] BEAM.
Accessible activities using: mental maths, number lines and grids, calculators, objects, pencil and paper.

Ben-Hur, M. (ed.) (1994) *On Feuerstein's Instrumental Enrichment*. IRI Skylight.
A useful collection of recent work on Instrumental Enrichment which provides learners, especially the culturally deprived, underperforming and autistic, with the tools to become more independent thinkers. Avows that all children can learn.

Blinko, J. and Graham, N. (1994) *Mathematical Beginnings: Problem Solving for Young Children*. Claire Publications.

Burns, M. (1990) *A Collection of Maths Lessons*. LDA.
Classroom stories about using an investigative approach to maths with KS2 children, describes the class, task, teacher interventions and outcomes. Considers teacher's role, maintenance and assessment of children in groups.

Burton, L. (1995) *Thinking Things Through*. Nash Pollock Publishing.
A practical guide to problem-solving and investigations with 30 carefully selected examples.

Carter, R. (1998) *Mapping the Mind*. Weidenfeld & Nicolson.
A powerful and vividly illustrated account of current neuro-science. Expertly written, highly readable.

Chinn, S. (2004) *The Trouble with Maths*. RoutledgeFalmer.

Claxton, G. (1999) *Wise Up: The Challenge of Lifelong Learning*. Bloomsbury.
An important and often simple yet profound review and analysis of current ideas about the way we think and learn. Just the kind of clarity we have come to expect from this author.

Claxton, G. (2002) *Building Learning Power*. TLO Ltd.
How teachers can help young people become better learners, both in school and out.

Deboys, M. and Pitt, E. (1988) *Lines of Development in Primary Maths*. Blackstaff.
A complete course based on a structure with progression of practical activities which leaves the teacher still in control. A developmental framework in three stages packed with good ideas.

Dickson, L., Brown, M. and Gibson, O. (1992) *Children Learning Maths*. Cassell.
A summary of research findings on how children learn or fail to learn mathematics; examples of children's responses give valuable insights into the learning processes.

Harries, T. and Spooner, M. (2000) *Mental Mathematics in the Numeracy Hour*. David Fulton.
Useful research, summary of learning theory, innovative work and grids.

Hopkins, C., Gifford, S. and Pepperell, S. (1992) *Mathematics in the Primary School: A Sense of Progression* (2nd edn). David Fulton.
Much of value to the classroom teacher. Plenty of examples as short case studies, well illustrated.

Houssart, J. (2004) *Low Attainers in Primary Mathematics*. RoutledgeFalmer.

Mankiewicz, R. (2000) *The Story of Mathematics*. Cassell.
Catalogue of development of big ideas. Wonderful images.

Miles, T. and Miles, E. (2004) *Dyslexia and Mathematics*. RoutledgeFalmer.

Mooney, C., Briggs, M., Fletcher, M. and McCulloch, J. (2002) *Primary Mathematics: Teaching Theory and Practice*. Learning Matters.
Well set out with coherent examples and practical tasks, linking theory, research and children's misconceptions. 4/98 compliant.

Mooney, C., Briggs, M., Fletcher, M. and McCulloch, J. (2002) *Primary Mathematics: Knowledge and Understanding*. Learning Matters.
Practical, relevant, accessible and clearly related to primary practice. Partner 4/98 compliant book.

Mosley, F. and O'Brian, T. (1998) *Eyes Closed*. BEAM.

Mosley, F. and O'Brian, T. (1998) *In the Hall*. BEAM.

Mosley, F. and O'Brian, T. (1998) *On the Mat*. BEAM.

Mosley, F. and O'Brian, T. (1998) *Numbers in Your Head*. BEAM.

Nelson, D., Joseph, G. and Williams, J. (1993) *Multicultural Mathematics: Teaching Mathematics from a Global Perspective*. Oxford University Press.
Teaching maths from a global perspective. Exploits our rich cultural heritages to improve maths teaching and to educate our children for life in a multicultural society. Maths as an international language and field of study.

Nickson, M. (2000) *Teaching and Learning Mathematics: A Teacher's Guide to Recent Research and its Application*. Cassell.
An accessible synthesis and analysis of recent research, wide ranging, including social and cultural issues.

NNS (1999) *Mathematical Vocabulary Book*. DfEE Publications.

NNS (1999) *National Numeracy Strategy. Framework for Teaching Mathematics from Reception to Year 6*. DfEE.

NNS (1999) *Standards in Mathematics*. QCA.

NNS (1999) *Teaching Mental Calculation Strategies*. QCA.

NNS (1999) *Teaching Written Calculation Strategies*. QCA.

Parsons, R. (ed.) (1998) *GCSE Mathematics – The Revision Guide* (4th edn). CGP Books.
Very useful, colourful, pupil centred crammer; www.cgpbooks.co.uk for core subjects at KS1, 2, 3 and 4.

Pike, G. and Selby, D. (1998) *Global Teacher Global Learner*. Hodder.
Useful theory, background and practical ideas, leading teachers and children towards an informed world-view.

Pound, L. (1999) *Supporting Mathematical Development*. Open University Press.
An excellent, thoughtful, well-informed book. Essential easy 'early years' reading.

Rucker, R. (1998) *Mindtools: The Mathematics of Information*. Penguin.
A charming and challenging intellectual carnival covering Number, Space, Logic, Infinity and Information.

Sharron, H. (1994) *Changing Children's Minds*. Sharron Publishing.
Feuerstein's Revolution in the teaching of Intelligence. A full account of Feuerstein's work and impact. Mediated learning, dynamic intellectual potential and the power of Instrumental Enrichment.

Smith, A. (1998) *Accelerated Learning in the Primary Classroom*. NEP.
A straightforward Accelerated Learning (AL) Handbook packed with ideas. A good starting point for AL.

Smith, A., Lovatt, M. and Wise, D. (2003) *Accelerated Learning: A User's Guide*. NEP.
Latest offering which challenges you to take the ideas and turn them into your own success story.

Wahl, M. (1999) *Math for Humans: Teaching Math Through 8 Intelligences*. Livnlern Press.
An unusual book which investigates one teacher's development of Gardner influenced mathematics teaching.

Williams, E. and Shuard, H. (1996) *Primary Mathematics Today* (3rd edn). Longman.
An excellent, durable reference book for teaching primary maths. Piagetian in style.

Williams, J. and Easingwood, N. (2004) *ICT and Primary Mathematics*. RoutledgeFalmer.
Using ICT to enhance primary maths; covers databases, spreadsheets, LOGO and interactive whiteboards.

Windsor, K. (2004) *Primary Maths Problem Solving, Ages 6–11*. Scholastic.
A range of problems at three levels using everyday resources, practical floor and table-top activities.

Wragg, E.C. and Brown, G. (2001) *Questioning in the Primary School*. RoutledgeFalmer.

Bibliography

Askew, M. (1995) *Number at Key Stage 1.* [Another for KS2.] BEAM.

Askew, M. (1995) *Recent Research in Maths Education 5–16.* HMSO.

ATM (1985) *Notes on Mathematics for Children.* Cambridge University Press.

ATM (1987) *Away with Maths Pack.* Association of Teachers of Mathematics.

ATM (2004) *Developing Number 2* (software).

Aubrey, C. (1997) *Mathematics Teaching in the Early Years.* Falmer.

Beishuizen, M. (1999) 'The Empty Number Line as a New Model', in Thompson, I. (ed.) *Issues in Teaching Numeracy in Primary Schools* (pp. 157–168). Open University Press.

Ben-Hur, M. (ed.) (1994) *On Feuerstein's Instrumental Enrichment.* IRI Skylight.

Bettelheim, B. (1976) *The Uses of Enchantment: The Meaning and Importance of Fairy Tales.* Thames and Hudson.

Bird, M. (1995) *Mathematics for Young Children.* Routledge.

Bird, R. (2001) *Target Boards.* Claire Publications.

Black, P. and Wiliam, D. (2002) *Inside the Black Box: Raising Standards Through Classroom Assessment.* Kings College, London.

Blinko, J. and Graham, N. (1994) *Mathematical Beginnings: Problem Solving for Young Children.* Claire Publications.

Bloomfield, A. (1990) *People Maths.* Stanley Thornes.

Brown, L., Hewitt, D. and Tahta, D. (1989) *A Gattegno Anthology.* ATM.

Brown, T. (1998) *Coordinating Mathematics Across the Primary School.* Hodder & Stoughton.

Brown, T. (2003) *Meeting the Standards in Primary Mathematics.* RoutledgeFalmer.

Bruner, J. (1966) *Towards a Theory of Instruction.* Harvard University Press.

Bruner, J. (1974) *Going Beyond the Information Given.* Norton.

Bruner, J. (1986) *Actual Minds, Possible Words.* Harvard University Press.

Burns, M. (1990) *A Collection of Maths Lessons.* LDA.

Burton, L. (1995) *Thinking Things Through.* Nash Pollock Publishing.

Carter, R. (1998) *Mapping the Mind.* Weidenfeld & Nicolson.

Caviglioli, O. and Harris, I. (2000) *Map Wise.* Network Educational Press.

Clarke, S. and Atkinson, S. (1996) *Tracking Significant Achievement in Primary Maths.* Hodder & Stoughton.

Claxton, G. (1999) *Wise Up: The Challenge of Lifelong Learning.* Bloomsbury.

Claxton, G. (2002) *Building Learning Power.* TLO Ltd.

Cornwall Advisory Service (1996) *Developing Differentiation in the Curriculum.* CEAS.

De Bono, E. (1974) *The Dog Exercising Machine.* Penguin.

De Bono, E. (1992) *Teach Your Child How to Think.* Viking.

Deboys, M. and Pitt, E. (1988) *Lines of Development in Primary Maths.* Blackstaff.

Dehaene, S. (1997) *The Number Sense. How the Mind Creates Mathematics.* Allen Lane.

Dennison, P. and Dennison, G. (1986) *Brain Gym.* Edu Kinaesthetics.

Dickinson, C. (1996) *Effective Learning Activities.* Network Educational Press.

Dickinson, C. and Wright, J. (1993) *Differentiation: A Practical Handbook of Classroom Strategies.* NCET.

Dickson, L., Brown, M. and Gibson, O. (1992) *Children Learning Maths.* Cassell.

Donaldson, M. (1978) *Children's Minds.* Fontana.

Dryden, G. and Vos, J. (2001) *The Learning Revolution.* Network Educational Press.

Evans, Z. (1985) *Pattern for a Set of Snakes.* Mimeo.

Evans, Z. (2002) 'Attitude is Everything'. *Mathematics Teaching* MT 181 December.

Faux, G. (1998) 'Using Gattegno Charts'. *Mathematics Teaching* MT 163 June.

Feuerstein, R. (1983) *Instrumental Enrichment.* University Park Press.

Fielker, D. (1997) *Extending Mathematical Ability Through Whole Class Teaching.* Hodder & Stoughton.

Flegg, G. (1983) *Numbers: Their History and Meaning.* Pelican.

Gardner, H. (1999) *Intelligence Reframed: Multiple Intelligences for the 21st Century.* Basic Books.

Gattegno, C. (1963) *Cuisenaire News* No. 3, January.

Gattegno, C. (1985) 'Knowledge v. Experience', *Mathematics Teaching* MT 110 March.

Gattegno, C. (1988) *The Awareness of Mathematization.* Part 2B. Educational Solutions.

Ginsburg, H. (1977) *Children's Arithmetic.* Van Nostrand.

Goleman, D. (1996) *Emotional Intelligence: Why it Can Matter More than IQ.* Bloomsbury.

Headington, R. (2000) *Monitoring, Assessment, Recording and Accountability.* David Fulton.

Hughes, M. (1984) *Children and Number.* Blackwell.

Ifrah, G. (1998) *The Universal History of Numbers.* Harvil.

Jung, C.G. (1964) *Man and His Symbols.* Pan Books.

Krutetski, V.A. (1976) *The Psychology of Mathematical Abilities of School Children.* University of Chicago Press.

Lewis, A. (1976) *Discovering Mathematics with 4–7 Year Olds.* Hodder.

Liebling, H. (1999) *Getting Started: An Induction Guide for NQTs.* Network Educational Press.

MacGrath, M. (2000) *The Art of Peaceful Teaching.* David Fulton.

Mason, J. (1982) *Thinking Mathematically.* Addison-Wesley.

Menninger, K. (1969) *Number Words and Number Symbols: A Cultural History in Numbers.* MIT Press.

MEP (1986) *Blocks in Primary Maths Software Pack.* NCET.

Merttens, R. (ed.) (1996) *Teaching Numeracy: Maths in the Primary Classroom.* Scholastic.

Merttens, R. (1998) *Simmering Activities.* Ginn & Co.

Mosley, F. and O'Brien, T. (1998) *Eyes Closed.* BEAM.

Mosley, J. (1995) *Quality Circle Time.* LDA.

Nelson, D., Joseph, G. and Williams, J. (1993) *Multicultural Mathematics: Teaching Mathematics from a Global Perspective.* Oxford University Press.

NNS (1999) *Mathematical Vocabulary Book.* DfEE Publications.

NNS (1999) *Standards in Mathematics.* QCA.

NNS (1999) *Teaching Mental Calculation Strategies.* QCA.

NNS (1999) *Teaching Written Calculation Strategies.* QCA.

Novak, J. and Gowin, V. (1984) *Learning How to Learn.* Cambridge University Press.

Nunes, T. and Bryant, P. (1996) *Children Doing Mathematics.* Blackwell.

Nunes, T., Schliemann, A. and Carraher, D.W. (1993) *Street Mathematics and School Mathematics.* Cambridge University Press.

Papert, S. (1980) *Mindstorms*. Harvester Press.

Parsons, R. (ed.) (1988) *GCSE Mathematics – The Revision Guide* (4th edn). CGP Books.

Piaget, J. (1952) *The Child's Conception of Number*. Routledge & Kegan Paul.

Pike, G. and Selby, D. (1998) *Global Teacher Global Learner*. Hodder.

Polya, G. (1957) *How to Solve It*. Oxford University Press.

Pound, L. (1999) *Supporting Mathematical Development*. Open University Press.

Rhydderch-Evans, Z. (1993) *Maths in the School Grounds: Learning Through Landscapes*. Southgate.

RNLI (2004) *Mayday: Action Pack for 9–12 Year Olds*. RNLI.

Rucker, R. (1988) *Mindtools: The Mathematics of Information*. Penguin.

Scott, N. (2004) *Reduce, Reuse, Recycle*. Green Books.

Sharron, H. (1994) *Changing Children's Minds*. Sharron Publishing.

Shuard, H., Walsh, A., Goodwin, J. and Worcester, V. (1990) *Children, Mathematics and Learning*. Simon and Schuster.

Skemp, R. (1989) *Mathematics in the Primary School*. Routledge.

Smith, A. (1998) *Accelerated Learning in Practice* (2nd edn). Network Educational Press.

Smith, A., Lovatt, M. and Wise, D. (2003) *Accelerated Learning: A User's Guide*. NEP.

Sylwester, R. (1995) *A Celebration of Neurons*. ASCD.

Thompson, I. (ed.) (1997) *Teaching and Learning Early Number*. Open University Press.

TTA booklet (n.d.) *Using ICT to Meet Teaching Objectives in Mathematics*. TTA.

Vitruvius, P. (1960) *The Ten Books on Architecture* (M.H. Morgan, trans.). Dover.

Vygotsky, L. (1978) *Mind and Society*. Harvard University Press.

Wahl, M. (1999) *Math for Humans: Teaching Math Through 8 Intelligences*. Livlern Press.

Walkerdine, V. (1998) *The Mastery of Reason: Cognitive Development and the Production of Rationality*. Routledge.

Watson, A. and Mason, J. (2004) *Primary Questions and Prompts for Mathematical Thinking*. ATM.

Williams, E. and Shuard, H. (1996) *Primary Mathematics Today* (3rd edn). Longman.

Windsor, K. (2004) *Primary Maths Problem Solving*. Scholastic.

Zaslavsky, C. (1979) *Africa Counts*. Lawrence Hill Books.

JOURNALS AND MAGAZINES

Child Education and Junior Education (teacher magazine from Scholastic): www.scholastic.co.uk

Educational Studies in Maths (international journal): www.kluweronline.com

For the Learning of Maths (international journal for maths education): www.flm.maths.ca

Mathematics Teacher (journal of the National Council of Teachers of Mathematics, US): www.my.nctm.org

Mathematics Teaching (MT) (journal of the ATM)

Maths in School (MIS) (journal of the MA)

Micromaths (ICT journal of the ATM)

Primary Maths & Science (teacher magazine from Questions Publishing): www.education-quest.com

ORGANISATIONS

Association of Teachers of Mathematics (ATM): www.atm.org.uk
Mathematics Association (MA), *Maths in Schools* (journal): www.m-a.org.uk
Micros and Primary Education (MAPE) (some downloads): www.mape.org.uk
National Association of Mathematics Advisors: www.nama.org.uk
Open University (OU): www.open.ac.uk
Open University broadcasts on the BBC: www.open2.net
Portal for the gifted and talented: xcalibre.ac.uk
SMILE (KS2, 3 & 4 resources and software): www.smilemathematics.co.uk
Standards Site: Numeracy, also gender, parents, EAZ (Education Action Zone):
    www.standards.dfes.gov.uk/numeracy
Teacherline 0800 0560561: phone up about any problem you are having 24/7.

SOFTWARE

BECTA Educational Software Database: besd.ngfl.gov.uk
Developing Number 2: 'Powers of Ten' and 'Complements', 'Numbers' supports
    making and saying numbers (N2), 'Tables' supports children learning multiplica-
    tion facts (C5). www.atm.org.uk
Interactive Maths (also from ATM) 16 programs on a CD for IWB. Supports work on
    many topics including: all number grids, dotty paper, pinboards, visualisation and
    probability: www.atm.org.uk
LOGO software from Logotron: www.logo.com
Now three Zoombinis packages: www.mindscape.co.uk
Research Machines site (e.g. Easiteach Maths for IWB): www.rm.co.uk
Software eligible for 'e-Learning Credits': www.cirriculumonline.gov.uk
Two sets of maths games software for use and purchase: www.primarygames.co.uk

TV PROGRAMMES ETC.

BBC's excellent materials: www.bbc.co.uk/learning
Channel 4's impressive site: www.channel4.com/learning

EQUIPMENT, MATERIALS AND RESOURCES

We have mentioned numerous new and old resources in this book. Try using Google
or another search engine to find suppliers. We have listed some web sites. For government approved retailers and even subsidised resources, look for the Cirriculum
Online logo.

The ATM (originally formed to design, develop and disseminate innovative mathematical resources) continues to offer a huge range of exciting classroom resources, books,
booklets, games and software.

BEAM (Be a Mathematician) (superb resources): www.beam.co.uk
Claire Publications (an inclusive, thoughtful supplier): www.clairepublications.com
Numdrum (a new cylindrical number grid): www.numdrum.com
Polydron International (not cheap, but durable resources): www.polydron.com
Tarquin (unusual and interesting resources): www.tarquin-books.demon.co.uk

USEFUL WEBSITES

ambleweb.digitalbrain.com: new Ambleside School site – a must see.

mathforum.org.alejandre/magic.square.html: magic squares from Mathforum.

mathforum.org/sum95/suzanne/tess.intro.html: tessellations from Mathforum.

mathworld.wolfram.com: encyclopaedic mathematics resource.

numbergym.co.uk: new site for mental arithmetic.

pass.maths.org/index.html: plus magazine – a career in maths?

perso.wanadoo.fr/une.education.pour.demain/articlesrrr/sw/rose.htm: Caleb Gattegno's Silent Way.

users.argonet.co.uk/oundlesch/mlink.html: Butler's wonderful set of mathslinks.

www.actden.com/index.htm: Digital Education Network.

www.alite.co.uk: accelerated learning.

www.angliacampus.com/: major provider of online service to education.

www.atm.org.uk: ATM site. Good source of books, resources and software.

www.bbc.co.uk/webguide/schools/subcat.shtml?maths/ks12/0: why re-invent the wheel? KS1 and 2 sites.

www.beam.co.uk: BEAM impressive useful resources.

www.braindance.com/homepage/htm: Tony Buzan home page.

www.braingym.org: Brain Gym site.

www.ceismc.gatech.edu/busyt/math.html: K-12 Mathematics US.

www.censusatschool.ntu.ac.uk: promising resource for data handling.

www.cict.co.uk/software/maths/index.htm: creative technology, virtual images.

www.cleo.net.uk: Cumbria and Lancashire education online.

www.colormathpink.com/: US site to encourage girls and women into maths.

www.counton.org/: good free maths site, was Mathsyear2000.

www.dfes.gov.uk: Department for Education and Skills.

www.digitaltelevision.gov.uk

www.ed.gov/pubs/parents/Math/index.html: helping your child learn maths.

www.educate.co.uk: support for parents, teachers and children.

www.education.bham.ac.uk/subjects/maths/links/default.htm: link sites full and advanced with annotations.

www.edwdebono.com: Edward De Bono home pages – thinking skills.

www.elib.com/Steiner/: Rudolph Steiner archives.

www.etacuisenaire.com: Cuisenaire Rods and materials, US supplier.

www.eurolog.org/: Eurolog.

www.globalfootprints.org: steps towards a sustainable future.

www.highscope.org/: Highscope early years longitudinal research.

www.iaaf.org/statistics/records/index.html: athletic data source.

www.ictadvice.org.uk/index.php: BECTA – using web-based resources.

www.indiatimes.com: an amazing diverse and eclectic source.

www.kidsdomain.co.uk/index.html: lots to do for kids – materialist.

www.le.ac.uk/education/resources/curres.html: link sites – try theirs.

www.learningalive.co.uk: research machines, goodies for sale.

www.mathsite.co.uk/Home: curriculum online maths resources for sale.

www.mathsnet.net: an every-trick-in-the-book resource and still free.

www.mathsoline.co.uk: maths subscription website.

www.mathsphere.co.uk: software and worksheets some free resources.

www.mathszone.co.uk: teacher recommended maths site.

www.mav.vic.edu.au/PSTC/: Problem Solving Task Centre, Australia.

www.mcs.surrey.ac.uk/Personal/R.Knott/Fibonacci/fibnat.html: exemplary site.

www.microworlds.com/library/math: LCSI software online.

www.motivate.maths.org.uk: maths videoconferences for schools (5–18).

www.naffcaff.co.uk/anorak.html

www.nasen.org.uk/links/home.htm: special education needs links and information.

www.network.press.co.uk

www.newhorizons.org: neuroscience and education, must see.

www.ngfl.gov.uk: national grid for learning.

www.nrich.maths.org.uk/primary.index.htm: outstanding mathematics enrichment.

www.open.ac.uk/framed.html: The Open University.

www.pacificnet.net/-mandel/index/html: teachers helping teachers.

www.parentcentre.gov.uk: new parent centre, up to date.

www.primaryresources.co.uk/: Edelston Primary, good design, resources and links.

www.qlsi.com/educate_direct/ie/: QLSI and instrumental enrichment overview.

www.rigb.org/events/programmeformaths_primary.html: Royal Institute primary
    masterclass programme.

www.rm.co.uk: cirriculum materials online. Software.

www.rmplc.co.uk/eduweb/sites/ufa10/index.htm: Birmingham's schools maths site.

www.sapere.net: home of philosophy for children.

www.skypublicity.co.uk

www.smilemathematics.co.uk: pedigree resources and software.

www.softronix.com/logo.html: MSW Logo, good and free.

www.standards.dfes.gov.uk/numeracy/publications

www.sunriseradio.com

www.swopnet.com: starter activities, lots of resources (US).

www.teachernet.gov.uk: major government portal.

www.teachers.ash.org.au/teachereduc/default.html: Aussie Schoolhouse, links,
    resources and pedagogy.

www.teachingideas.co.uk: some numeracy resources for each area.

www.thebigbus.com: subscription and CDs, was Argosphere.

www.thebritishmuseum.ac.uk/: a huge resource. Children's Compass.

www.thehopecharity.org.uk/reuven.htm: Professor Reuven Feuerstein.

www.theinternetforum.co.uk/bbc/

www.thelearningweb.net: learning revolution website.

www.think.com/: free site run by Oracle, 7–14 years. Must register.

www.think-energy.com: energy saving. Think energy and talk energy.

www.tooter4kids.com/weather/weatherindex.htm

www.topmarks.co.uk/: free respected site, searching and links.

www.traidcraft.co.uk: Fairtrade. Fighting poverty through trade.

www.tut-world.com/: worksheets/tutorials.

www.uneeducationpourdemain.org: UEPD Caleb Gattegno, Silent Way etc.

www.upmystreet.com: local information and maps with your postcode.

www.vedicmathematics.co.uk: so what is Vedic mathematics? Find out here.

www.wiredforhealth.gov.uk/: starting point for health education issues, 250+ links.

www.wwflearning.co.uk: WWF site, lifelong learning for a sustainable future.

Index

Lightning Source UK Ltd.
Milton Keynes UK
13 April 2010

152724UK00007B/19/P

9 780415 252089